Days of Destruction

DAYS of DESTRUCTION

Augustine Thomas Smythe *and the* Civil War Siege *of* Charleston

Edited by
W. Eric Emerson and Karen Stokes

The University of South Carolina Press

Published by the University of South Carolina Press
Columbia, South Carolina 29208

www.sc.edu/uscpress

Manufactured in the United States of America

26 25 24 23 22 21 20 19 18 17
10 9 8 7 6 5 4 3 2 1

ISBN: 978-1-61117-770-1 (hardcover)
ISBN: 978-1-61117-771-8 (ebook)

Library of Congress Cataloging-in-Publication Data
can be found at http://catalog.loc.gov/

This book was printed on a recycled paper with
30 percent postconsumer waste content.

CONTENTS

ILLUSTRATIONS

ACKNOWLEDGMENTS

The fascinating Civil War story of Augustine Thomas Smythe is documented in a significant number of letters that he wrote to family and friends during the conflict. This correspondence has survived for more than one and a half centuries because Susan Smythe Bennett, Smythe's daughter and the wife of the Charleston Renaissance author John Bennett, realized the letters' intellectual value and donated them to the South Carolina Historical Society. For several decades they have been preserved and made available to the public as the Augustine Thomas Smythe Papers at the Society's Robert Mills Fireproof Building. Recently the Smythe Papers and the majority of the Society's collections were moved to the Addlestone Library at the College of Charleston. At this new location, researchers can delve into the lives of this Irish immigrant family, whose lives helped to shape the future of their city and state.

The publication of this volume would not have been possible without the assistance and support of a significant number of people. The editors would like to thank Faye Jensen and the Board of Managers of the South Carolina Historical Society for allowing these letters to be annotated and published and also for their previous support of the publication of other letters found at the South Carolina Historical Society, which appeared in two Civil War documentary editions that preceded this volume. Taken together, these three collections represent a very small but historically significant portion of the rich and vast collections of South Carolina Historical Society. The editors are honored to have had an opportunity to make these letters more accessible to the public. The editors also would like to thank their colleagues at the South Carolina Historical Society and the South Carolina Department of Archives and History for their assistance during this process. In particular, we are grateful for the efforts of Ehren Foley and Wade Dorsey, both of whom took time to read parts of the manuscript and provide their thoughts and suggestions. Many thanks are due to Nic Butler, Robert B. Cuthbert, and B. Powell Harrison (an Adger descendant) for helpful information and to George W. Williams, former historiographer of St. Michael's Church, for an interesting tour of the steeple. The editors also would like to extend a special word of thanks to Alexander Moore, acquisitions editor at the University of South Carolina Press, who played a pivotal role in the publication of this volume and of two previous collaborative editions produced by the editors. Alex Moore has been both an accommodating editor and a friend to the editors, and we are grateful for his support and words of wisdom. Finally, the editors would like to thank their families for their patience during this and previous editing projects. As with all projects of this nature, the efforts of many combine to produce a work that, it is hoped, will enlighten and withstand the scrutiny of future readers. The editors take complete responsibility for any errors or oversights found within this volume.

EDITORIAL METHOD

The editors transcribed the letters in this volume as they were written. No changes were made to spelling or abbreviations. Obvious mistakes are indicated by *sic* within brackets. The only significant changes made to the correspondence were to adapt names and dates within the dateline to a particular form for consistency. All omissions within quotations and extracts are indicated by ellipses. Words or brief passages that are bracketed represent the transcriber's best interpretations of the material in question.

Introduction

This photograph of Augustine Thomas Smythe is dated 1863. His letters of November 1863 and later mention having his photograph taken by Mr. Cook in Charleston. Courtesy of the South Carolina Historical Society.

On June 2, 1864, a young lance sergeant in the Confederate Signal Corps penned a letter filled with the timeless hope and frustration of youth. To a close relative he confided that his experiences in the nation's bloodiest war, which had raged for more than three years, were a source of great disappointment and disillusionment. "Aunt Janey you know I am ambitious & it does gall me & cut me to the quick to hear of my companions rising in rank, while I remain here wasting abilities which I know to be naturally good & with no prospect of being any higher than I was when I entered the Corps over 18 months ago. . . . I am not satisfied here, nor am I satisfied with my part in this war, so different from what I hoped or planned."[1]

Sergeant Augustine Thomas Smythe's "part in this war" was different from that of his companions on duty in Virginia and undoubtedly different from anything he could have imagined when the war began. In fact, Smythe's duty station in June 1864 was dramatically different from that of all but a handful of participants in the American Civil War. It was not a place of death or destruction, although it provided a bird's-eye view of both. It was, instead, a place of stature and majesty. From the unique vantage of Smythe's post, he could witness the Union siege and bombardment of Charleston, South Carolina: the city of his birth, his youth, and his home even during a time of conflict.

As a sergeant in the Signal Corps, Smythe was destined to spend many days and nights in the 186-foot steeple atop St. Michael's Episcopal Church. There he and a handful of soldiers would pass signals to other posts located around Charleston Harbor. The steeple, however, was more than a signal station. It was an aiming stake (or reference point) and target for the Union artillery bombarding Charleston. William Gilmore Simms made this the subject of his war poem "The Angel of the Church," in which he envisioned the church and the city as under the protection of the archangel Michael. From his "lofty perch," Smythe could observe Union guns located on Morris Island as they fired round after round at the city. He could discern the smoke of the cannon fire and then watch as each round lofted toward Charleston. Most veered to the right or left of the steeple, but some fell short. After serving in the steeple for some time, he could discern the eventual impact point of artillery rounds on the basis of their trajectory as they approached his post. Eventually he came to view the Union rounds in an almost detached manner, even as they crashed nearby or onto the homes of family and friends on Meeting Street below him.

Smythe's letters are significant for their depiction of an unusual wartime perspective on the bombardment and destruction of much of Charleston. Smythe's viewpoint was the result of his service in the Signal Corps, a branch of the Confederate army that has received little attention in the seemingly endless trove of scholarship that historians have produced since the conclusion of our nation's most destructive conflict more than 150 years ago. The Confederate Signal Corps played a vital role in the defense of Charleston and its environs, and Smythe's letters, perhaps more than any other first-person account, detail the daily lives and service experiences of signalmen in and around the city during the war.

The letters that Smythe sent to family members also are notable for the picture they painted of the bombardment's effect on the city, in particular its lower sections and the society that dwelled there. One of the city's oldest and wealthiest communities, Smythe's neighborhood south of Broad Street was abandoned by the great majority of its residents for more than eighteen months. Smythe's letters provide the reader with an almost postapocalyptic perspective of the often quiet and frequently lawless street where he resided before and during the siege of Charleston.

More than one and a half centuries after they were first written, the letters of Augustine Thomas Smythe remain relevant for those who strive to understand our nation's bloodiest war. They are notable among the vast abundance of correspondence produced by nineteenth-century youth who witnessed the death and destruction of the Civil War and left a record of their experiences. From these records we can learn much about how that conflict in particular, and war in general, shapes and often defines the postwar lives of combatants. We also can learn much about how societies respond to the cataclysm of war.

Despite the passage of so much time, we are still responding to that great American cataclysm, wrestling with the war's causes, its outcomes, and our memory of the conflict. Each generation believes that it has the correct answers to the great questions surrounding the American Civil War. Subsequent generations always seem to disagree. As Americans, we are left grasping for the "true history" of "The War," and yet we never are satisfied with the history that we find.

The story of Augustine Thomas Smythe (1842–1914), like most American stories, is a story of immigrants. He was born in Charleston on October 5, 1842, to a family of Scots-Irish descent, and as a young man he added an "e" to his Smyth surname. His father was the Reverend Dr. Thomas Smyth, a native of Belfast, Ireland, and his mother, Margaret Milligan Adger, was the daughter of James Adger, a prominent Charleston merchant, who also was born in Northern Ireland. Augustine's father, Thomas Smyth, was born on

June 14, 1808, one of twelve children, eight of whom survived to adulthood. Weak and sickly as an infant, he grew into "a feeble child and delicate boy." Like his mother, Ann Magee Smith, Thomas was religious from an early age, though not immune to worldly distractions. Having inherited from his mother "a tender sensibility" and a "susceptibility to deep emotion," he later confessed that he was subject to many romantic infatuations as a boy. "Youth to me was a wild and feverish romance," he later recalled.[2]

Thomas Smyth, D.D. This portrait is from an engraving made in Edinburgh in 1851. It appeared as the frontispiece for his book *The Unity of the Human Races.* Courtesy of the South Carolina Historical Society.

In 1827, Thomas Smyth attended Belfast College, where he excelled in the debating society. While there he became engaged to Caroline Spear, who embodied, as he described it, "my ideal form of love and youth and beauty." Two years later, he entered Highbury College in London to study theology. He had a passion for books and learning, and while at Highbury he spent so much of his money on books that he passed two or three winter months "without a cent." His health suffered as a result of deprivation and from "excessive habits of intense study."[3]

Controversy eclipsed Smyth's time at Highbury. Accused of misconduct by another student (unjustly, Smyth maintained), he found his engagement to Caroline Spear ended. Depressed by this turn of events, he decided to join family members who had immigrated to America (his parents had settled in Vincennes, Indiana). Smyth traveled to New York and then to New Jersey to study at Princeton Theological Seminary. In 1831 he accepted a call from Second Presbyterian Church in Charleston, South Carolina, to "supply on trial," or act as a temporary pastor. When he arrived in Charleston, he was befriended by James Adger, a wealthy Charleston businessman and a fellow native of Belfast. At the time, Adger ranked among the wealthiest men in America. He had business connections in a number of large ports and operated a line of ships that regularly traveled to New York. He welcomed Smyth into his home and treated him as an adopted son. Soon thereafter Smyth developed an attachment to Adger's eldest daughter, Margaret.[4]

Margaret Milligan Adger was a devout, earnest young woman who taught Sunday school at the Charleston Orphan House and aspired to become a missionary to foreign lands. In February 1832 she wrote to her brother John B. Adger, who was a theological student at Princeton, and urged him to consider becoming a missionary to Liberia to minister to freed slaves who had left America and settled there. She had a special concern for Africa and expressed a desire to join her brother John in foreign mission work there and thus devote her life to teaching Africans "about Jesus." She considered colonization of America's freedmen the only way to ensure their future welfare and happiness, writing, "[I]n our country the free negro never can take that place he is entitled to, in Society—in Africa he will be on a level with all around him." Thomas Smyth shared her concern for the spiritual welfare of slaves, and during his college days (he was a Congregationalist at this time) he had likely been in sympathy with the abolition movement in Great Britain, which in 1833 resulted in the abolition of slavery throughout the British colonies and compensated British slave holders for their financial losses. Some of Smyth's good friends and associates, including John Stoughton and Robert Halley, were certainly supporters of the British antislavery movement. One of his Highbury College friends, William J. Unwin, wrote to Smyth in 1830 about an "Anti-Slavery Meeting" at which William Wilberforce and other notables were present, expressing his hopes that "it may lead to some favourable result."[5]

Margaret Milligan Adger Smyth, Augustine T. Smythe's mother.
Courtesy of the South Carolina Historical Society.

Margaret Adger's letters to her brother also reveal her deliberations concerning another matter. Smyth had proposed to Margaret, an offer that she did not immediately accept. In the spring of 1832 she wrote, "I told him [Smyth] candidly that I felt it my duty to engage in Foreign Missions & had determined to go with you—this did not satisfy him—he has examined the subject in all its bearings & concludes my influence with him & through him exerted at home for the heathen would be more than I could exercise *alone.*" Margaret asked her brother to "tell me what I ought to do—what is my *duty*?—& I will pray to be enabled to suppress every feeling that would rise in opposition to it." In a subsequent letter written to John, she was still wrestling with the question of marriage to Smyth, remarking, "I am not blind to his defects, I know he has many—& some *great* ones." Margaret also was being courted by another Presbyterian clergyman, John Leighton Wilson, a native of Sumter District who later would become a noted missionary to Africa and an outspoken opponent of the international slave trade. Margaret turned down Wilson's proposal of marriage because she did not love him and feared she never could. Despite her reservations regarding Smyth, she decided in his favor and became his wife in July 1832.[6]

Margaret did not specify the "defects" she saw in her future husband, but it is possible she was thinking of some faults that Smyth later confessed to in his *Autobiographical Notes,* in which he admitted that he was "naturally ambitious" and that in his work as a minister there had been "pride and self-seeking vanity." Known for his strong will and intellect, he also was possessed of a somewhat domineering personality. In 1858 J. L. Kirkpatrick, a fellow Presbyterian clergyman, wrote to a colleague that Smyth had an "overbearing, dictatorial way."[7]

Second Presbyterian Church, Charleston, S.C. This photograph dates to the midtwentieth century. Courtesy of the Library of Congress.

After serving the congregation at Second Presbyterian Church for a period as a "supply," Smyth received "a permanent call to become their Pastor." He did not accept the position until December 1834, however, following further studies at Princeton and deliberations about his fitness for the position in view of his delicate health. Throughout his subsequent career, he dealt with many problems and doctrinal controversies within his church, in the Charleston Union Presbytery, and in the Presbyterian Church as a whole. He attempted to resign his pastorate on several occasions in the 1850s but was each time overruled or dissuaded, and though he was offered other opportunities—among them the pastorates of other churches and a professorship at South Carolina College in Columbia—he remained in Charleston and at Second Presbyterian.[8]

Smyth never enjoyed good health. He suffered many bouts of illness, some of which he attributed to the climate of Charleston, and in 1850 what he described as an "attack" caused a partial paralysis of the left side of his body for a while and left him with a pain in his left arm and hand that never went away. Another such attack came in 1853, leaving him "long on crutches," as he recounted. Before these serious physical afflictions, he was deeply bereaved by the loss of his first two children—two infant daughters who died within a week of each other in 1837—and then his second son (the first named Augustine), who passed away in 1841, having lived less than a year.[9]

While on a visit to Belfast, Ireland, in 1846, Thomas Smyth became involved in a dispute with Frederick Douglass, who was lecturing in that city. Lawyers representing the famous former slave and abolitionist claimed that Smyth had uttered libelous statements about their client. Smyth denied that he made the slanderous remarks they specified (that Douglass was an "infidel" and had been seen leaving a brothel), asserting that he had only repeated, in a private conversation, some "reports" he had heard about Douglass. The controversy was resolved when Smyth explained himself in a letter of apology, but Douglass would again be the object of scandalous rumors a few years later, when followers of the leading American abolitionist William Lloyd Garrison accused Douglass of adultery with a woman named Julia Griffiths, a British abolitionist who lived in the Douglass home for several years.[10] Smyth felt deeply wronged by Douglass, who had not only made legal threats against him but who also had injured him "in public opinion."[11] Douglass admitted as much in a letter to a friend in which he proudly related that he had been "playing mischief with the characters of Slave holders," specifically naming "Rev. Thomas Smyth" as one of his targets.[12]

During the spring of 1846, the same year as the Douglass controversy, Smyth led a "great revival" at Second Presbyterian Church, during which he added more than a hundred new communicants to the church, including sixteen black members. The total number of black members would eventually peak at 160 under Smyth's oversight, and he and other local clergy would work diligently to establish places of worship for Charleston's black population.[13]

When Thomas Smyth's brother-in-law John B. Adger returned to South Carolina from his foreign mission work in 1847, he dedicated his life to "the religious instruction of the negroes in Charleston." Citing an inadequacy in "church accommodations" for them, as well as "a want of suitable instruction," Adger, Smyth, and others advocated the establishment of a "separate colored church."[14] The Episcopalians in Charleston already had organized Calvary Church for this purpose, and, though it initially met with opposition from some of the city's white citizens, the congregation (which included white members) flourished under the ministry of the Reverend Paul Trapier.[15]

Zion Presbyterian Church as it appeared in 1900. It was the largest church edifice in Charleston at the time it was completed in 1859. Courtesy of the South Carolina Historical Society.

In 1850 Second Presbyterian Church established a mission church for the black people on Anson Street. Its first pastor was John B. Adger, followed by the Reverend John L. Girardeau in 1852. In 1858, with great support from Thomas Smyth and members of the Adger family, the Anson Street mission was transformed into "a self-sustaining church with white

Eldership and members of its own."[16] Under Girardeau's leadership, the membership increased until it became necessary to build "the largest church edifice in Charleston" to accommodate them. The church was named Zion, and John B. Adger wrote of it: "This immense building, costing twenty-five thousand dollars, was all paid for by the white citizens of Charleston, as an expression of their interest in the religious welfare of the colored people. . . . The main floor was occupied by negroes, for whom the preaching was chiefly designed; but there were galleries on three sides facing the pulpit for the white people."[17]

Gilbert R. Brackett, a fellow Presbyterian clergyman who knew Smyth in his last years (and succeeded him as pastor at Second Presbyterian), recorded his pride in the establishment of Zion. "Both as a preacher, and as a pastor, Dr. Smyth ever felt and manifested a deep and affectionate interest in the *coloured people,* who filled the gallery of his Church, and largely composed his membership. . . . He was a warm supporter of the Zion Colored Church. . . . He spoke of it as 'a noble and glorious enterprise in which he heartily rejoiced.'"[18] Brackett also explained Smyth's views on slavery.

> It was in the spirit of a Christian philanthropist that he cordially favored and zealously defended the institution of slavery, for "however it may be denounced as imperfect and attended with evil," he held that "it had been employed by unerring wisdom and an overruling Providence, as an instrument for the preservation, elevation, and conversion of millions who would have lived and died in heathen ignorance, superstition, and cruelty." He believed that in so far as masters rendered unto their slaves that which is "just and equal," in their condition and sphere of life, than involuntary servitude was for them that which is best fitted to promote their well-being and happiness. But while all his learning and ability were enlisted on the side of slavery, he was equally earnest and bold in denouncing the unnecessary evils, and reforming the abuses and perversions of that domestic institution.[19]

During the 1850s, Southern clergymen and laity responded to abolitionist attacks on slavery by urging reforms for the institution that would bring it more in line with Christian principles. At the annual conventions of the Protestant Episcopal Church in South Carolina in 1859 and 1860, for example, prominent laymen proposed resolutions concerning marriage, stating that "the marriage relation between slaves has the same divine obligation as that between masters and mistresses."[20] Because of his support for such reforms and his involvement in the establishment of Zion Church, contemporaries sometimes accused Smyth of being an abolitionist. Although he may have supported the emancipation movement in Great Britain, he did not espouse such views after adopting South Carolina as his home, perhaps because no similar program of compensated emancipation had been proposed in America. Like his brother-in-law John B. Adger, he took the view that "Southern slavery was just a grand civilizing and Christianizing school, providentially prepared," and that "the two races were steadily and constantly marching onwards and upwards together" to eventual emancipation, when the enslaved race was ready to "graduate."[21]

Smyth was a prolific and influential writer who published numerous articles and sermons and authored thirty books on theological subjects. In 1843 the degree of "Doctor in Divinity" was conferred on him by Princeton Seminary for his "attainments in Theological Learning" and his "labours in the cause of truth and righteousness."[22] Theology, however, was not his only intellectual pursuit. He also had active interests in science, medicine, law, art, and literature. For many years he was a member of the Literary and Philosophical Society, which Smyth's biographer described as being composed of "the most intelligent men of Charleston."[23] In 1850 Smyth published *The Unity of the Human Races,* which refuted the theories of Samuel George Morton of Philadelphia, his protégé Louis Agassiz of Harvard University, and others who believed that the races came from separate origins.[24] Smyth also had a passion for collecting books, and he amassed a library of nearly twenty thousand volumes. In 1856 the Theological Seminary in Columbia purchased eleven thousand volumes from him, but he still retained a substantial collection to which he continued to add. That same year, the Smyth family moved into a house at 12 Meeting Street (now 18 Meeting Street), where his library "was established in a large, lofty, many-windowed room on the second floor."

Smyth was invited to offer a prayer at the 1860 National Democratic Convention, which took place in Charleston from April 23 to May 3. Of this event his granddaughter Louisa Cheves Smythe Stoney noted: "This was the National Democratic Convention, charged with the responsibility of choosing a candidate to be opposed to Lincoln. The factions were too evenly divided to come to a decision, and after casting 57 ballots, the greatest number ever cast at such a convention, it adjourned to meet a little later in Baltimore." Stoney also added a humorous annotation about Augustine Smythe in which she described an incident that revealed his lifelong interest in politics: "Only ladies were admitted to the galleries of the Democratic Convention. Smyth's son, Augustine, determined to be present, and, unable to gain entrance to the floor, attended one evening dressed in the garments of his aunt, Janey Adger, which, as she was a tall woman and he a handsome boy, suited him well."[25]

After Lincoln's election, the South Carolina legislature passed an act on November 11, 1860, calling for a State Convention to deliberate the issue of secession. Soon afterward, South Carolina's governor proclaimed a day of humiliation and prayer, and on the appointed day, November 21, Smyth preached one of his most notable sermons. Printed under the title "The Sin and the Curse," it lamented the death of "this glorious constitutional union" and identified America's "true source of disunion" in the "infidel, atheistic, French Revolution, Red Republican principle" embodied in the egalitarian ideas of the Declaration of Independence. "All men are not born equal," Smyth contended. "The only equality is, that all men are born in sin."[26] The nation was divided, he argued, because of the influence of a group of Americans who rejected the divine inspiration and infallibility of the Bible (which did not condemn slavery) and developed their own code of morality, or "higher law principle." Of them Smyth wrote:

> In the overwhelming mass which, like an avalanche, swept away all existing landmarks and barriers, there was a conglomeration of all possible variety of materials,—atheists, infidels, communists, free-lovers, rationalists, Bible haters, anti-christian levellers, and anarchists,—many of whom had no interests at stake, and no principles to restrain them within the limits of constitutional truth, justice or propriety . . . on this higher law principle, a majority of his creatures can decide for God, and against God, that slavery is, in its essential nature, absolutely sinful; further, that it is so essentially and heinously wicked, that in order to overthrow it, compacts may be broken, and robbery, murder, arson, treason, rebellion and massacre with all the hellish crew of bigotry, hatred, uncharitableness, excommunication, calumny, opprobrious vituperation, are let loose to devastate and destroy.[27]

Some of the views set forth by Smyth in *The Sin and the Curse* echo those expressed by James Henley Thornwell, a celebrated Presbyterian clergyman from South Carolina who was acclaimed in his time as the "Calhoun of the Church." In a sermon preached at the dedication of the Anson Street mission church in May 1850, Thornwell expounded on the causes of the worsening sectional tensions in America, asserting that "The parties in this conflict are not merely Atheists, Socialists, Communists, Red Republicans, Jacobins on the one side, and the friends of order and regulated freedom on the other. In one word, the world is a battle-ground, Christianity and atheism the combatants, and the progress of humanity the stake."[28] The historian Eugene D. Genovese noted that many Southerners saw America's sectional conflict as a clash of cultures—essentially one of orthodox Christianity (in the South) against Northern liberals, "who professed Christianity while they did their best to destroy its central doctrines."[29]

This illustration from *Frank Leslie's Illustrated Newspaper* depicts a meeting at Institute Hall in Charleston "to discuss the question of secession" on November 12, 1860. Courtesy of the Library of Congress.

On December 17, 1860, South Carolina's Secession Convention met at First Baptist Church in Columbia and voted unanimously for secession before moving the convention to Charleston. On December 20 the delegates processed from St. Andrew's Hall on Broad Street, where they had composed the Ordinance of Secession, to Institute Hall, a vast venue on Meeting Street that was ideally suited for the signing and ratification of the document. The signing was witnessed by a standing-room-only crowd of officials and citizens. Young Augustine also was a witness to the proceedings and was eager to procure a souvenir. Thomas Smyth's biographer wrote, "Among the crowd in the galleries was Augustine Smyth, who, sliding down a pillar, possessed himself of a pen, blotter, and fragment of palmetto." All of these mementos later would be housed at the museum of the Daughters of the Confederacy in Charleston.[30]

Though Smyth regretted the dissolution of the Union, he believed that secession was necessary for the welfare and safety of the South. In a letter of December 24, 1860, written to a fellow clergyman, the Reverend David Magie, Smyth expressed the view, held by most South Carolinians, that the platform of the Republican Party was "sectional and destructive to any continued Union with the South," adding, "I have no sympathy with Secession *per se,* but be it death, it is better than degradation."[31]

During the secession crisis, Smyth received numerous letters from anxious friends and colleagues across the country. Some appealed to him to use his influence to oppose disunion and the resulting possibility of armed conflict. In a letter of December 21, 1860, M. W. Jacobus of the Allegheny Theological Seminary in Pennsylvania pleaded with him to speak out "in behalf of *Peace and Union.*" Later, on January 18, 1861, Jacobus urged Smyth to "counsel utmost moderation" and begged him not to "despair of our nation," adding, "You cleave to the Constitution. Why can we not live together under it as aforetime? Even *Mr. Seward* declares himself ready to go for an amendment prohibiting any *future* interference with slavery, where it exists."[32] Jacobus was referring to the Corwin Amendment, an amendment to the United States Constitution that was introduced in the House of Representatives by Representative Thomas Corwin of Ohio and eventually passed by a two-thirds majority of Congress. It proposed amending the Constitution to explicitly forbid any interference with the institution of slavery where it already existed and stated, "No amendment shall be made to the Constitution which will authorize or give Congress power to abolish or interfere, within any State, with the domestic institutions thereof, including that of persons held to labor or service by the laws of the State." The outgoing U.S. president, James Buchanan, supported the amendment, as did William H. Seward (who would become U.S. secretary of state). Abraham Lincoln, in his first inaugural address, commented that since the provision in the Corwin Amendment was already "implied by Constitutional law," he had "no objection to its being made express and irrevocable." After the amendment passed in Congress, the ratification process began in the state legislatures, and the Ohio General Assembly became the first to ratify it. Maryland was the next state to approve the amendment, but the advent of war brought an end to the ratification process.[33]

When war began, on April 12, 1861, Smyth wholeheartedly supported the newly formed Confederacy. Gilbert R. Brackett wrote that Smyth "espoused the cause of the South," because he believed he was contending for the principles of "civil liberty and free government."[34] Margaret Milligan Adger Smyth also supported the fledgling nation, and, like many Southern women, she devoted much of her time to war work in the Soldier's Relief Association.

As life in Charleston grew more dangerous, Smyth took his wife and other family members to Summerton, a pineland village located sixty miles inland in Clarendon District. There, Smyth preached in the area's Methodist churches, while his wife continued her work in the Soldiers' Relief Association. Following the war, the Smyths returned to Charleston, where they found their old home "in a sad state." Smyth's granddaughter Louisa Cheves Smythe Stoney recorded that "soon after the evacuation of Charleston, a surgeon in the Northern Army had taken residence and lived there for months, selling all the furniture he could before he took his departure."[35]

Smyth continued his ministry at Second Presbyterian Church until February 1870, when he was "stricken with paralysis of the vocal cords."[36] After a partial recovery, he returned to some duties, but by November of that year his declining health compelled him to write a letter of resignation to the church. In the spring of 1870 he also suffered a severe blow when a fire destroyed part of his library (about three thousand books). Smyth's health deteriorated further over the next few years, and although he continued to periodically take part in the life of the church, by the spring of 1873 he was confined to his home. He passed away on August 20, 1873. The *Charleston Evening Chronicle* reported of his funeral on August 22: "Impressive funeral services were held to-day, at 12 o'clock, in the Second Presbyterian Church, over the remains of the late Rev. Dr. Smyth, who was the beloved pastor of the Church for a period of over forty years. A large number of prominent citizens attended, and the sadness visible in the countenances of all present revealed how deeply was felt the loss of this noted clergyman and venerated pastor."[37]

Numerous letters and memorial notices written by colleagues and friends after his death offer ample evidence that Smyth was held in considerable esteem. His brother-in-law John B. Adger wrote the following tribute: "Dr. Smyth was truly a great man. He had his weaknesses, (and who has not?) but they were only specks. He was great intellectually, great morally, and great religiously. He had a clear, vigorous, active understanding; a warm, brave heart; a strong will; an eloquent tongue; his industry was untiring; his energy never flagged. . . . I have said that he was a great man religiously; I mean that he was an experienced and ripe believer, an old and long tried soldier of the Cross, who had passed through fire and water, both oftentimes, and been hurt by neither."[38] A number of additional eulogies published in a memorial to Smyth offer similar comments by fellow clergymen and include some truly affectionate remarks by his relations.[39]

Augustine Thomas Smythe was the product of his upbringing as the son of the Reverend Thomas Smyth. Like his father, Augustine was proud and ambitious, and these characteristics would shape his wartime attitudes and postwar accomplishments. Unlike the Reverend Smyth, however, Augustine seems to have shown no propensity to join the ministry.

Thomas and Margaret Smyth had six children who survived, and Augustine was the second oldest son. Their children's education was a priority for the couple, and Augustine Smythe attended Augustus S. Sachtleben's school for boys in Charleston before enrolling at South Carolina College in Columbia in 1860, as the sectional crisis was building to a crescendo. By January 1861, after South Carolina had seceded from the Union, Smythe was contemplating joining South Carolina College's Corps of Cadets. His decision to do so was a source of consternation for his family. His elder brother, J. Adger Smyth, who would later serve as mayor of Charleston, wrote to Augustine that he feared that once he had joined the unit, his younger brother would feel obligated to serve with the other cadets if the company enlisted for the war. Adger noted that he would prefer that his brother "go under the command of experienced officers, not of boys like yourself." His brother saw no problem with Augustine joining the corps of Cadets if he believed that he could leave the unit in the eventuality of actual service.[40]

Despite this letter and his family's concerns, Smythe joined the Corps of Cadets on January 25, 1861. The unit was mobilized for state service and traveled to Charleston prior to the firing on Fort Sumter. After arriving in Charleston, the company was stationed in Mount Pleasant, and it later moved to Sullivan's Island following the fort's surrender to Confederate forces. Soon thereafter Smythe returned with his unit to Columbia, where the cadets resumed their studies. The Corps of Cadets was recalled to duty once again in the fall of 1861 before being disbanded.[41]

Smythe returned home to Charleston, where he belatedly followed his brother's advice by enlisting in an established unit, the Washington Light Infantry, which became Company A of the 25th South Carolina Infantry on April 4, 1862. As a member of the Washington Light Infantry, he participated in the Battle of Secessionville on June 16, 1862. His account of that action, the first letter printed in this volume, demonstrates the extent to which he was affected by the brutality of combat. Though he would later decry his position as a signalman, his initial combat experience affected him deeply. In a letter to his mother he wrote, "Just back from such a scene of blood as I trust never again to behold." He concluded the letter by repeating, "such another scene I do not wish to witness."[42]

Four months later Smythe received a respite from his service as an infantryman. On October 20, 1862, he was detached from the Washington Light Infantry to serve in the Confederate Signal Corps. Five months later he was promoted to the rank of lance sergeant. His service as a signalman would afford him the opportunity to serve in various posts around Charleston Harbor while remaining close to his family's home at 12 Meeting Street. It did not, however, preclude him from taking part in other combat operations. In a letter dated February 5, 1863, Smythe related the story of the capture of the USS *Isaac P. Smith* and his role in the operation. The *Isaac P. Smith* was a Union gunboat that made regular forays up the Stono River, so Confederate lieutenant colonel Joseph A. Yates, devised a plan to ambush the ship on one of its trips. Yates organized a force of infantry, artillery, and four signalmen, including Smythe, and deployed his men and guns in hidden positions on James Island and Johns Island along the banks of the Stono River. Yates's plan was to wait for the Union ship to sail upriver and then open fire on it with the hope of sinking or capturing it. Just as planned, the *Isaac P. Smith* sailed upriver and anchored off the Grimball Plantation on James Island. Confederate artillery and rifle fire from both sides of the river battered the ship and killed a number of its crew members. With its engines disabled, the Union vessel surrendered to Yates and his men. This was supposedly the only time that a ship surrendered to land forces during the war. Of the action, Smythe later wrote, "It is a wonder that our loss was no greater, only one man, for we were totally unprotected on the bank, only 250 yds distant & and she was firing grape constantly."[43]

For a number of months thereafter, Smythe was stationed aboard the ironclad *Palmetto State,* which protected Charleston Harbor and supported Confederate forces at Fort Moultrie and Fort Sumter and on Morris Island. He then briefly served as a signalman at Fort Sumter at the height of the Union bombardment in 1863. Afterwards he was transferred to the steeple of St. Michael's Church, which afforded him the opportunity to serve even closer to home, while keeping a watch on other family property located nearby. In another remarkable posting, Smythe participated in a plan to use a captured Union balloon as an observation post. Though he was chosen to make the first ascent, the experiment proved impractical and concluded unsuccessfully.[44]

Although little known today, the Confederate Signal Corps played a vital role in the defense of Charleston, and it was the offshoot of a branch of the United States Army that had existed for less than a decade at the time of the bombardment of Fort Sumter. The father of the United States Army Signal Corps was Major Albert J. Myer, who, in the early 1850s, adopted a signaling system known as wig-wag signaling, or aerial telegraphy. In Myer's system, signalmen would use a flag (or, at night, a kerosene torch) as a means of communicating information between posts or of relaying information among detached elements of the army during operations. The system used a number of distinctive signs or symbols created by waving the flags, and these, individually or in combination with others, could communicate information to other signalmen.[45]

Myer's system was firmly ensconced in the Federal army at the beginning of the war, but the Confederate army's wartime use of signals can be traced to the First Battle of Bull Run (or Manassas), on July 21, 1861. Captain (later General) Edward P. Alexander had been Myer's assistant in the U.S. Army during the testing of the wig-wag signaling system, and he had resigned his U.S. Army commission on May 1, 1861, to join the Confederate army as a captain of engineers. At the time of Bull Run, he was the chief engineer and signal officer of the short-lived Confederate Army of the Potomac and oversaw Confederate signaling during the battle.[46]

On April 19, 1862, nine months after the Confederacy's first combat use of signals, the Confederate Congress authorized the establishment of the Confederate Signal Corps as an organization attached to the Adjutant and Inspector General's Department. In Special Orders No. 40, issued by the War Department on May 29, 1862, the organization was created. Captain (later Major) William Norris was placed in command of the organization. Five months later, the Confederate War Department provided for an excess of fifty signalmen to be assigned to signal stations in and around Charleston. The first commander of these signalmen was Captain Joseph Manigault, a Charlestonian, who worked to broaden the responsibilities of his small command. On November 6, 1862, he wrote a letter to the departmental chief of staff, Brigadier General Thomas Jordan, offering the Signal Corps in Charleston as "magnetic telegraph operators." This letter provides insight into Manigault's favorable opinion of the men under his command.

"The material of the Signal Corps . . . is of educated and reliable men" who were "thoroughly instructed in all the scientific methods for the early transmission of information." Manigault sought more than acknowledgment of the mental capabilities of his command. His aim was to offer his signalmen as a less expensive alternative to the civilian telegraph operators in use throughout the department. To make the offer more appealing, Manigault proposed his men as operators of torpedoes and electric lights around the harbor, since they were knowledgeable concerning galvanic batteries.[47]

The saltwater bathing house at White Point Garden served as the Confederate Signal Corps headquarters in Charleston. Courtesy of the South Carolina Historical Society.

The Confederate Signal Corps in Charleston was based in a bathing house that jutted into the Ashley River at White Point Garden. Deemed to be the geographic center of Confederate operations in Charleston, the bathing house was a logical location for Signal Corps operations. Signal stations fanned out from this location to fourteen points around the Confederate defenses. In addition, there were other Signal Corps postings. One was a lookout station in the steeple of St. Michael's Church. Another location, known as "Headquarters," was on the north end of Johns Island. There also was a lookout at Haulover Cut at the southern edge of Johns Island. The purpose of the Haulover Cut station was to intercept Union signals emanating from the Union army's signal station at Botany Bay, on Edisto Island, which was midway between Union forces on Morris Island and Hilton Head Island. Confederate signalmen would decipher these intercepted signals and forward them to the Confederate commander on Johns Island, who would forward them to headquarters in Charleston.[48]

For Confederate signalmen in Charleston, the most common means of conveying information was via a twelve-foot staff to which was attached a four-foot square flag, usually white with a red square, for use during hours of daylight. At night a copper-tube torch with a turpentine wick would be attached to the staff in place of a flag. Signals were produced by waving the flag (or torch) right or left in certain combinations, creating progressions of letters, numerals, and abbreviations that were known by members of the branch. Signals sent by either Confederate or Union signalmen could be viewed by signalmen at other stations, since each signal station was furnished with telescopes or spy glasses. For the purpose of scanning as much of the landscape as possible, signal stations usually were established in locations with an elevation of between fifty and one hundred feet. A number of signalmen would be on duty at each station, and a good signalman was expected to scan the nearest stations for potential signals every few minutes.[49]

Though Smythe would bemoan his wartime posting as a signalman to family members, it is difficult to overstate the value of the signal branch to the Confederate defense of Charleston. Captain Frank Markoe, who replaced Captain Joseph Manigault as signal officer in Charleston, wrote that the service sent thousands of messages during the siege, some of which had a significant impact on the outcome of the battle for the harbor. Markoe would later report that during July 1863, his signalmen on Morris Island had sent more than five hundred messages and that, perhaps more importantly, they had conveyed to Markoe the substance of the enemy's signals during the same period. Markoe reported, "I have read nearly every message the enemy has sent. Many of them of great importance. We were forewarned of their [Union] attack on the 18th, and were ready for them, with what success is already a part of history." Word leaked out, however, that the Confederates were deciphering the Union signals, and Markoe was forced to change the Confederate signals when his personnel discovered that Union commanders were asking their own signalmen to decipher the Confederate messages.[50]

The Confederates would continue to read the Union signals into September 1863. Markoe related, "On the night of the 5th, the enemy made an attack on Battery Gregg, which failed, and was repulsed by the timely notice from Sullivan's Island Signal Station . . . which read 'To Admiral Dahlgren—I shall try Cummins Point to-night and want the sailors again early.'" Three days later, an attack on Fort Sumter was foiled when Confederate signalmen intercepted a Union message that stated, "The senior officer will take charge of the assaulting party on Fort Sumter, the whole to be under the command of an experienced officer."[51]

Smythe's letters attest to his ability, and that of his comrades, to intercept and decipher the signals sent by the Union forces besieging Charleston. In April 1863 he wrote to his sister, divulging a military secret of considerable importance. In the letter he described his service at Fort Sumter at the height of the Union bombardment.

> As to what I did it is a great secret & one which I am hardly at liberty to divulge but I will tell you & trust to your discretion. Some little time back we captured some of their signal men & one of them divulged their system. This was of course sent to our officer & I was sent to Sumter to read the Yankee signals, which were being made from the fleet outside to the Ironclads inside the bay. This was successfully accomplished for every message which they sent & they were chiefly from the Ironsides was read by us & sent up to Head Qts. This should not be spoken of, of course, for if it was known by the Yankees they would immediately change & thus put us again at sea. So please say nothing of it.[52]

Even as late as 1864, Union signalmen continued to pass signals in a manner that was easily interpreted by their opponents. The Confederate signal station at Haulover Cut continued to intercept Union signals from Botany Bay until early February 1864, when Federal troops raided the southeastern corner of Johns Island and surprised the Confederate signalmen stationed there. As the Confederate signalmen retreated, they left a record book of all of the signals that they had intercepted from the Botany Bay station. Thereafter Union signalmen received orders to send all messages in cipher or code.[53] As a result of the Union's use of a new cipher and its capture of Savannah, Smythe traveled to the Savannah River in December 1864 in a vain attempt to establish signal stations between Savannah and Hardeeville. On December 19, 1864, he wrote,

> After spending four or five days tramping along the Savannah River, here I am back again in old No. 12 safe & hearty. Our objective going was to establish a line of signals from Hardeeville to Savannah, but it was impossible to be done. The Islands . . . were & are in the hands of the enemy, & of course not to be used for signal posts, while all the headlands along the bank which would have answered for that purpose are in such close proximity to the enemy that if we raised our flag there, they could run over in the night & take us without the least trouble, there only being at those points picquets of two or three men.[54]

Smythe's service as a signalman in and around the city of his birth was the result of Union attempts to capture Charleston, which the North viewed as the symbolic birthplace of secession and the site of the war's first shots. The capture of Charleston, therefore, was an important Union military objective for symbolic reasons. It would remain a theater of military operations from 1861 until the withdrawal of Confederate troops from the city on February 17, 1865. Land operations to capture the city began in 1862, when Union forces unsuccessfully attempted to seize the city by first capturing James Island. The largest engagement during the Union push was the Battle of Secessionville on June 16, 1862, in which Smythe was a participant. The following year, Union military operations around Charleston Harbor intensified when a Union brigadier general Quincy A. Gillmore, assumed operational control of the Department of the South and began a campaign with the goals of destroying Fort Sumter, gaining access to the entrance of Charleston Harbor, and allowing the Union fleet to steam in and capture the city.[55] The success of Gillmore's plan relied on Union forces first capturing Morris Island, and the struggle for Battery Wagner, the primary Confederate fortification on the island, would become the most intense and significant land operation during the siege of Charleston.[56]

When Union forces could not quickly capture Battery Wagner, they battered Fort Sumter with guns located in the middle of Morris Island.[57] At the same time, Union engineers constructed a battery, christened the "Swamp Angel," in the marsh between Morris Island and the Confederate earthworks on James Island.[58] Within this emplacement they positioned an eight-inch, rifled Parrott gun that was capable of bombarding Charleston. With the Swamp Angel in place, on August 21, 1863, Gillmore sent a letter to Charleston addressed to General P. G. T. Beauregard, the Confederate commander of the Department of South Carolina, Georgia, and Florida. Gillmore demanded the "immediate evacuation of Morris Island and Fort Sumter." If his demand was refused, Union forces would "open fire on city of Charleston from batteries already established within easy and effective range of the heart of the city."[59] On August 22, 1863, the Swamp Angel began the bombardment of Charleston. Beauregard would refuse to surrender any Confederate fortifications or the city. The bombardment of Charleston would continue most of the time until Union forces finally captured the city on February 17, 1865. The siege of Charleston therefore constitutes the longest siege of the Civil War.[60]

Federal artillery firing on Charleston from Fort Putnam (formerly Battery Gregg) on Morris Island. From the editor's collection.

On April 20, 1864, Major General Samuel Jones succeeded Beauregard as commander of the department and Charleston's defenses. Hoping to deter the continued shelling of Charleston's residential and business areas, Jones made the decision to quarter fifty captive Union officers in a house located at the west end of Broad Street. The house's owner, Michael P. O'Connor, was a prominent Charleston attorney whose home had survived the Great Fire of December 11–12, 1861. After the fire, he had moved his family to Columbia. When Gillmore's successor, Major General John G. Foster, learned there were Union prisoners in the city, he continued the bombardment and requested that an equal number of Confederate officers be placed in a prison on Morris Island, where they would be exposed to the fire of the Confederate batteries and forts.[61]

The captured Union officers quartered in the O'Connor house would be Smythe's neighbors for a brief period. Five of them were generals, and when they heard of Foster's intentions they sent him a letter on July 1, 1864, informing him that they were being treated well and urging him to treat the Confederate officers humanely. In it they assured Foster that they were "as pleasantly and comfortably situated as is possible for prisoners of war, receiving from the Confederate authorities every privilege that we could desire or expect, nor are we unnecessarily exposed to fire." The generals who signed the letter were Henry Walton Wessells, Truman Seymour, Eliakim Parker Scammon, Charles Adam Heckman, and Alexander Shaler.[62]

On June 27, 1864, Smythe wrote to his mother about these new neighbors:

> The Yankee prisoners are in Mr. Conner's house at the corner of Broad & Rutledge Sts. It is a splendid house & a delightful situation. They have a large yard & empty lot to walk in & the other day the Govt. sent round & had gas fixtures put up so that they might have light all at the expense of the Confederacy. They are on their parole not to leave the premises but there is also a guard stationed round them. Great many people go round to see them. They are quite a good looking set, & very well dressed. Have plenty of money which they spend for coffee & sugar etc. It seems a shame to treat them so well. As we have now got the credit of putting them in shell range, we ought to do so & not leave them out there where a shell does not drop once in two months. They seem perfectly well contented with their situation & well they may be for they are much better off than in camp.[63]

A few days later, on July 1, Smythe reported to his sister regarding the prisoners:

> The Yankees have made no reduction of their fire on account of the prisoners in the city, but in retaliation have sent to the North for an equal number of our men, of similar rank, who are to be

> placed on Morris Island. I doubt if they will be as comfortable as these are. We have them in a fine large house, at the foot of Broad St. with a large open yard for exercise. Yesterday as I passed they were all engaged in a game of cricket & seemed to be enjoying it exceedingly. . . . There is nothing very hard in their lot, as they are now situated.[64]

The Union officers did not remain in Charleston. In response to General Foster's request, fifty Confederate officers were sent to South Carolina from Fort Delaware, but an agreement of exchange was reached, and both groups of prisoners were freed within a matter of weeks.[65] Later in the summer of 1864, when General Jones was ordered to accept and incarcerate hundreds of Union prisoners of war in Charleston, General Foster placed nearly six hundred Confederate POWs on Morris Island, and Smythe observed them in their stockade prison through his telescope.

The continued bombardment of the lower portions of Charleston created a nearly deserted impact zone. Those who remained in the area included the Confederate provost and other military units stationed at the Guard House at the junction of Broad and Meeting Streets, a very small population of white and black Charlestonians, and roaming bands of thieves who pillaged abandoned homes.

Augustine Smythe would reside in this impact zone during most of his wartime service. From his parent's home at 12 Meeting Street, it was a short walk to the headquarters of the Confederate Signal Corps at the bathing house along the Ashley River. It also was a short walk past his uncle's home at 36 Meeting Street to his duty station at St. Michael's Church. As the war progressed he spent an ever-increasing amount of time attempting to make his uncle's home secure from prowlers, particularly Confederate soldiers who stalked the city south of Broad Street collecting house fixtures made of copper and other metals, which were sold to the Ordnance Bureau for the war effort. In mid-April 1864 Smythe wrote:

> I have had No. 36 nailed up to prevent any further incursions of the Soldiers. They just roam at will now thro' the whole of the lower portion of the City. Our house & Mr. Middleton's are the only two in Meeting St. below Broad which have not been entered. . . . The Soldiers the other day to spite me, pulled down all the Wisteria from the brick wall but I have fixed it up nicely again & trained it into both trees. . . . Our Stores on the wharf have <u>not</u> been seriously injured, but the soldiers have been in there

also. They have done three times the damage to the City that the shells have.[66]

By January 1865 order in the city's lower portion had broken down almost completely. Smythe wrote:

> Robbers plentiful as usual & despite all my endeavors, No. 36 has suffered severely. As fast as I would put up the fence or nail the windows, they would break them down. All the lead, etc. has now been taken out, & worse than that three of the mirrors. I found it out the next day & then they had one of the large ones from over the fire places, down by the window ready to carry off that night. . . . It is useless almost to attempt to stop those fellows. They live all around & as soon as night comes, they knock down the fence, cut open a window & go to work. No law down in this part of town now. Assaults every night or so. The other night they robbed a man here just at our door & another night pulled our courier off his horse, robbed him & then put him on again & sent him off. It is horrible, the lawless state now of all Charleston formerly so orderly.[67]

Smythe's letters demonstrate his obvious frustration regarding the destruction wrought by thieves and scavengers upon the homes of family and friends. Similarly, he would comment in an almost fatalistic and melancholy way on the devastation wrought by the Federal bombardment. His letters to family members contained a constant stream of news about houses or buildings that had been hit by Union shells. He also wrote frequently about the bombardment's human toll. In a letter dated November 20, 1863, he reported on the first casualty from the Union bombardment. "So far," he wrote, "I have heard of but one man killed." A few days later, on November 25, he wrote, possibly correcting the gender of the victim, "One negro woman has been the only casualty so far." In early December 1863 Smythe reported the deaths of two women and a man ("one man on East Bay").[68]

Official reports counted five deaths and eight persons wounded in the city as a result of the Union shelling as of January 6, 1864. The same report noted that the effect of the bombardment on military operations in the city had been "comparatively unimportant."[69] After January 1864 Confederate authorities ceased to count casualties resulting from the bombardment, as they shifted their focus to events outside Charleston.[70]

Casualties from the bombardment would continue to mount, however, as noted in newspaper accounts and in Smythe's letters. On August 4, 1864, he wrote of more civilian injuries from the shelling, and on September 2, 1864, he reported that "a colored man" was killed near the Citadel Green (now Marion Square) by a shell fragment, adding, "Casualties now are of daily occurrence, sometimes two or three per day." In late September he described how members of the Carr family narrowly missed being killed by a shell when one burst in their parlor. He also related that a man named Burgess was killed when a shell fell on his house. On September 28 he wrote: "Have been down stairs to get the Sergeant of Police to carry a letter up for me to the Office which Locke, my chum, forgot to mail this afternoon. He tells me that a shell went into Mr. Burckmyer's house in Charlotte St. this afternoon & wounded more or less severely all his family, five in number."[71]

While experiencing the death and destruction that accompanied his wartime service, Smythe became engaged to the young woman he would eventually marry. Louisa Rebecca McCord Smythe ("Miss Lou") first met Smythe while he was a student at South Carolina College in Columbia before the war. As Smythe was the product of a family of intellectual endeavors, so too was his future wife. Miss Lou was the daughter of Louisa Susanna Cheves McCord, who was a significant intellectual and writer during her time. Before the war she authored numerous essays on political economy and social issues. Her other writings included poetry, reviews, and a blank-verse drama titled *Caius Gracchus*. She also translated a book written by Frederic Bastiat, a French political economist, which was published in 1848 as *Sophisms of the Protective Policy*.[72]

Miss Lou's mother ceased most of her literary activities when war began in 1861. For the conflict's duration she focused her energies on the family's support of the Confederate army, and she became well known in South Carolina for her work on behalf of soldiers. She not only nursed the wounded in the military hospital in Columbia but also was devoted to feeding and clothing Confederate soldiers in the city and served as president of both the Soldiers' Relief Association and the Ladies' Clothing Association. The McCord house in Columbia, where Miss Lou resided with her sister and mother (her father, David J. McCord, had died in 1855), was adjacent to the campus of the South Carolina College, where the main Confederate hospital was located. In time, part of the home became a hospital ward. It also served as a dining hall that provided food daily for the ambulatory patients. The McCord plantation, Lang Syne, provided cotton and food crops for the Confederacy, and Mrs. McCord personally funded the uniforms and equipment for the company of soldiers that her son, Langdon Cheves McCord, led as a captain. This son died in 1863 as a result of wounds received at the Battle of Second Bull Run (Second Manassas), leaving behind a young widow, Charlotte (Lottie) Reynolds McCord, who gave birth to their only child less than two weeks after his death.[73] Mrs. McCord, however, carried on in her labors despite this devastating loss and took comfort in her new grandchild, a daughter that they named Langdon Cheves McCord. In her memoirs, Miss Lou recalled that "Through these days our one delight was the baby, little Chev."[74]

Louisa Rebecca McCord, who married Augustine T. Smythe in 1865.
Courtesy of the South Carolina Historical Society.

Miss Lou's memoirs, written for the benefit of her children in the 1890s, provide some details about her courtship and engagement to Smythe in 1864:

> About this time your father came to Columbia for a day—as usual in high spirits and full, as we used to say, of "his foolishness." We still had carriages and horses and I remember we were all sent up town for a drive to take a watch of Aunt Susan's—then only a mysterious Miss Adger to me—to the jewelers to be mended—or rather we were to get the watch from the jeweler's. We took the drive and got the watch and "Mr. Smythe" came home to tea, and we had a right merry evening. After he had gone we were sitting, girl-fashion, around the fire in my room chatting, when Lottie,

> looking so sweet and lovely in her widow's dress, said to me, "some of these days he is just going to blurt out, 'Miss Lou, will you marry me' and you will get up and go." I was struck dumb with astonishment, never having yet looked on myself in a marrying light. . . .
>
> A few days after Mama got a letter, with another inside for me—such were the good old fashions—which was to be delivered in case she approved. The letter asked me to marry him and said that he would come back in a couple of days for his answer. . . . I was a very girlish girl compared to the girls nowadays, and I was simply terrified and as I remember, went about the house like a ghost—neither eating nor sleeping.[75]

Louisa asked for more time—two weeks—to consider Smythe's proposal, and at the end of that period, when asked again, she said yes. In February 1864 Smythe wrote to his mother and other family members to inform them that he had become engaged to Lou McCord. In a reply of February 10, 1864, his younger sister Sarah began by offering congratulations and expressing eager curiosity about his fiancée, but she also informed him that she and their mother had serious reservations about his decision. Relating part of a conversation with her mother, Sarah wrote, "She & I had a long talk last night & both came to the conclusion that you were entirely too young to know your own mind. You just out of the nursery. It is absurd."[76]

After receiving a letter from Smythe, his aunt Jane Adger replied that the news of his engagement had taken her "completely by surprise," and she too expressed doubts, wondering whether he had chosen a suitable young woman.

> I had not the slightest idea that such a thing was going on. I knew you admired the young lady & thought much of her Mother but I was all taken aback when I read "you were engaged" to her. My dear Boy I can only say God bless you & make her a blessing to you a help asset indeed to you, a companion worthy of you, a comforter & a consoler in all times of trial, a participator in all your joys as well as your sorrows. I do not know the young lady therefore can give no opinion of her. . . . My dear Augustine this is a step which will either <u>add</u> to your happiness, or take much from it. You say you have loved her two years, therefore you have not acted hastily as regards length of acquaintance, but Augustine have

> you thought of everything. She is accomplished & all that, but is she a Christian. Is she one calculated to walk His path with you. Is she a humble follower of the Lord, one of God's chosen ones. Will she help you in this way? Or is she a gay fashionable worldling. If she is the latter, she will not be happy in our family circle.[77]

The aunt praised Miss Lou's mother but also characterized her as "eccentric," and Smythe's letter to his mother, dated February 17, 1864, reveals that Mrs. Smyth also held some mistaken ideas about Mrs. McCord, which he was prompt to correct. "I think you have been misinformed about Mrs. McCord," he wrote to her, assuring his mother that his prospective mother-in-law did not have a "domineering character" and adding, "She is much more of a woman than people give her credit for. . . . From my own observation & knowledge of her I have formed a very different & at the same time a very high opinion of her character as a woman. She is well read, but also seems to be a great housekeeper. She is kind, very kind, to all who claim kindness of her & the sick & wounded soldier is ever cared for kindly."[78]

Shortly after Miss Lou's engagement to Augustine in February 1864, she made a trip to Summerton to meet his family, who were living in what she described as "a little cabin in the pineland settlement." She already was acquainted with his young brother Joseph Ellison and some of his aunts, who had visited her in Columbia, but, as she recalled in her memoir, "all the rest were new to me." Lou was nervous about meeting Augustine's parents, but, after what she called "the first shock," she enjoyed her visit and was deeply impressed by Mrs. Smyth, "a very remarkable woman" who treated her with kindness and generosity. Lou described her as "a tall, handsome, dignified woman with a manner that gave at first a slight suggestion of fear, but she could also inspire the deepest love and respect."[79]

Their engagement would last for the remainder of the war and would coincide with the uncertainty and fear that accompanied Sherman's march through South Carolina and the collapse of Confederate resistance within the state. Smythe's letters to his family were replete with the rumors, miscalculations, and deluded hopes that plagued South Carolinians following the Union capture of Savannah in December 1864. When his mother inquired about items that the family had stored in Columbia, Smythe wrote, "As for Columbia I should not attempt to move anything. That place will be defended at all hazards, even Charleston will be given up to hold it & I don't see how you can move the things nor where. No one there to attend to it. . . . About this place I don't know what to think. . . . I have heard several times from other sources that Lee's army will be sent here & Richmond left rather than allow Sherman to devastate this State as he has done Georgia. So I am hoping for the best." Days later, Smythe again commented that Charleston, not Richmond, would be the focus of the Confederacy's military efforts in the future. He noted, "Gentlemen from Richmond tell me that the talk there is to give up Richmond to save Charleston & such is I suppose the case."

In Smythe's last letter of this volume, dated February 13, 1865, he presented his sister with the military disaster in South Carolina as Confederate troops prepared to abandon Charleston and Columbia. His fiancée, Miss Lou, and her family chose to stay in Columbia, though there was little hope that Sherman's inexorable march would stop short of the city. Miss Lou became anxious about her fiancée, since the mail service was broken between Charleston and Columbia as Union troops approached the state's capital. The McCord family made preparations for Sherman's onslaught, hiding provisions, burying the family silver, and creating a kind of "fortification" in the house by removing the steps of the back piazza and boarding up its entrance so that there was no easy access to the upper-floor bedrooms.[80]

When Federal forces descended on Columbia, General Oliver O. Howard, General William T. Sherman's second in command, used the McCord house as his headquarters during the occupation of the city. Just before Howard arrived, a crowd of Federal soldiers began ransacking and pillaging the place. One of them seized Mrs. McCord by the throat and tore a watch from her dress. When General Howard arrived, the soldiers were still at work, and he saw his men looting and later caught them attempting to set fire to the house.

That morning, before Howard's arrival, Mrs. McCord had received a note advising her to leave the city. She wrote of it:

> One of my maids brought me a paper, left, she told me, by a Yankee soldier; it was an ill-spelled but kindly warning of the horrors to come, written upon a torn sheet of my dead son's note book, which, with private papers of every kind now strewed my yard. . . . The writer, a lieutenant of the army of invasion, said he had relatives and friends at the South, and that he felt for us; that his heart bled to think of what was threatened. "Ladies," he wrote, "I pity you; leave this town—go anywhere to be safer than here." This was written in the morning; the fires were in the evening and night.[81]

Miss Lou gave further details about her family's experiences during the burning of Columbia in letters to Augustine and his sister Susan. In one of them, she marveled at how the Federal officers tried to pretend that the burning of Columbia had been accidental.

> Oh the hypocrisy of those Yankees! It was wonderful to see how the officers tried to make us think the fire accidental as if we had no eyes & ears to find out for ourselves. I could scarcely keep my countenance. When a piece of cotton was found burning in our entry, the General Howard commenced speaking of the dreadful wind & the strange way in which cotton had been blowing about all day. He tried his hand too to humbug us about the shelling.[82]

She was referring to a conversation that had taken place between General Howard and her mother when a wad of burning cotton was found inside an enclosed back entry of the house. He had commented at the time that it was very remarkable how the cotton kept "blowing about." Mrs. McCord answered him sardonically, "Yes, General, very remarkable, through closed doors."[83]

On several occasions that day, General Howard prevented his own soldiers from burning down the house, and because of his presence the McCord residence was not destroyed and still exists today as a historic property in Columbia. Most of the McCord family papers, however, did not survive. The guards who were left at the McCord house by General Howard to protect it after his departure instead looted the place and destroyed family documents as well as most of the library. Mrs. McCord's house at Lang Syne Plantation also was pillaged.[84]

Although neither Smythe nor his fiancée knew for certain of the other's fate, both survived the war's final months. Smythe moved north from Charleston when Confederate forces abandoned the city. He joined the 5th South Carolina Cavalry and participated in the battles in North Carolina that would precipitate the surrender of Confederate forces under General Joseph E. Johnston. Smythe returned to South Carolina, and on June 27, 1865, more than two months after the conclusion of hostilities, he married Louisa Rebecca McCord. Mrs. McCord conveyed Lang Syne Plantation (later the home of Julia Peterkin, South Carolina's only Pulitzer Prize–winning author) and nearby Goshen Plantation to the young couple for the sum of five dollars. Smythe traveled to Fort Motte, the location of the plantation, and found a Union gunboat nearby on the Congaree River.

He took the oath of allegiance to the Union and thereafter claimed Lang Syne and the rest of his nearby property.[85] Smythe's efforts at planting were unsuccessful, however, and after a year he returned to Charleston with his wife. There he successfully pursued the youthful ambitions of which he had written in his wartime correspondence.[86]

For several years after the war, his mother-in-law, Mrs. McCord, lived with various relations, and in 1871 she left South Carolina to reside in Canada. In 1873 she made a deposition for the commission investigating and adjudicating claims for war damages incurred by British and American citizens and gave her account of the burning of Columbia. In 1876 she returned to Charleston to live with her daughter Louisa and Smythe. She died three years later, on November 23, 1879, in Charleston and was buried in Magnolia Cemetery.[87]

Upon returning to Charleston, Smythe studied law under Charles Henry Simonton. He was admitted to the bar on November 28, 1866, and began a successful law practice in Charleston, during which he partnered with a number of local attorneys. His ambitions and his business ventures, however, took him to the state's northwestern counties. He acquired Woodburn farm near Pendleton and invested heavily in nearby cotton mills and businesses. He served as director of a number of companies, including the Southern Cotton Harvesting Company (1883), Charleston Bagging Manufacturing Company (ca. 1884–1893), Pelzer Manufacturing Company (1885), Cylinder Gin Company of Charleston (1887), Mason Cotton Harvester Company (ca. 1888–1891), Coosa Company (1892), and Anderson Phosphate and Oil Company (1901).[88]

His postwar achievements were not limited to business. In keeping with his childhood interest in politics, Smythe was elected to the State Senate, where he represented Charleston County as a conservative Democrat from 1880 to 1894. As a senator he served on or chaired a number of committees responsible for a wide variety of functions, including charitable institutions, railroads, and internal improvements. He resigned his seat in May 1894 to concentrate on his business ventures. He also served as trustee of several colleges and universities, including Converse College, the University of South Carolina, South Carolina College, and Clemson College.[89]

In keeping with the prominent position that he had assumed in his home city, Smythe was an active participant in Charleston's fraternal and social organizations. He was a Freemason and served in leadership positions in a number of orders and lodges. In addition, he was an officer in some of Charleston's oldest organizations, including the Hibernian Society, the

Carolina Yacht Club, the St. Cecilia Society, the South Carolina Society, the Charleston Ancient Artillery Society, and the South Carolina Historical Society. He also was a deacon and ruling elder of Second Presbyterian Church, where his father had served for so many years as pastor.[90] Smythe was not alone in accepting leadership positions in prominent organizations. In 1896 his wife, Louisa McCord Smythe, became the organizing president of the South Carolina Division of the United Daughters of the Confederacy. She would later rise to the position of president general of that organization, thus working to preserve the legacy of her husband and others who had served and sacrificed in an attempt to breathe life into a cause, a new government, and a new nation that ultimately would fail.[91]

CHAPTER I

A Taste of War and New Duties
1862–May 1863

Augustine T. Smythe to Margaret M. Smyth

Monday Eve
[June 1862]

Dear Mother,

Just back from such a scene of blood as I trust never again to behold.[1] Poor Taverner[2] & Fleet Lanneau[3] both dead! This morning I had just awoke late to reveille & was hurrying to dress when I heard the bugle sound the assembly & rushing out found that we were ordered off immediately. We were soon under way beating Hagood's regt. by about 100 yrds thus securing the post of honor. We marched on most of the way at "double-quick" stirred up & excited by the shells bursting thick over Secessionville. We hastened up to a hedge about ¼ of a mile from the village & the order was immediately given to us to stoop! Scarcely had we so done when a volley of balls swept over our heads killing five in Co. B & wounding 7 also wounding some 4 or 5 others in the regt. I never felt so ticklish in my life but, thank God I am safe & so is the whole of our company. This is almost a miracle for the balls fell among us & just beyond us by a few feet. The worst of it all was that the Yankees were right in front of us not far off & yet our officers thinking they were friends ordered us not to fire. This was obeyed by most of us but some of the company fired & killed 7 or 8. Two of our men were in their places when the bush in front parted & out came two men one of them asked who he was. He answered, "Friend, dont shoot for God's sake!" "Where from?" "Rhode Isl." They immediately raised their guns & fired killing one & wounding the other. Immediately after the discharge they retreated & commenced to shell us but tho' these fell all around us we did not mind them for we had seen shell before. After a while when all our wounded &

dead had been removed they detailed a squad of ten (10) men to go on the field & get arms. I was one & such another scene I do not wish to witness. In grt haste

Good bye,
Augustine

The Battle of Secessionville, which Augustine T. Smythe described as "a scene of blood," on James Island. From the editor's collection.

Augustine T. Smythe to Jane A. Adger

Tuesday morn
17 June 1862

Dear Aunt Janey,[4]

We have been in our first fight & have met the Yankees at last &, thank God! we are not only safe for the most part but have driven back the enemy with great slaughter. I was awakened yesterday morning at daybreak by the sound of the bugle calling us to "fall-in" & hurrying out found that we were to march off immediately to meet the advancing Yankees. We quickly fell into line & started off hurried on by our own excited feelings & by the sight of the shell bursting round Secessionville. We marched out "quick" for some time but as we neared the battle ground we could stand it no longer but giving a shout marched on at "double-quick." As we passed Hagood's encampment we found them drawn up & ready to march but quickening our pace a little we got ahead of them & thus secured the post of honor. As we were within a mile of Secessionville we turned off from the road & running across a long field, then thro' a creek, then thro' another field in which the shells were falling & bursting we marched our position behind a hedge where the order was given immediately to lie down. Scarcely were the words uttered & the men down when volley after volley of bullets flew around us cutting off the branches in front of us & falling behind us & in front of us. It was a trying moment for we none of us knew but that the next bullet would finish us, yet the men behaved with the greatest coolness fixing their bayonets & getting ready for the charge. Now occurred the mistake which sacrificed Co. B. We heard & could see men moving on the other side of the hedge but just as we were about to fire an order came from Col. Haygood [*sic*] that it was his men, not to fire. This was repeated by our officers & believing them friends we held back. This delusion was increased by the Yankee officers on the other side continually crying out "Dont fire we are friends, you will kill our own men, &c." Whether this was a mistake or a trick is not known. Soon, however we found that they were firing at us & shortly the trees opened & four or five came right upon us. One man singing out "Who are you?" "Friends! for God sake dont shoot?" "Where from?" "Rhode Island." Hardly had the words been uttered where they fell pierced with balls. Just then the firing ceased for a moment which the Lieut. in command of Co. B came to Col. S. who was standing behind us & with tears in his eyes informed him that his men were cut to pieces & asked leave to remove them. Our company immediately offered to spread out & protect their line while they removed their dead & wounded. Oh! the anxiety of that moment! not knowing which one of our friends was alive or dead! Soon there came a whisper along the line; "Serg. Lanneau is killed, Lieut Greer,[5] & Taverner." There was no outcry but you could see by the compressed lip that if the Yankees gave us another chance they would pay for their folly. Then came the sad spectacle of seeing the dead & wounded removed & the heartrending sight nerved many a man to greater strength. The Yankees now opened on us again with shot & shell which fell & burst over & around us but killing only one man. Soon all was in a measure quiet & then a squad was detailed to go out upon the field and gather up arms, look after the wounded & with this detachment I was sent & such a scene I wish never again to witness. Twenty or thirty men lay stretched out on a small field, wounded, dying & dead. One man must have been in the act of loading his gun when a grape shot took out the whole small of his back for he lay dead with his hands raised just as if he was even there loading. Another one lay close by with his leg entirely shot away & only a piece of skin connecting his knee & his thigh. Many were in the water dead, in a small creek between them & Secessionville. One poor fellow wounded in the back & throat lay in the water close to the bank but unable to get out, while tide was up to his shoulders & continually rising. We helped him up, gave him water & left him on the field for the litters to carry off. We gathered upwards of 60 guns, five Enfield & Minie Rifles, on our side of the marsh, many of which had been thrown down by the Yankees in their flight. Haversacks, canteens & cartridge boxes were also found in great numbers "considering" that they only received the fire of a company & a half. These we brought in & they are now stowed away in the tent beside me. On the other side of the marsh where Lamar's battery could play upon them, the slaughter was of course immensely greater. After bringing in the arms we were again sent out with litters to bring in the wounded & we had to carry them nearly two miles to the ambulance. It was heavy work & occupied us until late in the afternoon when we were relieved. We started without breakfast & only had a floating battery & piece of bacon to go on all day. When I came home, I had to help Uncle Joe[6] arrange the Yankee guns & then before I got supper I went about a mile to the wharf to see Taverner but after waiting two or three hours had to return without seeing him. I sent him home to Mother to nurse with Uncle Joe's approval & therefore slept very well last night & ate a very good breakfast this morning. Call for letters. Good bye.

Love to Aunty, Sis & all in haste
Augustine

Augustine T. Smythe, Camp Pettigrew,
James Island, S.C., to Louisa S. McCord, Columbia, S.C.

19 June 1862

Dear Madam,

I am almost ashamed to write you again after leaving your last kind letter so long unanswered, but not only the old saying, "Better late than never" urges me to go on but also because I have for the last three weeks or month been so busy that, tho' I have often thought of you & intended writing, this is the first good chance I have had. While at Goat Island[7] we had little or nothing to do & tho' at Secessionville they were a little harder on us, still it was not until our arrival here that we knew fully what pleasant times we had been having. We have had nothing but marching & picquetting, sometimes running off at false alarms & then really going after the enemy. We have been under shell several times & have now got so used to it that we can stand without dodging even. For two or three weeks past we have not slept, on an average more than two nights a week in our tents & yesterday was the second day only since we came to this place that we have been quiet in camp & drilled regularly. I have got so accustomed at last to sleeping in the woods that really I can get as good a night's rest there as in my tent. On Monday however, we had a march to some purpose for we really met & drove back the Yankees. We were around early in the morning & double-quicked to the place of action, where our position was assigned us behind a hedge with the Yankees on the other side. Scarcely had we got into our places & the order given & obeyed to crouch down when a volley of balls past over our heads & continued for nearly three quarters of an hour, & which killed four & wounded seven or eight in our company alone, besides knocking up the dust around the rest of us. I could see several fall & bury themselves not six inches from me in the ground. The worst of it was that Hagood thinking Stevens'[8] men were in front ordered us not to fire & it was not until some of the Yankees had come thro' the hedge that we discovered our mistake & fired a volley killing & wounding some twenty or thirty. The Yankees now commenced their favorite work of shelling us but tho' they burst above & around & round us, they killed only one man. The enemy, a N.H. regt., soon retreated leaving us in possession of the field & of nearly 100 arms. The loss on the other side of the marsh, at Secessionville was much greater. There nearly three hundred, dead, wounded & prisoners were found, several among them officers. The men were nearly all intoxicated with whiskey given them the night before & had fifty or sixty rounds of cartridges in their boxes expecting to march on to Charleston the same day. Yesterday a flag of truce was sent over asking for the dead or if they had been buried for the number of them.

It is nearly breakfast & drill time however & I must close. Please excuse this shabby note but you know the inconveniences of camp life. I thank you much for the kind offer which you made me in the young ladies' name & if I am in want of anything I shall not scruple to ask for it. Please give my kindest regards to Miss Hannah[9] & Miss Lou & assure them that I have not forgotten them. Did they not promise to Mr. Houstoun[10] & myself, some geranium leaves after our first fight? I think so.

With the highest respect I remain sincerely your young friend
Augustine T. Smythe

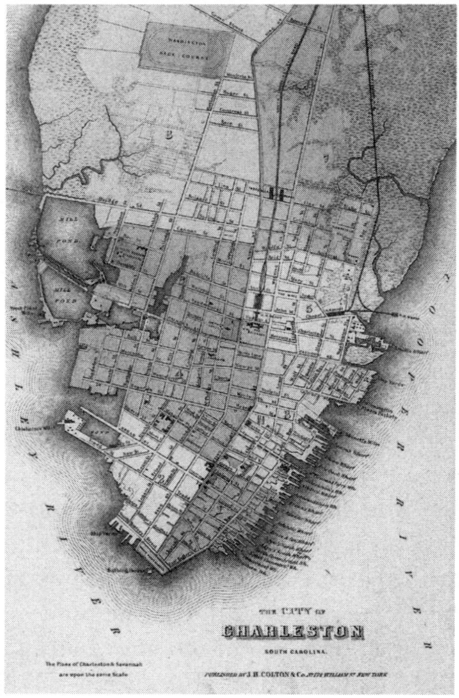

An 1855 Colton map of Charleston showing the location of the bathing house at the tip of the peninsula. From the editor's collection.

Special Orders, Head Quarters Eutaw (25th) Regt. SCV, Camp Stono, James Island, S.C., to Augustine T. Smythe

Oct 22nd 1862

Special Order No 79

In Pursuance to Special Orders No. 199 Paragraph VIII from Hd Qrs Dept So. Ca & Ga the following named Privates are hereby detailed on extra duty in the Signal Dept & will report to Capt Joseph Manigault[11] in the city

RE Pennall Co A, WLI., 25 SCV[12]
A T Smythe " " " "

By order
Lt Col Pressley[13]
GH Moffett[14] Comdg
Adjt 25th

Augustine T. Smythe, Charleston, S.C., to Jane A. Adger

Saturday night
1 Nov. 1862

Dear Aunt Janey

I have just finished some copying for Father & while Mother writes to Uncle R.[15]. . . I shall occupy my time in writing you a few lines merely to inform you that I am still in the land of the living & that I have not entirely forgotten you. . . . I have been up now for over a week & so far I am much pleased with the exchange. I have not yet been assigned to any station but trust to be kept at the Bathing House.[16] My business hours now are from 9 A.M. to 1½ P.M. & from 4 to 6 P.M. The manual labor is quite hard as the flag & staff are pretty heavy but then there is not very much of it & besides there is more interest in it than drilling. As to the accomadations [*sic*], they are <u>much</u> better than in camp as we all stay in houses except those stationed on James Island & they have a large tent. On Sullivans Island we now occupy Mrs. Glover's house[17] (Dr. Gilman's) but expect probably to move into Mrs. Ross' shortly as the other one is to be pulled down, it being in the way of a battery on the beach. All of the houses from there nearly up to the Church have been torn down & batteries erected on their sites. These are very heavy, their armament consisting of ten, ten inch Columbiads, of which seven are mounted & the other three are lying there ready to be placed on their carriages. There is also a new & very heavy battery, from the Moultrie House extending along the beach & bearing directly on Maffit's Channel, consisting for the most part of heavy Columbiads. In Ft. Moultrie we have fourteen eight-inch Columbiads mounted & in Ft. Sumter there is scarcely a casement without its gun. We have also quite a heavy fortification on Morris Island & and new & strong one at the mouth of Wappoo[18] called Ft. Waddy. The gun boats too, are finished at last so that, in my opinion, we are pretty strongly fortified & Charleston is not to be taken by the Yankees easily, if at all. The impression here now is that the attack will not be made until the spring time & perhaps not at all, to which latter opinion I hold. The guns have nearly all been taken from the Battery & sent to other parts as Beauregard[19] says that he does not expect to use it to fight from. He told Col. Keitt[20] however, so Col. K. says, that he intended to fight Charleston, street by street & not to surrender it. This came straight from Keitt & may be so. The reports of intervention & recognitions are again becoming rife here & many believe that the Govt. is in possession of certain intelligence on that score. The Govt. it is said will issue no more bills but make those now in circulation answer. This looks like peace in prospect. I was up to your house this morning in the garden & great house. Everything looked well especially the young geraniums. . . . But it is 10'c & I must stop. Love to Sue & Auntie & to Sarah R.

Your afft. nephew
Augustine T. Smyth

Augustine T. Smythe, Charleston, S.C., to his aunt

Thursday 5 Feb. 1863

Dear Auntie,

. . . We have had some exciting times here for the last week; the capture of the gunboat in Stono & the breaking of the blockade by our ironclads. I was fortunate enough to be one of four chosen to accompany Lt. Col. Yates[21] on his expedition. We started off on Tuesday morning on foot on our secret march to John's Island. On the other side of the bridge we took the cars to Rantowles Station, & being there some hours ahead of the waggons & artillery, we went to the camp of the Marion Artillery[22] & spent the night. In the morning we started off by day break in a snow storm so bitterly cold & regaining our "train" took up the line of march for Legare's distant 15 miles on John's Isl. passing over at Church Flats. We reached the place that afternoon & as soon as it was dark, arranged the artillery along the banks of the river in ambush. We had quite a force along. At Grimballs on Jas. Isl., three rifled 24 pdrs. & several other guns lower down. At Grimballs on John's Isl., & at Legare's lower down the river, we had concealed our guns, some in stables, some behind bushes, & one in the basement of Legare's house. Two of "us" were stationed at Legare's & the other two went to Legareville[23] to notice & report the movements of the boats. Then there were others at Grimballs on Jas. Isl. forming a line to town. The weather was intensely cold & we were allowed neither light nor fire, so that it was not very pleasant. Our rations were "floating-batteries."[24] I was one of those stationed at Legare's. This was our chief point, because the bank here was high & the channel only 250 yds from it, & then our best guns were there. Everything was quiet until Friday morning when the boat was seen moving about & firing, but she soon anchored again & all was still. The boat which the expedition was intended for was this very boat, the I. P. Smith,[25] as we had heard from a deserter who came in some days before of her heavy & valuable armament. About three o'clock the men at Legareville reported the boat coming up the river. We immediately dispatched a courier up to Col. Y. to bring down the men who were hid in the woods about a mile or so back. This was necessary because all along the bank was a perfectly open field with no cover. We then sent on the news to the other posts by signal and now came the exciting time for the boat steamed rapidly up the river right to the house, where a picket of five men & a Lieut. & ourselves lay concealed. If they had seen any of the guns or any of us by the house they could have landed & captured us & then retreated down the river in safety; as the men to work the guns were not yet in sight. But no, to our great joy, she saw nothing, but steamed up the river to Grimballs on Jas. Isl. & anchored. The officers say that they came up to have a quiet dinner & to kill some ducks. Just however as the dinner bell rang, our guns from Jas. Isl. opened on her & the first shot passed thro' the engine room tearing off the arm of the Asst. Engineer. By this time, our men had arrived & run the guns from their places in the houses to the bank of the river & the house & banks were lined with sharp shooters. As soon as she heard the shot she cut her anchor & came running down the river firing grape on both sides. It was a beautiful sight to see her steaming down the river with the shot plunging all around her. She passed without material harm by all the batteries, but one, & we gave her up as lost, when a well directed shot from Legare burst her steam pipe & she had to stop & surrender. Col. Y. immediately started us scrambling for steamers to tow her up to town & we did not stop until 4 next morning when everyone left. As soon as the boat stopped, we hailed her & ordered her to send a boat ashore as we had none to board her with. Luckily one of her boats was unhurt, & in this the 1st. Lieut. came & surrendered the ship saying that the Capt. was too badly wounded to surrender himself. This was false, for he came up afterwards with only a scratch on his head. Had this boat been injured, as the others were we could have had no communication with her. As soon as they heard the firing, two other gunboats came up the river but were driven back. It is a wonder that our loss was no greater, only one man, for we were totally unprotected on the bank, only 250 yds distant & she was firing grape constantly. As our ammunition was exhausted the guns were carried back, & preparations made to blow up the prize. Three times was the candle lighted for this purpose while we, torch in hand stood ready to give the appointed signal from shore, but fortunately a message came just there from Gen. Ripley[26] saying that there were boats on the way & not to blow her up. We waited until four in the morning & then the steam boat having arrived, left for town. The Smith is now left safely at one of our wharfs. I went onboard, Sunday & found her in a horrible state, covered with gore, brains & human flesh scattered broadcast by a shell which burst just in her ports. She had one 30 pdr. Parrot gun, & eight 9 in. Dahlgrens besides a quantity of pistols, rifles, stores &c., altogether making her a prize of great value. She was pretty badly hurt, several shots being put in her just above the water line. We took 117 prisoners; besides 25 killed & wounded. One shot entered her port, took all the men on one side of the gun there & flying across cleared one side of the gun opposite & then plunged into the water. The Smith is quite a large vessel, a propeller, & runs fast. She will be exceedingly useful to us in keeping our rivers clear of the abolition forces. That same night the iron clads ran out, sunk one vessel, crippled another & as they say, raised the blockade tho' there are now quite a number of vessels out there including one ironclad. We have had however very stormy weather, yesterday & to-day & she may & I hope is injured by it. . . .

Your affectionate nephew,
Augustine T. Smythe

Augustine T. Smythe, Charleston, S.C., to Captain W. F. Nance[27]

5 March 1863

Captain,

By a special order from your Head Quarters I have been appointed a Lance Sergeant in the Signal Corps. In the fulfillment of the duties incumbent upon that position, especially in visiting the posts inaccessible to boats, the services of a horse are indispensable, and I therefore make this my application to be allowed the same food & pay for a horse used in the service, as is granted to the other mounted men of the Corps.

Very respectfully
Yr. Obdt. Servt.
Augustine T. Smythe
Lance Sergt. Signal Corps
1st Mil. Dist.
Approved
By Command
Brig. Gen. Ripley
Wm. F. Nance
A.A.G.

This Currier & Ives lithograph depicts the ironclad attack on Fort Sumter on April 7, 1863. Courtesy of the Library of Congress.

Augustine T. Smythe, Charleston, S.C.,
to Hon. James L. Seddon, Confederate Secretary of War

April 1863

Sir,

I have the honor to make to you this my application for the position of Lieutenant in the Signal Corps of the Confederate States. I have been in the Corps here for the last seven (7) months, as an operator and then as Lance Sergeant, and being thoroughly and practically acquainted with the business in all its details, I feel fully competent to fulfill the duties incumbent upon a Lieutenant.

I have the honor to be
Very Respectfully
Your obdt. Servt.
Augustine T. Smythe

Augustine T. Smythe, Charleston, S.C., to Jane A. Adger

23 April 1863

My dear Aunt Janey,

I received your letter two or three days ago & hasten to reply now by Jane who leaves to-night.

Well, the long anticipated & talked off [*sic*] attack on Charleston has been made & has failed. The Monitors have been met & have been driven back leaving us one as a memento or sample on Morris Island. To us in the city it seemed but a skirmish but the walls of Sumter as well as her garrison bear testimony to the terrible conflict in which they were engaged. It lasted for only two hours but, entre nous, if they could have stood it for two hours longer the whole east or sea face of Sumter would have been cracked & perhaps beaten down. As it is she has been severely damaged, several of the solid 15 inch shot penetrating three or four feet into the solid brick walls. These have been mended of course & the wall really strengthened by removing the guns from the lower tier of casemates, & filling them up with sand. These guns were only smooth bore thirty-two pounders & were of no use against the Monitors. Thus the wall is really stronger than before. The guns on the parapet have also been changed & several nearby ones on the inner face have been moved to the other side, so that if they return they will meet from the same battery, a much heavier fire. The men & officers are both confident of their ability to cope with & drive off the Monitors whenever they come back. The Yankee report is very incorrect. The closest that they came was about 900 yards & they did not receive our heaviest fire as they were at one time directly between Sumter & Sullivan's Island. True Battery Bee[28] did fire, but only at the "Keokuk"[29] & one other & then at long range. Our gunboats did not fire a shot but waited quietly for them near Fort Johnson. As to their being able to shell the city, it may be so, but they were farther off than Sumter a good deal. Then as to their being hit by torpedoes, as is said of the "Keokuk" it is untrue. They did come up boldly to the fight but had to give it up. Their 15 in. shot & shell are awful projectiles. The officers say that they could be distinctly seen flying thro' the air & almost dodged. The authorities are hard at work trying to raise the "Keokuk" on account of her guns, boilers, iron, &c. & they hope to succeed. Our ironclads however have to go down to protect her from being blown up by the Yankees. None of the other fortifications were injured by the enemy & are all sporting for a fight. They are all hard at work fixing up & strengthening themselves in every way. The battery at Cummings Point has had a Brooks gun placed in position in it since the fight & is ready & waiting. You see we are very confident here but not blindly so. Our barrel & net obstructions were a great trouble to them. They were evidently afraid of these & fired grape at them constantly. When they come further up they will find more obstructions than mere net work. The Thistle[30] which tried to [negotiate] blockade night before last got into it & had to come back. She & the Beauregard[31] both tried it again last night, but failed again. They may be successful tonight. The Beauregard is going out to bring in a cargo solely of Government goods. The Thistle is owned chiefly by Gen. Ripley & Col. Keitt. These are the only vessels now in port. One of our signal men is going out on the Beauregard.

You asked me if I messed with the officers in Sumter & what I did there. Certainly I messed with them & associated entirely with them. As to what I did it is a <u>great</u> <u>secret</u> & one which I am hardly at liberty to divulge but I will tell you & trust to your discretion. Some little time back we captured some of their signal men & one of them divulged their system. This was of course sent to our officer & I was sent to Sumter to read the Yankee signals, which were being made from the fleet outside to the Ironclads inside the bay. This was successfully accomplished for every message which they sent & they were chiefly from the Ironsides was read by us & sent up to Head Qts. This should not be spoken of, of course, for if it was known by the Yankees they would immediately change & thus put us again at sea. So please say nothing of it.

I wish very much that you & Auntie would come & pay us a visit now. The gardens are in all their splendor & the weather is so delightful. There are a great many ladies in town & you would find it very pleasant. Do come & see us if only for a week or so. I begin to think you don't care about us now. . . .

Write soon. Love to all & much to yourself from

Your affectionate nephew,
Augustine T. Smythe

Captain James Alexander,[32] *Charleston, S.C.,*
to Captain John M. Otey,[33] *A.A.G.*

20 May 1863

Captain,

I have the honor to request that Sergt. A. T.Smythe, Signal Corps,1st Milty. Distr. may be ordered to visit the Hd. Qrs. of the Signals Officers of this Department at Tallahassee, Savannah & Pocotaligo,[34] on the public service and under such confidential instructions as I shall give him.

I am Capt.
Your Obt. Servt.
James Alexander
Capt & Chf Signal Officers
Dept. SC, Geo & Fla

CHAPTER 2

Aboard the CSS *Palmetto State*
August 1863–November 1863

Augustine T. Smythe, Charleston, S.C., to Jane A. Adger

8 Aug. 1863

My dear Aunt Janey,

. . . First let me thank you for your very acceptable present of the cologne. I am extremely fond of it & am quite a connoisseur in the article. This is very nice & I am much, much obliged to you for thinking so much of my comfort. (Excuse all bad writing, for there are four (4) of us writing at this table & it is very rickety & shakes at the least push. I am just in the thoroughfare too & have to move every minute or two to let some one pass.)

We have had two quite pretty little affairs here during the week. The first was on Tuesday night. Three boats from the Gun boats & two filled with men from the Eutaw Regt. started just at dark to surprise the enemy's pickets. They went to within a short distance of them, when the soldiers landed & the boats went on round to cut off their retreat. The soldiers came upon men entirely unawares & fired on them killing two & wounding the Capt. & Sergt. & one other man. They took immediately to their boat & pushed off but our boat coming up just then they were fairly caught. They had a fine boat which we now have. The whole number caught was ten. The other affair was on Wednesday night. The Juno,[1] a blockade runner, rigged up with a torpedo & under the command of Lt. Porcher[2] of the Navy went out by Battery Wagner to reconnoitre. She went down to within 300 yds of the Monitors & there met up with the 1st Launch of the Wabash acting as guard boat. The Juno tried to run her down or strike with her torpedo. Luckily however the boat sheared out of the way but just as she was going under the wheel of the Steamer where she would certainly have been sunk, the anchor caught her & towed her along. Twelve of the men jumped overboard with the oars but the other ten with the officer surrendered. Two of these men were afterwards picked up on Sullivan's Island. The boat is a splendid launch with a 12lb. howitzer & had a crew of 22 men fully armed. Considering that the steamer had only ten men armed with rifles, the launch should have whipped her but the men behaved very cowardly. This is a great prize & is the very thing we wanted. Lt. P. behaved bravely & is much commended. Besides this there has been nothing except that every other night we go down to Fort Sumter to protect the communication with Morris Island. This is very laborious as the night that the ship does not go down the men have to man small boats to carry troops to & fro. This keeps them up nearly every night & will soon break them down unless some other plan is devised. We have not yet given up Wagner but have increased its armament by another 10 in. Columbiad & a 32 rifled & banded. The whole South face of Sumter has been filled with sand strengthening it exceedingly. We are hard at work building batteries all round Morris Island & have now some very heavy ones particularly one at Legare's point on James Island which mounts or is to mount 21 guns. The Yankee prisoners say that they are daily expecting 10,000 reinforcements & then they will renew the attack, & this time differently from last. They do not want Wagner now, so they say, but can do without it. Their opinion of the Monitors has fallen very much & they regard the Ironsides[3] as worth the whole of them. She is certainly by far the most annoying to our batteries. Her commander is Stephen D. Rohan.[4] It is said that Beauregard considers the destruction of the Ironsides as necessary to the safety of Charleston but this is mere outside report. Another report is that Gilmore & Dahlgreen[5] have fallen out & are now at loggerheads & therefore the attack is not resumed. Certain it is, that everything now is very quiet with the exception of a little shelling now & then, & the regular shelling which one of our batteries keeps up every night to annoy the Yankees. It is a beautiful sight to watch the shells go up like rockets, up, up, up & then stop for a moment in mid air as if considering where they should drop & then fall fast, & faster until within a few feet of the ground, when there is a bright flash, a report, & all quiet. This is our principal amusement at night. They fire at intervals of about 10 minutes, more for the purpose of annoying the Yanks than from idea of really damaging their works. Life on board[6] still goes on as monotonous as ever. Nothing to do except read. Now & then however I have a treat in the way of a days fishing. To-day I got some bait but could not get a boat so I fished from the shield. We were quite successful however & caught a nice mess of fish which I hope to enjoy at dinner-time. We go bathing very often tho' for the past two or three days the tides have been unfavorable & the excitement on board has prevented our going after dark. I am getting used to this kind of life & almost fond of it. It is very cool here generally. The climate reminds me very much of Sullivan's Island. Even now I have to put a weight on the paper to prevent its being blown away.

One of our chief plagues here are the cockroaches which infest every thing every place. The drawers are full of them & where you take up a towel to wipe with you must first shake out the roaches. I have several tame ones in my room who bring me my shoes, &c. & throw empty my basin. This is accomplished in a very curious & really unique manner. The roaches assemble on the edge of the basin & jump in one after another until they crowd out the water entirely. This is the aspect of the basin generally when you look at it. These are all we do have tho'. Mosquitoes are unknown & fleas are rare. Altogether I am tolerably comfortable barring the heat at night & the leaks when it rains. But I must close. Love to Aunty. Love also to Aunt Nancy & all in the house. Write to me when you get a good chance. I shall be very glad to hear from you. Believe me, till I write again, in much love

Your very affectionate nephew
Augustine T. Smythe

Augustine T. Smythe, Charleston, S.C., to Margaret M. Smyth

Monday night
7 Aug. 1863

Dear Mother,

I have thought much of you to-day & of your sad departure from Charleston[7] & home but have felt relieved to know that you are no longer exposed to the dangers which encompass our loved city. I was unusually congratulated by the officers when I informed them that you expected to leave this A.M. They had all expressed surprise at your not going before & kept advising me to urge you to leave. No one here has any relative or friend in the city. Those who did have, have sent them away with only a single trunk many of them. You were highly favored in having a car, wagons & a son at your disposal to assist you in moving. I shall feel anxious to hear from you about your arrival in Clarendon. How you traveled.

I reached the Bathing House just in time last night but made Holmes wait until I could send back for my coat which I had forgotten. Readied the ship all night & in due time I am now regularly in harness again (It has been very pleasant all day, & quite comfortable but to-night about 6:30 P.M. it commenced to rain very hard & then our discomfort commenced. As there was not any place on deck I had to come below into the Ward Room to write where tho' I have removed my coat & collar, & opened my shirt, I have to keep a handkerchief going to maintain a dry face. There are two others writing at the table with me. Mr. Ward[8] our 1st Lieut. & Mr. Jordan,[9] our Chief Engineer) Besides writing we are kept busy driving off the cockroaches which in goodly numbers & of all sizes large & small, keep running over the table & even across the sheets on which we are writing. Our favorite amusement here of which I forgot to tell you is to make two rings on the floor one inside the other & putting two roaches inside the inner one have a race between them, as which one will first get out of the outer ring. Those who are hard up for sport & find themselves the unhappy victims of ennui, consider this as an unfailing source of amusement. . . .

I have just heard of a way to get letters thru the blockade. Enclose them opened as they must be read, with $1.00 to pay the postage to Gen. J. H. Winder[10] Richmond & they will be forwarded. It will in all probability be read by him so you must write suitably. I shall write to Auntie in a day or two & will tell her of it. (No news to-night except a rumor that the rifle pits have been recaptured. I do not vouch for the truth of it.) . . . It is very hot & getting late so I must stop. . . .

In much love to all
Yr. Afft. son, Augustine

Louisa S. McCord,[11] *Columbia, S.C., to Augustine T. Smythe*

20 Aug. 1863

My dear Young friend

I thank you for your letter & feel the kindness which does not forget us in the midst of your present perils. I have often thought of you, for the greater the trouble we go through, (and I have had, as you probably know, very heavy ones to meet, even since I last saw you,)[12] the more it seems to me do we cling to what is left behind; and when our nearest & dearest are torn from us we turn to those whom our minds associate with them.

You mention that all your Father's family has left, or is leaving Charleston. If they are out of your reach, I hope you will keep in mind that in case of your being sick or wounded, you will always find a room & a welcome with me. My vocation is to help soldiers, & when the soldier is a friend, I am only the more ready for my duty. Come to me therefore (if need be) to be nursed; though I trust that God may protect & keep you from the need.

My Daughters send their kind remembrance & best wishes to you. They call themselves well; though in truth the only bright one of my household is Baby,[13] who grows fat & laughs as if there was no such thing as war. The rest of us think only of making sand bags for the forts, listening for the guns which we hear from Charleston, watching for the last war news, & I go to the hospital; and thus the dreary days go on.

Goodbye. Again & again, may God bless and take care of you.

Always most truly,
Your friend
Louisa S. McCord

Augustine T. Smythe, CSS Palmetto State, *to his aunt*

30 Aug. 1863
Sunday Night

Dear Auntie,

I have been wanting to write to you all day but the table has been employed, or rather occupied, until now, by the Purser, making up his accounts & I have been unable to get to it. Now, however, supper is over, & the table has been put down in the Ward Room & I can write in peace. Up above & even here however, there is considerable bustle & excitement preparing for a trip to Morris Island in the small boats. This we have to do every two or three nights in order to keep up the communications. It is impracticable for the steamers to go down as the Yankees would see & fire at them & we have no steamers to spare. Transportation now is very limited & it was really a God-send to us when the other day a small steamer, the Spaulding,[14] formerly on the line between Savannah & St. John's, ran in. The Govt. seized her immediately & she is now running about the harbor as a Govt. boat. This night boating is very hard as it has to be done in all weathers & often under fire. Still it is the only way of re-inforcing our men on the Island & supplying them with commissary & ordinance stores.

Word just came over from Commodore Tucker,[15] not to let the men go down in the small boats but to keep them on board. This is in anticipation of an attempt by the Monitors to run in during the night & shell Morris Is. & the city. I think they have been expecting something of the sort for some nights. We are always lying ready with steam on & our anchor buoyed, & ready to ship at a moment's notice. We have had several alarms & are now quite practised in getting up in a hurry. I & several of the officers sleep in hammocks swung on the gun deck & when the alarm is given, we must be up & dressed, our hammocks stowed away below & we ready for duty in five minutes. Pretty quick work. We never "turn in" of a night without expecting & preparing to be called up at any moment. I, in particular, am thus exposed, as I am liable to be required for signalling at any time of the night & am very frequently.

Last night at 1 o'c I had to be up for an hour or two, as we expected the Ironclads, & to-night already I have been working some & expect to work more. . . . More orders. No one allowed to sleep on the gundeck to-night but must move their hammocks below. Something is in the wind. An expected attack. I have got so used to these preparations etc. now that they scarcely excite me at all. Every three or four nights the ship herself goes down about Fort Sumter, to be ready, whenever there are any suspicious appearances. Our life here is full of anxiety & disquiet (as well as discomfort), as you may see by this rambling letter which I have written amidst a great many interruptions & much bustle & confusion, & fear may be incoherent. Affairs on Morris Island remain in status except that Battery Gregg is being very much strengthened in order that even if Wagner should fall we may make a stand there & at least give us more time to fortify behind. If they had been as busy before as they are now, the Yankees never would have gotten Morris Island. They are building two batteries on Jas. Island, one by the old Martello tower,[16] & the other higher up. These are to be or are armed with the guns from Sumter. They are surrounding Castle Pinckney[17] with sand, rendering it a second Wagner. They are building a battery on the East End of Mt. Pleasant to protect the rear of Sullivan's Island & keep the communications with it open. They are also taking away the guns & ammunitions from Sumter nightly & sending them to the different batteries. When the Yanks have got Sumter & Morris I. even their task has just begun. The gunboat Charleston[18] is ready for work tho' she has not all her guns in. She lies at the wharf still, tho with steam up, & they are putting the guns into her rapidly. The torpedo boat is ready to do her part. We had quite a sad accident yesterday. A "machine"[19] we had here & which carried eight or ten men by some mismanagement filled with water & sank, drowning five men, one belonging to our vessel & the others to the Chicora.[20] They were all volunteers for the expedition & fine men too, the best we had. It has cast quite a gloom over us. Strange isn't it, that while we hear with indifference of men being killed all round us, the drowning of one should affect us so.

Mother & Father left town Friday for Clarendon where they expect to spend the winter unless disturbed by the Yankees. They were very much favored as Father got a car & carried his buggy, horse, cow & some baggage. Adger brought up his wagons & helped them move & there thru Father & Gen. B. got a furlough of seven days & so went up with them. This is a secret tho'. Thus they will get up very comfortably in comparison but oh! how uncomfortably in reality. Poor Mother, my heart bled for her. It was a heavy trial & affliction to her to leave home & go among strangers, as it were. Then she did not want to leave us boys & me in particular as I was by myself, & this seemed to worry her more than anything else . . . she was ready to risk it all only to stay. . . .

Your afft. nephew,
Augustine

Augustine T. Smythe, CSS Palmetto State, *to Jane A. Adger*

Thursday night
3 Sept. 1863

My dear Aunt Janey,

. . . Sunday night as you may have seen by the papers the steamer Sumter[21] was sunk by the Sul. I. batteries. She had on board 900 men just relieved from Morris I. Of these 5 were killed, several wounded, & a number (unknown) drowned. Our men were roused up at 4 A.M. & sent to their relief & succeeded in saving them all but not their arms nor accoutrements, most of which were lost. It was a sad accident & a heavy blow to our transportation already very limited. She sank soon after the last boat load of men left her as the tide was rising on Monday afternoon at 1 P.M. two Monitors came up & opened on Ft. Sumter but soon after retired. About three o'clock however four of them came up & renewed the attack. Our batteries on Sull. I. & Battery Gregg opened on them with full blast & then firing was excellent as a shot struck one of them the steam was seen issuing in clouds from her & she immediately retired, tho' firing, & was towed down by a tug. Another was pretty badly struck. Their aim seemed to be Fort Sumter & the demolition of its E. & N.E. walls. The bursting of their shell make a report louder than that of any of our guns. They fire about once every six minutes. On Tuesday we went up to town to have our boiler mended. There was no commotion below except slow firing on Sumter from the Yankee land batteries. On Tuesday night about 11 P.M. I was on deck still talking to some of the officers, when we observed the signal below of the approach of the enemy. All hands were immediately called to quarters, the hammocks stowed below & everything made ready for a fight! We soon observed five Monitors loom up slowly round the point of Morris I. & approach the S. Our batteries on Sull. I. & Gregg[22] opened on them again & the firing was for some time then was an incessant roar of artillery. About 12 o'c the Ironsides & the sixth Monitor came up & joined in the chorus. They paid most of their attention to Fort Sumter trying to batter down its wall but occasionally throwing a shot at Sull. I. We lay ready with steam up, guns loaded, anchor ready to slip & waiting for them but they were evidently disinclined for close quarters as they did not pass by Fort Sumter at all. About 4 A.M. they hauled off one of them apparently injured. It was a bright moon light night & the same was grand beyond description & I shall never forget it. At times the whole horizon would be one flash of light from the cove to Morris I. & again there would be flash after flash & report after report in rapid succession as if it was merely a salvo of artillery. Distinct amid all the fire however could be distinguished the sharp crack of the 15 in. shell as they exploded over Sumter, louder & more terrific in their reports than anything else. The men slept at their guns all night. These alarms are now the rule not the exception. Yesterday & last night nothing occurred except the ordinary firing but we were called up about 3 A.M. as the ship was dragging her anchor & we had to get up steam & move higher up. To-day our batteries have been busy shelling the Yanks; they firing occasionally at Sumter. (The Charleston is now ready & keeps guard out there with us. This is a great help to us & we shall give the Monitors a heavy tug now. They are hard at work on the big gun[23] but we will not have it mounted until Saturday. Then the Yankees will see sights when they arrive.) The Antonica[24] tries to run the block to-night. . . . Much love to Auntie & yourself from

Your own boy Augustine

Augustine T. Smythe, CSS Palmetto State, *to Margaret M. Smyth*

Saturday night
5 Sept. 1863

My dear Mother,

. . . We are all again in a state of excitement (tho' it can hardly be called excitement exactly as it is a much more quiescent feeling) but preparation to-night as information has been recd. of an expected attack. The Charleston has gone down the harbor already & we are waiting further developments & orders to follow her example. The attack it is anticipated will be made on Cummin's Point in barges from Moultrie in the Monitors. We are cocked & primed for them if they do come up. We are so used to these nights of expectancy however that they do not worry us much. Gen. Ripley sustained a serious loss last night in the capture of his fine sail boat in which he used to visit the posts. He sent it down to Morris Isl. on business which it had accomplished & was returning, bringing up also Maj. Warley[25] who was wounded slightly at Wagner, when a Yankee barge fell in with it & grabbed it up. This is very unfortunate as the crew are very well acquainted with all the fortifications &c. & will be able to give much valuable information. A flag of truce boat was sent down this afternoon to inquire about it but she had scarcely got below Sumter when the land batteries (Yankees) opened on her, knocking off one man's hat & striking the main top while the wind from another ball struck a man down. They (the boat) stopped of course but the naval officers who boarded her to receive the dispatches apologized saying that the land commander could not have seen the white flag. Fortunately no one was hurt. No other news to-night except that the big gun is all ready. . . .

Sunday night

The blow has come at last! To-night Morris Island is to be evacuated & given up to the Yankees. All our men have gone down in small boats to assist in removing the troops & the Charleston has gone down to Fort Sumter to protect [it] in some manner. I have been expecting this all day as I had an intimation this A.M. from official sources that if the firing at Wagner was continued to-day the place would have to be evacuated, the joint opinion of both the Engineers & the Commandant of the post, but still when I heard it positively this afternoon that we were to give it up to-night, it came over me like a pall. I had hoped that as we had held out so long we should be able to bid them defiance, but it has turned out otherwise. The worst trouble in the case is that there are 125 sick & wounded in Wagner who are to be brought off besides the well garrison & we have only 14 small boats carrying about 25 men apiece to transport them. The steamers will be unable to go to the Island. Already there is one Monitor now at the point of Morris I. firing away so that besides this unpleasantness there will be great risk. The Ironsides too is shelling & the rest of the Monitors which the land batteries keep up an incessant din. Besides the Yankee launches are prowling around & may just as likely as not pick up one or two of our boats. I wish it was safely accomplished & the men all back again. The Eutaw Reg. is there & has been there for some days tho' I only heard it to-day I do not know whether Uncle Joe is with the Regt. or not. I have heard of but one casualty so far & he not a particular friend. Firing still going on. Our batteries on James Is. are busy firing on them & they replying. Above all the din can be heard the loud booms & the sharp stunning crack of the 15 inch guns & shell as they are hurled at our poor men while noise from the fragments of shell can be distinctly defined striking the water, sometimes in close proximity to us. This evacuation has cast a gloom upon us but more a further dislike to yield anything or any more soil to the accursed Yankees & especially a place which we have defended so bravely & until so much loss to the enemy & ourselves as Morris I. than from any feeling that our city is gone or that the place will have to be surrendered. They have made preparations to blow up the magazines both at Wagner & Gregg, & Fort Sumter is also ready for the same fate as soon as they have determined that it is untenable. It is all undermined & the application of the torch will render it useless to the enemy & harmless to ourselves "they say." Perhaps it is better to give (it) (Wagner & Gregg) up now than to be driven from it as we would probably be in a few days & then be unable to remove our men or anything else. The enemy had advanced their [sap] [26] to within 75 yrds of the fort & in a short time would have come up within the battery itself. We are stronger however to-day than we were when the Yankees first attacked us. Battery Wagner, since it could not save Sumter, has done its part well & has gained us time to erect batteries & mount guns which will render the taking of Charleston no child's play. Still poor old Charleston may & most probably will be laid pretty low as from Cummin's Point they can easily reach it with their 200 pd. guns. We too shall see a few more shell tumbling round us than heretofore tho' they have been shelling Ft. Johnson all afternoon, & their shells have been falling near us. I was over at Johnson this morning. They have a splendid 4 gun battery there. The guns are not mounted on the surface but below so that their muzzles are on a level with the ground. Between each gun there is an immense traverse making each gun in a separate battery as if were while passages all below the surface lead from one to the other & to the magazine. The guns are old pattern 10 inch Columbiad & new pattern ditto, & one rifled & banded 8 inch Columbiad. They had a 7 in Brooks rifle gun which they were carrying to Mount on Battery Wampler,[27] between the Martello tower battery & Battery Glover[28] & a double-banded rifled 24 pdr. We shall make a hard fight here. The attack on Battery Gregg in launches was made last night. We were prepared for them, (as thro' the agency of the Signal Corps the intention to make such an attack had been discovered) & whipped them back tho' they did have two or three Monitors to help them. No attack was made on Wagner but shelling was kept up all the time. They have been shelling Gregg all day in consequence & I only pray that they have stopped it now tho' the firing down there is very heavy. We can form no idea of their loss last night. Col. Keitt is now in command of the Island & he will conduct the retreat to-night. Fort Moultrie opened on the barges last night besides the light artillery on shore so we hope that some were sunk. . . .

Give my best love to Father. Tell him the description of the batteries & guns is for him. I trust he is getting on better. Love to all the dear ones with you. God keep & bless you & all of us dear Mother.

Good night. Your own boy,
Augustine

Augustine T. Smythe, CSS Palmetto State, *to Margaret M. Smyth*

8 Sept. 1863
Wednesday 8:30 A.M.

My letter did not go off this A.M. by day break as I expected & I now have a chance to give you the result of the fight last night, glorious to our side. We captured 7 launches, 19 officers & 100 men who expecting to find only a small guard in the Fort to protect provision were completely surprised at finding the Charleston Battalion[29] & were easily caught. The Chicora who was down on guard opened on them with grape & cannister & made fearful havoc among them. They were so certain of success that they even brought two launches of provisions along to last them for two or three days. Among them was the first Lieut. of the Ironsides who was in charge of the party. We also obtained two flags one small & the other large.

This is a great haul. Old Sumter is glorious even in her ruins. The Charleston Battallion [*sic*] was in the Fort. Besides those taken prisoners there were a great many killed & but few escaped. Early this A.M. a flag of truce was sent up by the Yanks but I have not heard their message.

Beautiful clear, cool morning. How I should like to spend the day with you in the country instead of being cramped up in an Iron coffin here. Love to all. Mail going & must stop.

Yr. afft.
Gus

Augustine T. Smythe, CSS Palmetto State, *to his sister Sarah A. Smyth*

Tuesday
8 Sept. 1863

My dear Sarah Anne,

We are in the midst of shells & shot now. The evacuation of Batteries Wagner & Gregg was successfully accomplished on Sunday night in small boats under the charge of Mr. Ward, 1st Lieut. of the Palmetto State, manned in some measure with Soldiers men from town rather but mostly by the crews of the Chicora & Palmetto S. The Charleston went down to Fort Sumter to protect the moving as far as possible. The soldiers behaved splendidly. They were marched from Wagner to Gregg & there drawn up in line along the beach waited the orders to get in the boats. No hurry, no confusion, no panic, tho' the shot & shell were raging round them, from the Ironsides, Monitors & land batteries. Capt. Huguenin[30] & 20 of his men were left in Wagner as a guard until a courier should go to him informing him of the removal of all the troops from Gregg, when he deliberately fired the magazine & retreated. Think of his position, left in the fort by himself with only 20 men, & the Yankees within 40 yds., his only hope of safety being in their ignorance for if the attack had been made no help could have been afforded him. He spread out his 20 men along the parapet & kept them firing all the time in order to deceive the Yankees & the ruse was successful. By some mishap neither magazine exploded, owing it is thought to the dampness of the train which had been laid sometime. We lost three boats, one with the crew only in it, belonging to the Chicora & the other two with soldiers manned by the men from the city in all under 30 men. They were captured by the enemy in launches in which they were coming up to make another attack on Gregg. The enemy did not discover their mistake in firing on deserted fortifications until nearly two hours after when they slowly felt their way up the Island. The gridiron now floats over both Batteries. They have not yet got any guns mounted there tho' hard at work, but will soon have them up & then look out for shells both here & in Charleston. Yesterday the quiet was broken only by a shot every quarter of an hour or so from our batteries at Morris Island. Yesterday afternoon just after dinner four Monitors & the Ironsides came up to Sumter & opened on Moultrie & Sullivan's Island in general. They were answered with spirit from our batteries & the heavy booming of their guns could be heard until long after midnight when they retired & all was quiet except the continual shelling. Shortly after dark we got up anchor & went down to Sumter to protect the netting &c. This prevented my writing. Yesterday morning the enemy sent up a flag of truce an acct. of which you will see in the papers. It was met by Lieut. Bowen[31] of our ship, & is considered more as intended for a chance to reconnoitre than anything else. . . .

I did not turn in this morning until 4 A.M. when we anchored back in our old place. This morning again the Ironsides & three Monitors came up & commenced firing on Sullivans Isl. The Ironsides kept off at a respectful distance but the Monitors came up beyond Sumter. They fired slowly but with great precision.

Just called off to send a message for Commodore Tucker & shall only have a chance to add a few lines. The Ironclads have left. Gone back again. One appears aground off Cummin's Point. There is a large fire on Sullivan's I. I dont know what it is. The Charleston just gone up to the city for coal. . . .

In haste,
Yr. afft. brother,
Gus

Augustine T. Smythe, CSS Palmetto State, *to Louisa R. McCord*

30 Sept. 1863

Many thanks, Miss Lou for the splendid pair of gloves which I recd yesterday by mail. They are beautiful & you have excelled yourself in them for they are much nicer than the other pair you made me. They fit me exactly & will be very comfortable during the cold weather which we feel coming on, especially in this exposed situation where I almost expect to spend the winter. I am the subject of much envy on account of them, as they are admired by everyone & justly, for such a pair I could not get in the city for love nor money.

The Yankees have woke up a little from their long silence. Yesterday and today before they were busy at Sumter, from the same battery which they used before; firing on Monday 37 shots of which [26] struck the Fort, killing one negro & wounding another, but doing no damage of actual consequence to the Fort. This morning they have commenced shelling Ft. Johnson, & the pieces fly all around the ship, making it rather unhealthy on the upper deck. They have not fired at the gunboats yet, but we are expecting them to do so as soon as their fortifications are ready. Their Ironclads are still quiet.

We in the meanwhile are busy working. They are putting up a three gun battery on the James Isl. shore about a mile above Ft. Johnson & the guns for which they are expecting daily. They are also mounting guns at three or four points to protect the channels of the river. These guns are principally 10 inch Columbiads from Richmond. The Big gun has been dismounted as useless & the other is still at the North Eastern R.R. Depot, where it will remain for a while, I am told, as the authorities consider it hardly worth the trouble of mounting. In its place on "The Battery" they are putting three 10 in guns & the 11 in. "Keokuk" gun from Ft. Sumter.

I am quite well but very uncomfortable in this Metallic Coffin of ours. I only wish the Yankees would hurry up & let us be done with the job, for I believe we shall whip them. We have no conveniences on board here & when it rains the deck leaks so that we have hardly a dry place to stand in. The war cant last always however.

Please give my best regards to Mrs. McCord & remember me kindly to Mrs. McCord & Miss Hannah. [Accept] my sincere thanks for the gloves which you may think of as keeping me comfortable during the cold nights & days believe me.

Very respectfully & truly,
Augustine T. Smythe

Augustine T. Smythe, Charleston, S.C., to his sister

Oct 4, 1863
8 p.m. Sunday Night

. . . This is a lovely night. Just cool enough to be pleasant, clear & bright but not moon-light. The moon rises now about 11 P.M. I have been walking on the shield[32] for more than an hour thinking of you all at home & wishing myself with you if only for an hour. It makes one home-sick just about twilight & early dark & I have had quite a fit of it to-night. It isn't right however & I dont often give way to such feelings but to-night, out there by myself, they would come.

There is an expedition on post to-night wh. promises very fairly a success but I can only tell you that it is a little torpedo boat,[33] a steam one this time, which is going to try one of the Monitors. They went down last night but the Yankees had all their launches strung across the channel & they could not slip by so to-night they are going to run over the bar & come in the rear of them. I hope they will succeed but am not very sanguine. We have failed so often that it seems fated for us to miss. This is a little craft built like a cigar & is the fastest thing in the harbor her speed 14 knots. She is no larger looking than a row boat & only carries 4 or 5 men. She is just the thing for the purpose & if there is any truth in torpedoes, this is their chance to prove themselves. Dont say anything of these particulars however as they should not be spread about & I only tell you as you like to hear the news. I shall write again to-morrow & tell you the result, if I hear it. The news from the West is that Gen. Polk is suspended & Gens. Hindman & Jones are under arrest for disobedience to orders. This is the sum total. All quiet around here. It would be a shame to be fighting on such a lovely night, Sunday too. You see I ain't altogether a barbarian yet tho' fast becoming one. I am quite well only a little blue. One of our Pilots has gone down in that craft & as he is a prime fellow I feel quite anxious to know how he gets on. I hope to get up to the City on Tuesday but am not certain. . . .

Good night. Love & a kiss to Mother & all.
Your brother
Augustine

Augustine T. Smythe, CSS Palmetto State, *to Margaret M. Smyth*

Monday
5 October 1863

My dear, very dear, Mother,

Twenty-one to-day! How the time does fly! Yesterday I was a careless boy frolicking away the time & to-day I wake up to find it my twenty-first birth day, when I am to be a man, to act for myself, to shoulder my own responsibilities & to carve out my own way in the world. I should fain put it back if I could, for I am not ambitious to be my own master. I take upon myself all the cares & troubles incident to it. My mind has been very busy to-day thinking of the past, of my happy youth, joyous boyhood & pleasant childhood. I shrink from looking into the future. All my plans are so vague so uncertain, even my tenure of life is so risky that I have no base to start from, no point, no certain date, from whence to begin. I feel very sad to-day & very thoughtful. It may be owing in a measure to the circumstances in which I am placed, in the midst of strangers, with no one to sympathize with me, no one to wish me "happy returns" even, no exercise to take, but my thoughts run wild over the past, & memories of the older time well up in my heart filling my eyes with tears. I cant help contrasting myself now, with myself of a few years back & wondering if ever again I shall see such happy times & then I turn away from the prospect sad. All seems dark before me. Yet I should not yield to such feelings & it is very unusual that I do, for generally I am hopeful & happy as possible to be in my position, but to-day I cant shake off this sadness. How I should like to see you to day, to receive your birthday kiss & to sit down & talk with you till all this heaviness was gone. Instead of that I am surrounded by a crowd laughing & talking & telling their jokes but little in accordance with my feelings. Yet they are pleasant enough generally, only to-day I am in no humor for such things.

Twenty-one years old, but how differently I am situated to-day from what I formerly expected. Truly "L'homme propose mais Dieu dispose,"[34] for that I should be to-day out in an Ironclad, separated from all my friends & dear ones, never entered into my calculations. Do you remember the birth-day, my 7th I think, which I had a party up home? I went out with you in the morning & you bought a book as a present for Ellen[35] to give me. How distinctly I remember all those pleasant days. How when the feast was over we all went into the yard & had such nice plays. I seem to be living over my life to-day.

I am quite well & getting very fat, as much so almost as I was about this time last year, when you nursed me so well thro' the typhoid. Poor Dr. North![36] He is one friend less in the world to me. Those days spent up in that room tho' days of sickness had their seasons of pleasure & then the time of convalescence! I should be almost willing to try it again if I was certain of getting thro'. I should like so much to get off for about three weeks to run up & see you all, but I dont see any chance for it at present. I expect I shall have the pleasure of wintering it down here in this narrow little craft, dark, cold, & damp as they say it is in cold weather, with no employment for the dark long nights, for our supply of candles & oil is very limited. Still I must not complain for every place has its trials & they must be borne patiently. I get on pretty well. I have books to read &, when I can get to the table, letters to write & this is employment for the day. My relations with the officers are very pleasant & some of them are very fine gentlemen. The great trouble is the close confinement, which is very trying as we have no place for exercise except the small deck. Our fare is pretty good, plain but enough of it. Davie has not yet returned but is sick in town so I am by myself. I expect him down in a day or two & then I can get a chance to go up to the city for a day. I wish the Yankees would settle the matter, either by going off & leaving us alone or coming in & getting whipped, as I believe they will be. They are very quiet now & have been for two or three days. We are busy at our fortifications & are even mounting some guns at Sumter. They have two or three put up already but cant mount many more as the Fort is two [*sic*] ruined. I have not heard anything of the little torpedo boat which went down last night but hope she accomplished something. . . .

I have written to you just as I felt, Mother, sadly. This is not the usual tone of my feelings for I am generally cheerful & contented but to-day the sad thoughts will come. It is such a lovely day too. Beautiful & clear, with not a cloud in the sky. May it be emblematical of my life! I have been interrupted very often during this letter, having had to signal two or three times & must stop. Love to all the dear ones & a kiss to all. Write to me often as you can. Love to Father, Ellen & all.

With much love to yourself, dear Mother.
Your absent boy Augustine

Augustine T. Smythe, CSS Palmetto State, *to Jane A. Adger*

Monday October 5th 1863

My dear Aunt Janey,

Can you realize that to-day is my twenty-first birthday? It is very hard for me to do so. It seems but yesterday that I was a little boy playing about & now To wake up to the idea that I am a man, to act for myself, & to be responsible for my own actions! I have never been anxious for this day to come, & now that it is here I would fain put it back & still remain, as I have always been, a careless happy youth. Do you remember the summer that I was left in your care by Mother? How distinctly all those memories of old times come up to-day, those happy days of boy-hood, when I played about under the old trees up town & when my hardest task was to go to you for my daily lesson, or a little later, to study with you my Sunday School lesson every Saturday. The [*sic*] recollect those Saturday mornings in the lime stone room in the old house & what a job it was for me to learn my hymn & the passage of scripture under my Question Book? Shall I ever again see times as happy as those were? I certainly have not for the last two years since I have been engaged in this abominable war. Then again those two pleasant trips to Georgia taken in your & Auntie's company. Some of the pleasantest portions of my life, indeed most of them are those spent in the company of Auntie & yourself. I have always looked upon you both as second Mothers almost & to-day after writing home to Mother it seemed as if the day required equally as much a letter to you. Let me now then, Aunts, just on the threshold of my life, as it were, tell you how grateful I am for all the kindnesses which I have ever experienced at your hands, & if I ever can do anything to conduce to your happiness or well-being, I shall always be glad, very glad to do so, to the extent of my power. My heart is full to-day. It seems to me such a severing of ties, a breaking loose as it were, from the free & happy time of youth & am entering into the dusty arena of the worlds on my own account, to sink or fall for myself, or by myself to win fame or distinction. I am a man & tho' actually no freer than I have been for years past, still I am now legally & virtually my own master, to take care of myself & to bear all responsibility on my own shoulders. I am perhaps more thoughtful on account of the circumstances in which I am placed, but as I lay in my hammock last night & this morning I could not help thinking busily, busily & my thoughts irresistibly went back to the past, to the scenes of my boy-hood & youth, to the memories, pleasant memories of the "good old times of yore" & now I cannot help writing in the same strain. The future is as dark & troubled, so uncertain that I dread almost to look forward & have no foundation to go on, even my own life is exposed to so many risks that it would be folly almost to form any plans. My past has been so pleasant & I wanted to write & tell you & Auntie how much you had contributed to its pleasure, how the memories of my happy youth are entwined with thoughts of you both & to assure you how grateful I am for all your kindnesses.

The weather here to-day is beautiful. Clear, bright, autumn days & lovely nights. How should I like to see you all to-day, to meet you once more all together at home or even to be with you anywhere. This life here is horribly confining. No change, no chance for exercise, except by pacing up & down on the small shield & that is so monotonous and yet it is about as good as any for there are the trials & privations to every station & we must only submit quietly. It is a dreary prospect tho' to look forward to spending the winter down here, in this cold damp ship, without lights, which cant be had, & no fire save under the boilers & I do not think that the Yankees will come in here for a long time yet & we are all making up our minds to winter it here. I wish the enemy would hurry up & be done with it, as I believe we shall whip them if they come, but this waiting is horrible. We are looking every day to see them open on the city as they no doubt will do in a week or so. We in the meanwhile are still going on with our fortifications. They have just mounted a 10 in. Columbiad on the battery opposite us on Jas. Isl. & expect to mount two more. I do not know how they are getting on in the city with the batteries but hear that the big gun is mounted & has been fired several times successfully. We are all in good spirits for the fight & confident of success. They are re-mounting guns in Sumter & have one or two up already. They cant put more than 3 or 4 there. . . .

I am quite well & getting very fat. You would hardly know me. I do not know my weight. It is late & I must stop. Excuse this bad writing but my pen is bad & my table rickety. I have written just as I felt to-day. I feel more lonely than I have for a long time. No one here to sympathize with me, no one to offer the ordinary wishes of a birth-day, no one, in fact, to care to-morrow if I am drowned to-day. This is not right tho' I should be thankful that I am as well off as I am & not complain. . . . With much love
Your affectionate boy,

Augustine

Oct. 5 '63
8 P.M.

J.A.A.

Such a glorious day as we have had & now the sun has set behind a cloudless horizon with a cloudless sky. I have taken it as a propitious omen & it has stirred up resolves within me to rise up to the responsibilities & troubles that may come & to prove myself a man, capable of overcoming or enduring them. Longfellow's grand psalm of life runs in my head. "Act,—act in the living present Heart within & God o'er head."[37] Even if my future is dark & gloomy now should be the time of action & God grant that I may ever be where duty, honor or my country call me ready to do my duty at all hazards & at all risk. Pray for me, dear Aunts, that I may have strength given me always to do my duty & to do it well.

Your affectionate
Augustine

The torpedo boat did not go down last night but has gone to-night.

A.T.S.

Augustine T. Smythe, Charleston, S.C., to his sister Susan D. Smyth

6 Oct [1863]
8 A.M.

Gloriously did our little boat do its duty last night, if the report from town is true; striking the Ironside[38] & tho' not sinking her at once, injuring her seriously. The way we hear the story is that she ran down to the neighborhood of the Ironsides, when they opened on her with their great guns & small, at the same time calling to them to surrender. Lieut. [Glazal][39] or someone cried out "We surrender" & then Lieut. G & the fireman of the craft jumped overboard. The Pilot & Engineer kept on & succeeded in striking her with the torpedo & then escaping & coming back safely. They could not stop to see the damage done but observed the Ironsides signalling [*sic*] at a great rate all night & this morning she is seen busy pumping & with several boats under her bow & stern & plying to the other vessels around. The supposition is that she is very badly injured. Lieut. G. & the fireman have not been heard from. Oh for a blow to sink her at once! The exhaust of her pump can be plainly heard at Ft. Johnson. Boats are busy working under her starboard bow. No other news-mail time. Good bye.

Augustin

Augustine T. Smythe, CSS Palmetto State, *to his sister Sarah A. Smyth*

Sunday
11 Oct. 1863

Dear Sarah Annie,

I am very much pleased to hear of your rides which you seem to enjoy so much. I should like exceedingly to accompany you but it cant be yet a while. I want you all to learn to ride well & fearlessly. . . . I am glad you will have the chance to see a Camp Meeting.[40] It is a sight worth seeing & remembering. There again I should like to go with you. When will this war end & we can be free once more to go & do as we please. I wish it would hurry up & stop. I for one am tired of it. . . .

I destroy all your letters so you need not be afraid of the Yankees getting them. . . . I am not well to-day & feel too badly to finish this now, so shall wait till this P.M.

4 P.M.

I shall try & complete this letter to you now which I started this morning. I am not feeling well at all to-day & am doctoring myself a la Ellen viz by starvation & keeping quiet. I ate only a piece of bread for breakfast & tho' I did eat two or three cakes when I opened the box from Aunt E,[41] I made up by eating no dinner. My cold is broken & I hope to be all right again tomorrow . . .

The weather is clouding up & I expect we shall have some dirty weather. It is not too late for our equinoctial gale yet. I wish it would blow all the Yankees ashore & stop this mess.

The Yankees are quiet to-day. Yesterday afternoon they shelled Ft. Johnson pretty severely tho' not doing us any damage that I know of. Their fleet is undemonstrative still. There is a report to-day that we exploded a torpedo under one of their blockaders last night but I have not heard any of the particulars yet. Gen. Ripley's boat captured a Yankee launch last night but all the men had left but two when it was taken. These torpedo things will scare the Yankees badly any how even if they do not hurt them materially & will give them a wholesome respect for the difficulties of entering this harbor. When they do try to come in they will find it a hard road to travel sure enough. We have now three guns mounted at White Point garden, one 11 inch & two 10 inch Columbiads. The whole Green is cut up & dug up to furnish dirt for the traverses &. They are using St. Lukes chapel, the wooden one corner of Chapel & Alexander Sts. as a commissary Depot. The whole of the street there just back of our Church is being dug up to furnish earth for the beast works & batteries round the city. The big gun is a complete success the 2nd one I mean. The story goes & I believe it is true that Gen. Beauregard has turned it over to Col. Yates to put where he pleases & they say that he wants it to go on Fort Johnson. There are a great many who think it much the best place & I am among them. When it was on the Battery, we were just in the range of it & as likely to be hit as the Monitors. At Johnson it can be used against Morris I. & will command the channel for a long distance up & down. We are getting stronger every day & the hope is growing up in many of us that we shall get thro' it all right yet & that even the city may be saved. The Yankees sent away some troops the other day but this may not mean anything. Anderson's brigade[42] has left here for the West where we all expect the big fight. They are still working at the battery near us but have not mounted more than the one gun. The berm of Castle Pinckney, that is the rim round the lower part of the Fort, the edge as it were, on which were piled the sand bags has given way under the weight & they have taken all of them away & left the fort as before. The casemates however are still packed with sand & they intend to slow fight them at any rate. The two (2) 10 inch guns there & the one at foot of Laurens St. will command that narrow channel pretty well. We have been expecting a fight for the last week on John's Island as the enemy are in Legareville on the Stono, but so far all has been quite there. In fact all round here is quiet except the continual shelling which our batteries keep up on the enemy & to wh. they now & then reply. They did not open yesterday as they promised. . . .

Much [love] to Father & Mother & all the other dear ones at home & with much love to yourself. Your afft. brother

Augustine

Augustine T. Smythe, CSS Palmetto State, *to Margaret M. Smyth*

25 Oct. 1863

My dear Mother,

No letter to-day from home nor anywhere else & I certainly expected one at least from you. I wrote to Sue yesterday & a long letter to Aunt Janey to-day & now to-night write only a few lines to tell you that I am feeling much better to-night & shall be quite well again in a day or two. The diarreioea has stopped all afternoon & the fever has entirely left me so I am in a fair way of recovery. I have had a splendid walk on shore & have just got back quite tired. We ran, jumped & hulloed like school-boys going home from school. We must have walked some 5 or 6 miles & it has wearied me considerably. I weighed this afternoon 140 lbs., more than I ever did before, then it was 150 lbs last year after the typhoid. This is healthy tho' I think & not blubber for I exercise all I can & go ashore two or three times a week. When I dont go ashore, I walk the shield or deck.

No news to-night. Last night we heard that the Yankees were to open on us to-day or to-morrow but they have not done so yet. They were not to open on the city but on James & Sullivan's Islds. We are looking for them to begin soon for apparently they have finished their batteries & are ready to begin. Gen. Ripley has been removed from Charleston & sent to Mt. Pleasant to command there. Col. Rhett takes command in the city meanwhile. His friends are trying to have him made a Brigadier General & Col. Keitt aspires to the same dignity I hear. We captured two days ago at Waccamaw Creek just above Georgetown, a Yankee schooner & 14 men including one officer. They are all safe. This is <u>all</u> the news to-night. . . .

Your own boy,
Augustine

Augustine T. Smythe, CSS Palmetto State, *to Margaret M. Smyth*

28 Oct. 1863

My dear Mother,

. . . Well! they shelled the city again yesterday, that is commenced to do so, tho' only one fell in the city. This one struck the Union Bank[43] & after tearing up a great hole in the wall & floor fell luckily into the cistern & so did no damage. Another fell in the water at Adger's wharf[44] & a third fell further out in the stream. After this their gun burst but a boat just from town reports that they shelled it again last night but I have not heard any particulars of it. The Yankees yesterday afternoon seemed to be turning all their guns on the city & we are looking for a warm time soon. This morning they are hard at work firing on Poor Sumter. Last night a boat from their reported that the Fort was not materially injured but only slightly so. There are three Monitors up there firing on her also & they seem determined to knock her flat. They occasionally throw a shot up in this direction or toward Johnson but their chief aim is Sumter. . . .

Real winter. No frost yet on acct. of wind. I shall finish to-night. Till then good bye. Love to all & much to yourself from

Augustine

Augustine T. Smythe, CSS Palmetto State, *to his sister Sarah A. Smyth*

Tuesday
3 Nov. 1863

My dear Sarah Anne,

I have owed you a letter for some time & would have answered before but really did not know where to find you whether in Pendleton or Clarendon. I wrote to Sue in Rivoli[45] but then found she was in Summerton, so when your time came, I waited till I could be certain of your whereabouts. Now too, I am not sure that this will reach you at all but I am tired waiting so here I thank you for your kind letter which I recd some time ago. I am glad you have had the chance of going to Camp Meeting as it is one of the institutions of the South & one that we all should see, tho' we may not all be believers in its benefits & excellences. They are very pleasant tho' & the best place for good feeding in the country. I have enjoyed myself very much at some of them.

I have been in town to-day. I went up yesterday at dinner time & as a special favor got permission to stay in town last night & until to-day at dinner time when I came back. We had great doings in town yesterday. The President, you know arrived & they made a great fuss receiving him with soldiers & bands of music & speeches. He is a fine looking man with a very intellectual countenance but only one eye.[46] He spoke very well his delivery clear & emphatic. To-day he visited Sullivan's Isl. & the Charleston.

To-morrow he goes over to James Isl. & there is to be a grand review. I should like very much to see it.

We are now lying about 400 or 500 yards from Sumter & the reports of the Yankee guns & the explosion of their immense shell jar the whole vessel. The Yankees attempted to attack the Fort on Sunday night, but it mis-carried before they reached the fort. Last night they tried it again & one of their boats landed on the berm & the Lieut. in charge even reached the parapet but being shot at by the rifle men they hastily retreated to their boat & pushed off. We are on the look out for another to-night. The Yanks still keep up their heavy firing from Morris Isl. & the Monitors. The Fort however is still pretty strong tho' their continual fire is beating it away. The men are closely confined to their hiding places. They have to lie quiet all day & only when night comes & the firing slackens a little can they venture out. They cant cook their food, but eat cooked provisions sent from town. Four men went out to cook the other day but two were killed & two wounded. The Yanks fire at Sumter alone tho' some shots drop pretty near us now.

The old yard home looks as natural as ever. The Night-blooming [Series][47] bloomed again last night with five (5) blossoms. It was magnificent. Robt. McNeil[48] has trimmed all the rose bushes & fixed up the garden very well. Most of the geraniums are dead but Robt. is to set out a lot of cuttings for me from his plants. He has a splendid show of geranium plants & if the Yankees let us alone they will be a sight worth seeing in Spring. His Japonicas are also very fine & they will be some beauties there this winter. Daddy Philip & Maum Sarah[49] are pretty well. They still occupy their old room but Daddy P. uses the Wash Kitchen as Kitchen & brings Maum Sarah down there every day to sit. They are very comfortable, more so than I am by a long shot. Fields & Wilkinson still stay in the yard at night. Fields was not expected to go up until near Christmas.

They are working away at the cracked gun in Charleston. The plan is to fill it with iron & bore it over & they seem to be sanguine of success. The other one is to be put on Central Wharf.[50] They are still digging dirt on the Battery. They have a very large bomb proof there, big as a house, & there five large guns. I dont think the Yankees will ever get into Charleston. They may shell it, tho' that even is doubtful, & then they are at the end of their tethers & as Jeff said yesterday, shelling is very much overrated. . . . Love to all at home & a kiss to Baby & Sarah. Write soon to

Your brother,
Augustine

I had quite a fall last night. My hammock gave way at the front & let me down on the deck. Fortunately my head did not strike & I only got a bruised thigh. It might have been much more serious as I was up 5 ft. 3 in. in the air [on] rope [wire].

Augustine T. Smythe, CSS Palmetto State,
to Thomas Smyth, Summerton, S.C.

18 Nov. 1863

My dear Father,

. . . I do <u>not</u> believe that the Yankees can ever take Charleston nor Sumter either, certainly not with their Ironclads. If they are so badly damaged in an encounter with Moultrie as to necessitate a trip to Port Royal for repairs, I dont see how they can stand the fire of our batteries inside. As to their destroying the city they may do that in a measure only, for shelling from Morris I. is rather dangerous on their guns. They commenced yesterday as you see in the papers, about 10 A.M. & kept it up to 2 P.M. throwing 15 or 20 shell. They fell mostly in the neighborhood of Elliot St. & Broad. One knocked down the house on the corner of that & East Bay. Another entered the telegraph office, another struck the City hall or two in fact, not doing much damage. Another fell on the North wharf tho' I dont know how much hurt it did, if any. The Greek fire[51] part was all a humbug, as they did not set fire anywhere. The people were very much frightened they say & ran all about the streets hunting for some safe place. There is one consolation & that is their guns cant long stand firing at such range.

They still keep up their firing on Sumter tho' now principally from mortars, & seem to be saving their heavy guns. The old Fort still stands, waving her flag in triumph, tho' it is over ruins, & firing her evening gun in defiance. We have communication with it every night by steamer, tho' the full moon now interferes considerably. The Yankees too have a powerful calcium light,[52] with which they threw a ray on the very wharf & hinder our safe passage to & fro considerably. Moultrie the other night put it out twice, with her guns. We had a brisk little fight with the Monitors the other morning in which I think one was injured. Since then they have been very quiet. They now number five. The Ironsides on Monday had upstream [*sic*] & was moving about for the first time since she was struck. We think here that she has probably been repaired but she has made no hostile demonstration yet.

I was over on James Isl. this morning & had a long walk, from the effects of which I am now quite sleepy. The batteries there are the same as I have written about before, except that they have been & are being continually strengthened by the addition of covered ways, traverses etc. Fort Johnson is now a regular Fort enclosed by breastworks etc. in front & rear. The bomb proofs there are very large & strong & they are still working on them & constructing what seems to be a breastwork or protected way from there to the Battery Martello. I went up into the lookout there, about 100 ft. high & had a magnificent view of the harbor & could see the Yankees walking about on both Gregg & Wagner watching the effect of their shot on Sumter. One of the Monitors lies around the Point all the time as a lookout, & I could see the men walking on her turret & decks. There were a great number of vessels, wooden ones, of all sorts & kinds lying about. We are looking for an attack either on Sumter or James Isl. & are preparing to give them a warm reception if they come. One of the gun boats goes down every night to Sumter & another below Ft. Johnson to protect Shell Pt. To-night is our rest & we are quiet at our anchorage. They are moving the big gun & have got it down nearly to the wharf, I hear, tho' not mounted yet. At Castle Pinckney, since the berm gave way, they have tried another place. They have built up a wall of sand inside the Fort ten feet from the outer brick one. On this are mounted the guns & all the space between is packed with sand forming a pretty good wall. The David is still quiet, as the nights are too clear for her to operate successfully. The two new ones are going on bravely. The Yankees still keep up their continual firing but we are quiet & have not fired a shot I think since the engagement with the Monitors. This is all the news. I looked thro' the glass from the Observatory at Sullivan's I. to-day & can't see our house, so they must have pulled it down. I am so sorry. My eyes are hurting from this light. I am in good health & getting on very well. The Yankees have been quiet to-day except at Sumter. We are working away on our Ironclads but I dont know when they will be done. I must stop. Love to Mother & all at home. Write often. I did not get any letters to day.

Your affectionate son,
Augustine T. Smythe

Augustine T. Smythe, CSS Palmetto State, *to Margaret M. Smyth*

Friday
20 Nov. 1863

My dear Mother,

. . . I went down to the East End of Sullivans Isl. to Trusedell's place[53] but was not very successful, only being able to get some Raccoon Oysters & none of the planted ones. It is true! Our house has been pulled down & all the others on the front beach from the Cove up to the Fort have shared the same fate while there place is supplied by batteries. I did not have time to land but only took observations wile sailing past. The church is down. The Episcopal one[54] is used for a Commissary store & the Catholic one[55] stands but is shut up. The whole Island or rather that part of it comprising the village looks desolate & rather the worse for wear. The Moultrie House[56] stands but no longer a house. All the weather boarding, floors, piazzas, roofs etc. have been taken away, most probably by their soldiers for fire wood or to build their shanties & there now remains only the gaunt frame work. It looks so deserted & made me so sad to look at it & then think of its former days, when it was the gay fashionable resort. Many of the houses are riddled with cannon balls & but very few I fear will ever be habitable again. The Island is full of soldiers & the whole face from the Fort to the Cove is one long battery mounting the [heaviest] guns. I do not think now that I shall ever live there again since the dear old house has gone, but it was a plan of mine to live there one of these days when I was rich. I had no time to land. Battery Marshall[57] at the East end of the Isl. where I went for the oysters is a splendid fortification. It is to protect the end of the Isl. from an advance from Long Isl.[58] which you know is only separated from it by a narrow creek, Breach Inlet. It also protects the entrance to the creek which runs back of the Isl. & by which they could turn the rear of our batteries. As it is to guard as well against a landing & charge of infantry, as boats & artillery, it is a mixture of breast works & battery & a fine work it is. I have a memorandum of the armament eleven (11) guns & shall add it for Father. Beginning Northward we have first a 30 pd. Parrot rifle, then breastworks & there a rifled 32 pdr. mounted in the center of a high sand hill formed into a battery & wh. gives it a very long range; there breastworks & two 12 pdr. rifled guns; then one 8 in. Columbiad, then one 8 in. howitzer & then two 12 pdrs. smooth bore to sweep the beach. All these are scattered along the line of breastworks & each one is ensconced in a separate battery of its own with five traverses etc. Then at the South end of the line is another little battery for four guns but only three are there now, one 42 pdr. smooth & 2 8 in. howitzers. This protects from an attack by the creek back of Long Isl. & is a complete battery of itself & quite strong. There are a good number of troops there the whole under the command of Col. Hamilton[59] of the 1st S.C. Vol. The fourth gun for this latter battery is there & will be mounted in a day or so. Below Battery M. down the beach is a two gun battery but I did not have time to go there. From there down the whole beach is studded with batteries. All this is for Father who likes data. The Battery is about ¼ of a mile long.

Since my last to Father they have continued to shell the city daily throwing in about 10 or so daily. They do not shell constantly but for an hour or so in the morning & then again in the P.M. To-day they have thrown in quite a number. I have heard where some of them have struck four persons from the city & give them [*sic*]. One struck the City Hall not doing much damage. Another went into the City Square. Another struck the Guard House (lower) nearly smothering two guardmen in the dust, but not injuring them. Another went into Ladson's Court but did no harm. Another entered the tenement house in Tradd St. opposite Scotch Church, went thro' both tenements, & struck against Mrs. King's house. This turned it back when it went down into the cellar of the house & burst throwing up a piece of the wall about 14 lbs. thro' the floors to the 3rd story. Another went into St. Phillip's church yard. Another struck Crane Boylston & Co.'s corner Meeting & Market Sts. making a hole in it.[60] Several have gone into Elliott St. & Broad & around there. None have gone farther down than Ladson's Court. Another one burst in King St. opposite Enston's, marking the house prettily. So far I have heard of but one man killed. Several shells have fallen in the burnt district & some around the Mills House but none have struck it. They are quiet now but will probably commence again in the A.M.

Well Sumter has again been attacked by boats & been again victorious. This morning about 3:30 A.M. we were waked up by the cry of "All hands to quarters" & hastening upon deck found that the signal had been made that the enemy's boats had assaulted Sumter. We slipped anchor & ran down to the Fort in a hurry but when we got down they were already off as the defeat was easily accomplished. The Charleston was down there on guard & she had all the sport to herself. They were in small force, not more than 12 barges, they think, & the opinion here is that it was a feeler or else a feint & that the real attack was to be made on some other point. I have heard no particulars. . . . The Moultrie[61] is ready to run the block but is waiting a dark night. We all think her certain to be captured as her speed is hardly

3 knots. The weather now is delightful. Clear, calm & pleasant & we are enjoying it very much. The shells going to town pass just over us & make a mighty ugly whizzing, I tell you. Tell Powell howdye for me & all the other darks. Love to Sis, Ellen, Father, Adger & a kiss to both babies. Write often.

Your own boy
Augustine

Hibernian Hall (at left) was built between 1839 and 1841. The building immediately to the right clearly shows shell damage. Courtesy of the Library of Congress.

Augustine T. Smythe, CSS Palmetto State,
to Thomas Smyth, Summerton, S.C.

Wednesday
25 Nov. 1863

Dear Father,

. . . I . . . saw Mayor Macbeth[62] & gave him your message of congratulations. . . . I met him accidently in the street for I could not find him. He has moved his office to the Orphan House[63] & his residence up to Cannon St. but I could not meet him there but stumbled on him on my way down town. The Guard House has been struck by a shell, on the East side & a considerable hole made in it, so they have moved the whole establishment up to the Orphan House except the Rouge's [*sic*] Gallery, which still remains in town. . . . I went over to the Church yard for a moment from the Treasury Office but on a message for Aunt Janie but had no time to go into the church. The yard is in very good order, neat & clean & they are putting up a new stone in it to Jas. A. Duffers[64] & also fixing up the square at the N.E. corner of the church just by our enclosure there. They seemed to be straightening the stone or fixing a new one. I did not see as the yard is full of doves & other little birds. . . .

I was very agreeably disappointed at the appearance of the city after the shelling it has endured. Instead of having the debris of houses staring one in the face you have to hunt up the resting places of the shells & many of the stories I have written to you are exaggerated. The one about the shell in Tradd St. is all bosh! as I gave it to you. The shell merely went thro' the West wall in Barbot's yard & lodged in an out building in Pringle's yard only going thro' one side of this house & making even there quite a small hole. There was but one that went into Ladson's Court & it fell harmlessly into the yard. One fell in Mr. Barnwell's yard opposite No. 36[65] but did no damage. One or two fell near Lamboll & Legare Sts. but were not injurious. The worst hurts I saw were: the house corner of King & Horlbeck's Alley opposite Enstons, which was the receptacle of two shells, one of which burst inside & shattered it pretty badly; the house N. corner Elliot & E. Bay which has quite a hole in it; the Guard House which has a large hole in the E. wall & the S.C. Hall in which shrapnel shell burst, peppering the walls & breaking out the windows. I could not see the damage done to the City Hall nor to the Hibernian Hall so it must be slight. They say one fell in St. Phillips churchyard, but tho' I passed by it, I could not see any signs. One fell in the middle of Broad St. near State & burst without doing any damage. So one fell in King St. near Enston's just in front of it, but hurt nothing. This all proves how much more damage shelling actually does on paper, than in reality. One negro woman has been the only casualty so far. They will have to shell a few times more before they lay old Charleston in ashes. To knock down the city even would require four or five shells to a house. Every body is moving up above Calhoun St. tho' & all the drays & carts in the city have as much as they can do at $5 pr load & they are hard to be got at that. Still if I was living by myself at home I should feel perfectly satisfied, but am so glad you & Mother are not there. They have not shelled now for two or three days. Dont believe all you hear about the shells or you will swallow as I have done, some big stories. The Yanks have been keeping up their regular fire on Sumter. Yesterday tho' they opened also on James & Sull. Isl. We replied & there was quite a brisk artillery drill all morning. In the afternoon they threw their shell at Ripley,[66] one passing over & the other two falling short. We think they are going to open all around soon & are only getting the range now. To-day they are not firing so much at Sumter but shelling James Is. with a vengeance. You are mistaken. Beauregard visited the Fort but Davis did not as there was no call for him to expose himself so either. We are getting along so so & tired of waiting for the Yankees. I wish they would come & be whipped as they certainly will when they try to run in. Love to all at home. Write when you have the time & believe me

Your afftc. son,
Augustine T. Smythe

CHAPTER 3

Duty at Fort Sumter and an Engagement
December 1863–February 1864

Augustine T. Smythe, Fort Sumter, to Margaret M. Smyth

1 Dec. 1863
Tuesday

My dear Mother,

I dare say you will be very much surprised at the date & heading of this letter. I have been here since Friday evening when I came down in a small boat. I have been thinking whether to write & tell you I was here or not but having a chance now to send this up to town I thought it best to tell you candidly. I wrote you from the gunboat telling you of my expected temporary removal from it & stationing at some other post. This turned out to be Sumter & here I am now, alive & kicking & very well off except for the dirt which does not aid my comfort at all. This is the first good chance I have had to write you & must hurry now as the boat will soon be returning. I did not know whether it would be better to wait until I got out of the Fort before I wrote & or to write immediately, but have come to the conclusion that you ought to know that I am in here tho' it is only for a short time. This is the first letter I have written since my advent to this abode of happiness. I have not had the chance of informing you sooner. I am quite well & hearty & very glad that I came down as the Fort is worth seeing & being in now. The Yankees have slackened their fire very much for the last day or two & to-day they have been firing quite heavily on Moultrie & James Isl. They still continue to throw mortar & Parrott shell at the grand old fortress tho' the only casualty since I have been here has been one negro who was killed Sunday night. The Fort is much stronger than I expected to find it & cant be easily taken. On the N & E. angle in the casements we have three heavy guns mounted & ready for action manned by one company of the Fort

Sumter troops. There are about 350 men in the Fort altogether & 150 negroes (about). We are hard at work building bomb proofs & strengthening the different points exposed to attack & I dont think the enemy ever can get the old place. I fired the evening gun Saturday night just for the sake of doing it. I have command of a squad of sixteen (16) men who take charge of the hand grenades & greek fire. This is in addition to the Signal duty which is very light. They are stationed on the only two remaining points of the parapet, the S.E. & S.W. angles & are to hurl their missiles on any advancing party. The fort is a complete mass of ruins to look at it but there is many a safe nook & casemate yet left untouched. I am quite comfortable & quite well. They have been shelling the city several times lately. Our on Friday fell in Barker's lot but did not explode. Another burst in Tradd St. This P.M. they killed a woman in the city so the report is. I am so so glad you are not there. . . . Now Mother dont worry about me. I am as safe here as in the gunboat for in the bomb proof there is no danger. The weather is quite pleasant, tho' bitter cold. Clear frosty. This A.M. the inside of the Fort wh. is a regular lake was completely frozen over. I must stop, as the boat is nearly ready & there is such a crowd of men round me knocking my elbow & the table that I cant write. Love to all at home. I shall write again my first opportunity but as the boats are irregular so may be any letters. So dont be anxious. I expect to be out by the time this reaches you. Much love to yourself dear Mother from your own boy

Augustine

Augustine T. Smythe, Fort Sumter, to Margaret M. Smyth

Thursday
2 Dec. 1863

My dear Mother,

I wrote you a letter last night wh. I hope you have recd safely. I now have another chance to get you off a line as the quarter master boat has come down as I know you are anxious to hear from me. . . .

The Yanks shelled town yesterday afternoon again, killing one man on East Bay & one woman in Church St. Most of them fell around Cumberland St. One struck in St. Mary's church yard in Hazel St. & a fragment struck a coffee pot in a man's hand driving a dray in the street, without hurting the man. Did I tell you that one struck in Barker's lot the other day but did not burst? Some also struck in Tradd St. around Legare St. They have not shelled town to-day. We have got a band down here to-night & shall have some music so that will help to pass the evening. I am quite well as I told you except a little sore throat wh. I am going to doctor to-night with some cotton oil. You see I tell you even my slightest complaints so you are well posted & need never fear I am sick because you dont hear. . . . I enclose a piece of the old flag staff wh. has been shot away many times & of the flag wh. is full of shot holes. These are all the relics to be got except brass from the Yankee shells of wh. I have secured enough to make me a pr. of spurs. I must stop as there is such a crowd & so much confusion I can hardly write. Besides the boat will leave soon. I expect to be out by the last of this week, ere this reaches you, then I shall go back to the gun boat I expect.

Love to all at home. One shot to-day covered over the head of our remaining with sand & rubbish but their remaining quiet now gives us a chance to fix them up again. This is all the damage done to-day. They have hurt the fort now nearly as much as they can do. Music by the band so I must stop as this will make confusion worse confounded.
Much love to all at home & much to you Dear Mother from your own boy

Augustine

Augustine T. Smythe, Fort Sumter, to Margaret M. Smyth

3 Dec. 1863

Dear Mother,

I have time to write you a line wh. Lt. Swinton[1] who goes up to night will mail for me. I am quite well except my throat wh. is still sore. The Yankees have been firing to-day altogether at our corner of the Fort, the S. W. angle & have thrown down quite a pile of bricks but done no damage. This morning we had the band on the outside of the Fort & were playing for the benefit of the Yankees when they threw a shot knocking about a cart load of bricks over us but not hurting any one seriously. The Band finished their tune & then adjourned inside. This afternoon they went out again & played Dixie. Hon. Edward Ruffin[2] is down in the Fort to-night on a visit. This is regular Fort paper as my supply is very low so you must take it as it comes. They have been throwing mostly Parrott shells to day & all at our angle of the Fort. They shelled the city again last night but they fell mostly around

Southern Wharf & around there not doing much damage. When I go to town I am going to dig up the one in Barker's lot & keep it as a curiosity. No more news. Love to all.

Your afft. boy
Augustine

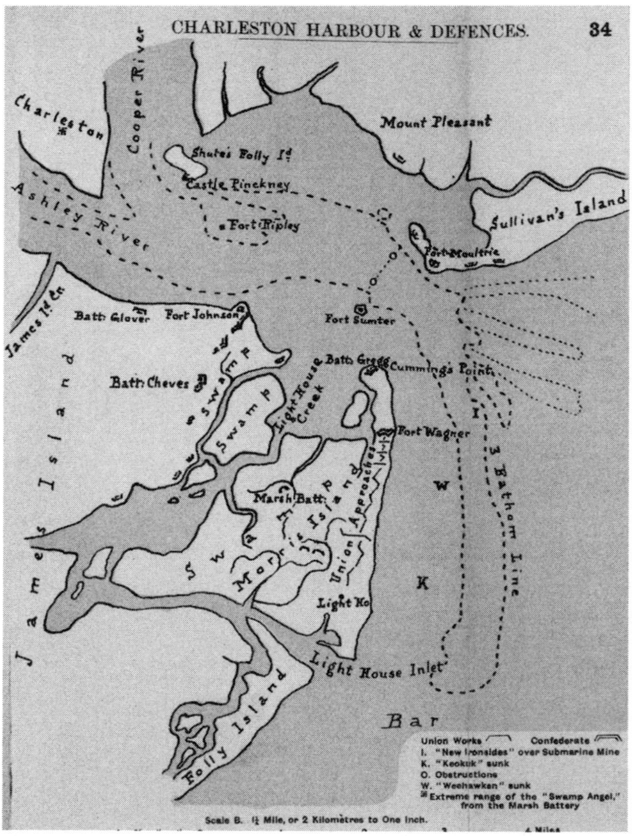

Map of Charleston Harbor, from a 1910 book of maps by John Formby.
Courtesy of the Library of Congress.

Augustine T. Smythe, Fort Sumter,
to Margaret M. Smyth

5 Dec. 1863

My dear Mother,

The Yankees have been very quiet to day scarcely firing at us at all. They kept up a slight bombardment last night firing about every 10 minutes or so but slackened off considerably since day light. There is now going on a brisk artillery duel between Moultrie & Ft. Putnam[3] but of course we dont know of any damage being done tho' they make some splendid shots on both sides. The Yanks seemed to think it better to save their ammunition by day & pitch in at night & they are not far wrong for they cant hurt the Fort much more by all their shells & they can hinder us working at night. There is a large gang of negroes constantly going & the Fort is now stronger than it ever was. There are quite a number of howitzers in the Fort some of wh. are kept in safe positions in the day, but at dark they are placed where they can rake an assaulting party. Others are regularly mounted in the bomb proof, so as to sweep the interior of the Fort, should the Yankees succeed in gaining it. We are all ready for an assault & prepared to whip them back to their hearts content. I am quite well, except my throat & it is much better. Tell Father I have doctored it with raw cotton & it has helped it considerably. I am looking for relief nightly as my week is out & I expect soon to leave these quarters. They have not shelled town to-day to my knowledge. One burst in Gov. Allston's house[4] the other day & another fell in Mr. Desaussure's yard. Close for No. 36. Tell Adger Capt. Sellers[5] & Mazyck[6] & their companies came over last night to stay three weeks I think. There is no news here. Am fully well, so excuse this short letter. I write merely to relieve your anxiety for I have no news to give you. Now I must go & see to fixing my hand grenades. Love to Sis, Ellen, Father & all at home & a kiss to the babies. Have not heard from you for several days.

Ever your own boy
Augustin

*Augustine T. Smythe, 12 Meeting St.,
Charleston, S.C., to his sister Sarah A. Smyth*

10 Dec. 1863

My dear Sarah Annie,

I have been wanting & intending to answer your letter which I recd. the day I left for Fort Sumter for some time but down there I was only able to scrawl off a few lines occasionally, & I wanted to write you a nice, long letter, & this is the first chance I have had since my return from the Fort & my abode here. I came up safe & sound on Monday night, being relieved rather sooner than I expected as two of the regular men there were sick, tho' I only went down for a week & should have been brought away on Friday by rights. . . . I am glad however that you are not here for they are still shelling the dear old city. They commenced yesterday afternoon, throwing some five or six, merely to get the range & be ready for the night. What brutes! & cowards! To wait until the dead of night when everybody is asleep in their beds & then throw in their horrible missiles of destruction. One of them yesterday struck the rear of the Mills House,[7] destroying three rooms, but not injuring anyone nor the house itself seriously. Another struck Mr. Grimballs house next door to Grandfather's not hurting it very badly I hear. Another struck a woman in Elliott St. near Church, wounding her dangerously, perhaps mortally. No. 36 has had some close shots to it . . . and another struck old Maum Hardgraves shop, going thro' the house & into the street just in front. . . . Several have fallen in Tradd St. . . . Last night just as I was going to bed, about 10 P.M. they commenced shelling again. I heard two come & then went to sleep & did not hear any others tho' they threw about 10 I think. Then again about 3A.M. they opened & threw some five or six but I did not wake in time to hear them for I did <u>not</u> wake till nearly 7 o'c. & that was too late you know. I am so used to shells now that they dont keep my eyes open at night time easy. One fell this morning in the cellar of the Guard House, but I have not heard of any others. It is a shame that these scoundrels should outrage humanity to such a degree as to fire thus on a city, with women & children in it, at night. Our batteries however, keep them from firing very long, that is one consolation. . . .

I am getting over my cold rapidly & shall soon be able to return to duty. . . . The yard & garden look very nice. Robt. has taken up all the pinks & reset them & also given it a thorough weeding & cleaning so that it looks very well. The roses are all trimmed, still the flowering & little red roses are in full bloom & so the jonquils, & I have quite a nice bunch on my bureau. There was a very severe frost the other night, which killed the tops of the hibisci & of the scarlet geraniums but has done no damage to the popinac trees except killing the flowers. The orange trees bore well, but nearly all the fruit has been pulled off & I have made several orangeades up here since I have been sick. The yard, Phillip keeps very nice & clean, almost as much so as Sam used to. My two turkies are growing fine & fat & I hope to enjoy one of them on Christmas, tho' the other will not be fit to eat till spring. Phillip comes to me now in great tribulation to show me $1 worth of lard which he bought to fry me some fritters in the morning & which he declares "aint wat was tree cent wut, fust time," so you may judge how you would live here with fat $4. pr. lb. & bacon "berry high."

One would hardly recognize town now. To go along the Bay & Broad St. it seems like Sunday. Every store is closed, & no one is to be seen except some stray straggler who may chance to pass along, while uptown is the business part entirely. There all is life. All the head quarters of the different departments are up there, around & above the Citadel, & the old city is turned upside down. Nobody is considered safe below Wentworth St. but I reckon they wont hurt me so I shall risk it & stay. Tattoo down on the battery so I must hurry up. . . . I send this to Summerton as you may be there. Whew! here comes another shell. Gone up about Broad St. I think. Now they will keep this up for an hour or two. Love to all in Summerton. Write soon to

Your affectionate brother
Augustine

P.S. Now you can say this letter was written under fire.

Augustine T. Smythe, 12 Meeting St., Charleston, S.C., to Margaret M. Smyth

Friday
11 Dec. 1863

My dear Mother,

. . . I have just come from the Bathing House & Markoe[8] says I must go down to the boat tomorrow so I suppose it will have to be done. My cold is pretty well broken & I feel much better than I was, tho' I am not quite over it yet. Still as he is very short of men & anxious for me to go down I think

I shall try it. If I get worse why there may be a chance for a sick furlough. I wish so much that I could get off to spend Christmas with you. (Whew! here's a shell) but it is out of my power. . . .

The Yankees shelled again last night at three intervals 8 P.M. 2 A.M. & 4:30 A.M. Again this morning & they even threw one just now. I have heard only where a few went. One corner Pitt & Beaufain, one corner Rutledge & Beaufain, one in Elliott St. near Church & one on Vendue Range. They all pass above me here & I now hardly stop writing when they pass over. It is a horrible thing this shelling the city at night, & with pauses between as if to catch unawares, when they know that there are women & children in the city. This morning there was quite an excitement down the harbor. Fire & smoke was seen issuing from Sumter & the Yankees were firing at her with a vengeance while our batteries replied with equal vigor. . . . I heard afterwards from a boat which has been sent there that the ammunition for small arms had taken fire & exploded but not seriously injuring the Fort. Several were killed & wounded by it tho'. The Yanks did pour in the shot when they saw the smoke. No other news. . . . Mail time so I must stop. Love to all at home. Oh how I should [*sic*] to see you all again. Write often to your own boy,

Augustine

Another shell just gone over.

The Mills House wagon has just come to move Fields up Bee St. I think when all the Mills House has gone with private quarters.

Augustine T. Smythe, Charleston, S.C.,
to his sister Jane A. Smyth

5 Feb. 1864

My dear Janie,

. . . Do you know the Legare St. house has been struck?[9] I heard so I got the key from James to go in & examine it. The shell entered in the angle of the slate roof at the S.W. corner of the wooden house & went thro' without breaking into the school room, to the entry below, where it burst just at the window. Two or three pieces went thro' to the lower story & one went thro' the basement floor into the ground. The house is very little damaged. The plastering is broken in some places & most of the glass in that neighborhood has shared the same fate. A piece went thro' the window & struck the greenhouse, cracking a portion of the frame work & breaking several panes of glass, but not wounding it seriously, only very slightly. The plants are all in there & look very well. I forgot to tell you that all the glass in the aquarium was broken, whether by a piece of a shell or by the concussion I cant say tho' more likely the latter. The hole in the roof is very small as the shell was not one of the large ones. It has hurt the house very little. Another shell fell in the garden in the extreme East end, in the large flower bed, or rather walk in front of the trees where the bend used to stand, but it went into the ground without bursting & only dug up a few violets. A third struck the wall just west of the greenhouse & sent thro' into the Dutchman's shop, doing no harm to your house except throwing a few bricks over the grass plot. This is all so far, that have fallen in the lot. James tells me tho' that some one entered the house in the day time some weeks ago, but that he did not miss anything & thought the person could find nothing handy. He says he watches there every night to protect the yard & pumps &c. & to catch the thief who stole his revolver & some other things at the same time. Some one broke into Mr. Bowen's yard the other day & tearing down the pumps, tied them up, preparatory to carrying them away at night, but Robt. McNeil found it out & carried the things to the Guard House for safe keeping & I think caught two of the thieves also. A shell struck his kitchen the other day, entering at the S.E. angle of the roof & bursting in that room. It did pretty considerable damage to the up stairs arrangements. Another carried away one half the top of the east house chimney but none have struck the house itself. Seven (7) have gone into the lot at No. 36 of which one entered the house, bursting in Aunt's room, another demolished the green house & a third set fire to the negro quarters, which were burned. The others fell in the garden & did no damage. The one in the house, broke a good deal of glass but did not materially injure the house itself. None have struck our house yet, tho' the other morning as I was at breakfast one burst in the Alley & a piece knocked off a slate from the roof. The houses all round tho' have been hit often.

There is no news at all to-night. The Yankees are very quiet firing in no direction, neither at the city, Sumter, nor the wreck. This is their first cessation from firing on the city since last Saturday. The shells have been coming at the rate of one every 10 minutes & the evening of the fire they threw thirty (30) in one hour. Now everything is quiet & I who am on duty to-night & have to sit up all night, am very sleepy. My turn comes round once every four nights & now I expect once every three nights, as one man leaves to-morrow. It is horrible work & of that sort that I see no fun in. . . .

Write soon to your affectionate
Gus

Augustine T. Smythe, Charleston, S.C.,
to Jane A. Adger and Susan D. Adger

Private
7 Feb. 1864

My dear Aunts,

I have a new niece picked out for you! or in other words I am engaged to be married! The young lady, as you may guess, is Miss Lou McCord of Columbia, my fondness for whom you have often spoken to me about. It is not a sudden thing with me, for I had a strong partiality for her long before I left College, & intended then to address her at some future time. My plan was to propose to her when I graduated, go to Europe with you, & if she consented, be married on my return. But man proposes & God disposes, & this with, with all my other plans, has been thwarted by this war so that now, I suppose, after it is over, I shall have to go to work. I kept quiet a long time, over two years, hoping that it would end soon enough for me to resume the College Course, & continue in the line I had projected, but this is now impracticable & so when I was on furlough the other day, & did not, nor could I reasonably expect another for a year at any rate, I could be still no longer, but had to speak my mind. She asked for a little time to consider, & it was only a day or two ago that I received my answer in the affirmative. I have told no one as yet except Mother, who knew all about it when I left, & this is the first opportunity I have had since of writing to you about it. . . . She is a sweet girl & I know you will like her, but there is no use for me to say anything on this subject as I know you will only laugh at it. Of course, (tho' I do not think her perfection), I do think she will be one to make me happy & one who will be welcome in the circle. She is emphatically not a fast girl & this is no small recommendation in these times. I have not chosen in a hurry. My mind had long been made up & the only question was as to the right time to speak. I was over there a great deal when in College, tho' as she heard shortly after I left that I was engaged she did not expect my addresses. I do not anticipate of course, the consummation of this thing until after the war & I am settled in some business but I should not like to have heard when far away of her engagement to anyone else.

I have thus written freely to you, dear Aunts, for you know I look upon you both as my second Mothers, & those to whom I owe a son's respect & love & I should not feel right to keep this longer than I could possibly help concealed from you. Still I must ask you to keep it a secret, for a time at any rate & also to consider this a letter confidentially to yourselves. I have told no one yet but Mother & Sue & shall not for a while make it public. I must write to Father soon which I dont exactly know how to do, inasmuch as he gave me a long talk on matrimony before I left. Still I must face the music. The others can wait a while as there is no hurry to tell them & I should rather not. You & Mother & Father are all that I feel I ought to tell at once & I have done or shall do so.

Public

There is no news at all to-night except a story which I have just heard that in a house in Coming St. this morning a woman was found hung while the house had apparently been robbed & rifled of every thing of value. I shall not vouch for the truth of this statement but do not think it unlikely. The enemy have not shelled since Friday when I last wrote except a couple to-night. At No. 36 things remain in status quo. . . . The garden is looking very well but oh! the greenhouse! it makes me sad to look at it. Still it died in a good cause. If we have unusual seasons I hope we shall have some unusual flowers, for the yanks have been kind enough, you know to plant in the garden, three very unusual seed, which I hope however will not burst up suddenly, but come gradually to the service. The Guard House has I think recd one more shot since my last report, making four holes now in its Meeting St. side. I do not know whether I told you that the Lecture Room to the Baptist Church by 36 has been struck & that three or four have gone into the grave yard. There are six in St. Michaels yard & two on the pavement outside, one of which came thro' the wall. God seems to be specially protecting that church. No less than some 20 shells have fallen within 100 yards of it & yet it has not grazed. Not many of those that fall in soft earth burst, so the graves are not much disturbed. The Scotch burying ground[10] has also received three or four but the church is untouched. So far the only one I know of is the Lutheran[11] which has been struck. The worst used up house I have seen yet is Harrall's store,[12] corner of Hazel & Meeting Sts. & this is very much shot up. It will have almost to be re-built. The burnt district has recd many a shell & when they fall there, dont the brickbats fly! Mr. Moffett's house (another shell, one an hour) opposite our church has been struck & one went into John St. They fly all round town now & I expect they will soon reach the upper portion of the old city. It is so queer to see all the business up there & all down town so dull. About here it is deserted & one might as well be on James Isl. for all the company one sees or all the people. No promenading on the Battery now I can tell you. Robt. complained to me the other day that some one had been in his garden & stolen some cabbages but that it was the first time. I hardly blame any one for taking them if they dont go into the house. . . . It is late & I must go to bed as I have to be up all to-morrow night. I have this to do every 3rd night now. Pretty tough! Give my best love to all at home, to Mother, Sue, Sis & all & please write soon to

Your affectionate boy
Augustine

Augustine T. Smythe, 12 Meeting St.,
Charleston, S.C., to Margaret M. Smyth

17 Feb. 1864
7 p.m.

Oh! Mother, dear Mother, you dont know how your letter has pained me, how sad I have been ever since I received it Monday night. The thought that I have hurt my Mother, her whose love has always been so very dear to me, for whose sake I have made & should make as many sacrifices whose smile of approval was always my highest reward, whose good night kiss was ever thought necessary for a night's rest, the refusal of which was always, even to the time when last we separated, the heaviest punishment she could inflict, the thought that I had pained her has been haunting me ever since. I have been so blue & wished so much that I could only see you once more & like a child, weep in your arms. Mother, it makes me very sad to think of it & the tears will come as the thought comes back again & again, throughout the day that my Mother, is displeased with me. I tried to write yesterday, tho' it came too late for the Monday's mail, but was on duty & could not do it, & this morning I was busy about Adger's salt & Father's things, & this is the first chance I have had. Here I am in dear old No. 12,[13] sitting where Father used to sit, alone in this big old house, with only the familiar tick of the clock to keep me company, with a fire which makes the room look oh! so natural, for it is quite cold & as I take my eyes from the paper, fancy is busy bringing up all round me the dear ones whom I have seen gathered about this hearth, now scattered & away, & then I feel so lonely & so homesick & above all the thought that my Mother, whom I have always cherished in my heart in its most sacred recesses, whose comfort & prop I ever sought to be & to be whose guardian & stay now in the evening of her life, was my purpose & highest ambition, to feel that she is pained & hurt! Oh Mother it makes me so sad. God knows that sweet as is the possession of the love I have just now, there would be an infusion of bitter at the knowledge that it was obtained at the price of a Mother's or even of the slightest portion of a Mother's love. I <u>know & value</u> my Mother's love & affection, its depth & unselfishness, & God knows, how loath I am to part with one iota of that which has always been my pride & blessing & which I have ever done my best to win & when won to cherish & perpetuate. Oh, Mother let not Lou come between us. It will not be my doing if so. I am too fully conscious of the worth & scarcity & a love like a Mother's to part with any of it or to have any of it weaned from me. My heart is full to-night, Mother, & I write just from its dictation. I am very lonely here. At the Bathing House there are uncongenial companions in the majority & an unpleasant atmosphere pervades the place which makes me glad to be away when I can. There is too much gambling & swearing there. Up town there are gambling saloons, & bar-rooms, & worse & a crowd always there. These are not to my taste, thank God! & my Mother's teachings! There are only two or three ladies here & not particular friends. So my only refuge is home & here it is so lonesome especially after dark when the outer world is shut out, when the hour comes for home pleasures & social happiness, then it does make me home sick to be in the dear old house, now solitary, stripped & deserted. You speak of coming down to see me. I wish so much that such a thing were possible. How I should like to see you in the old house once more! But I dont think you ought to expose yourself to the dangers attending. I should never forgive myself if anything should happen to you. Where would you stay? Not here in the house by yourself. That would not do at all.

I think you have been misinformed about Mrs. McCord,[14] certainly so as far as my knowledge of her goes. She has been a widow for some time & obliged to manage her own affairs. Still I have never seen any symptoms of a domineering character at all nor of one who likes to rule or bend to her will. She is much more of a <u>woman</u> than people give her credit for. Certainly she has done immeasurable good to the poor & the soldiers since this war. She is & has been unceasing in her visits & attentions to the College Hospital[15] & many a poor fellow owes his life to her care & her kindness as well as her supplies. The poor around all go to her in trouble & are always supplied. From my own observation & knowledge of her I have formed a very different & at the same time a very high opinion of her character as a woman. She is well read, but also seems to be a great house keeper. She is kind, very kind, to all who claim kindness of her & the sick & wounded soldier is ever cared for kindly. This is my opinion & such is what I have heard. Poor Sue! her letter brought tears into my eyes. I must write to her by this mail. I got your letters on my return from a short run to Cola. . . . I should be very glad if you could write to Miss Lou, but I do not wish to urge you against your own inclinations to do so, nor Sue either. If you prefer or think best not to, do not on my account what you had rather leave undone. If you do, the direction is, Miss L. R. McCord, Columbia, S.C., but again let me beg you not to write unless you are perfectly willing & feel it altogether right to do so. I leave it with you entirely. I am encouraged by my visit. She was glad to see me & I had an agreeable & pleasant trip. You ask me if I sought God's direction in this matter. It has been a subject of prayer with me since before I left College & when I got her letter with her answer, I received & acknowledged it as an answer to prayer. Daily & nightly with my other petitions to the mercy seat, there went up one, that if right in the sight of God, we should be brought together & love each other, & when I did hear from her, I went to my room & on my knees returned thanks to God & prayed for his guidance & protection to the end. I have sought him & his aid & now hope for his blessing. . . .

Now I shall leave the rest till next time as I want to tell you how my plans of going to Va. are getting on & it is very late & I have to sit up to-morrow night. I have for the present dropped Morgan,[16] till I hear more about him. I wrote some time ago to Mr. Venable,[17] asking him if he knew how I could be transferred from here to Va. giving my reasons etc. but have not heard from him yet. Then I wrote to Heart,[18] as Signal Sergt. at Richmond whom I knew here, to ask him about being transferred to the Signal Corps there. I have not yet heard from him either. I have heard from Capt. Barrows yesterday. He says the Engineer Corps is full now, but there will most probably be some vacancies at the opening of the Spring Campaign, where he hoped to get one for me. Another plan is to join a cavalry company of Stuart's Brigade,[19] which is here for two months recruiting & go to him with the hope of getting the position of signal officer on his staff, a place now vacant. This last I have not yet thought over but shall do so. It does not strike me very favorably just at present, but may do so. What do you think of it? I am more than ever anxious to quit here & go to Va. & am doing my best to accomplish it. When you write tell me which plan you prefer. . . .

Augustine

Augustine T. Smythe, Charleston, S.C., to Jane A. Adger

21 Feb. 1864

My very dear Aunt Janey,

From my heart I thank you for your kind letter of the 16th & the words of sympathy & congratulations you there speak . . . believe me that I value them very very highly. You ask me, dear Aunt Janey, if I have made this a subject of prayer. I answer, Yes. Daily with my prayers did the petition rise that if God saw proper I might be blessed with her love & when this thing was brought about, I recd & acknowledged it as a direct answer from above. I feel, as I said to Auntie, that the matter is in his hands, & that he who has so far, I trust, guided me, will lead me in future, to the end & that he will do what seems to him best. From what I have ever seen in her deportment & behaviour both in church & out of it, I can but believe that she is a Christian & in this hope I rejoice. Like you, I think that an irreligious worldly woman will not make me happy but this I believe firmly is not her character. I write all this in confidence to you, Aunt Janey, for except to Mother & Auntie I should not like at all that this should be known. This is my own private life. I dont exactly know how it would do to send up one of her letters. She might not like it & perhaps it would not be a fair specimen. . . .

There is very little news here & the town is quite dull. The Yankees have not been shelling the city to-day (or yesterday rather for it is now 3 A.M.), but occupied themselves occasionally with Sumter but not often. Their guns must (evidently) be wearing out. For the last week or so nearly all their shells have fallen short & the other day of 100 thrown at the city, only 12 came in. The others fell in the water between this & Castle Pinckney. They do not seem to know it or they would have stopped. A deserter just come in says that both Gilmore & his men are heartily sick of shelling the city. There will be no active operations here this summer everybody says. The Monitors are fairly backed down. They were expecting an assault on Sumter last week but no sign of it as yet appeared. Unless they bring 10,000 men & are prepared to sacrifice 5000, they had better not come at Sumter. . . .

The submarine torpedo boat,[20] the fish, which has been put in repair & been lying down at Sullivan's Island for some time, went out on Thursday night & it is supposed sunk a blockader, as one of them was seen to go down. This attack was unknown at the time even at Hd. Qtrs. they supposed it was the storm. Since then, however, nothing has been heard of her & she is put down as lost. The common name given her is "murdering machine." The Davids are ready for work & I hope will soon be put at it. It is time. . . .

I heard from Capt. Barrows the other day. There were no vacancies their [*sic*] but they expected some when he would try & get me one. I am more than ever anxious to be transferred to Va. or the West & am trying my best to accomplish it. I am endeavouring now to get on in the Signal Corps & then see when I am on there what I can do. . . .

Please give my best love to Auntie & all the dear ones at home. . . . In very much love to yourself, dear Aunt Janey, I am

Your afft Augustine

Augustine T. Smythe, Charleston, S.C.,
to his sister Sarah A. Smyth, Summerton, S.C.

28 Feb. 1864

My dear Sarah Annie,

I am going to tell you a secret but you must be sure & keep it to yourself now, as I do not want you to mention to to any body at all.

I am engaged to Miss Lou McCord of Columbia, a young lady whom I know you will love when you are acquainted with her. She is a little older than you are but I am certain you will like her. She has dark hair & eyes & a fair complexion & is about Sue's height.

Now Annie you must keep my secret as I am not going to tell any except my own family & Aunts & dont want the others to know.

Thanks for your letters. I shall write as soon as I get the chance but you must not get tired writing to your brother,

Gus

CHAPTER 4

A Lofty Perch in St. Michael's

March 1864–November 1864

Augustine T. Smythe, Dill's Bluff,
James Island, S.C., to Susan D. Adger, Columbia, S.C.

6 March 1864

My dear Auntie

Enclosed please find a photograph which you know I promised you some time ago. . . .

The house at No. 36 has been struck again. The shell came thro' the roof, into the same room as the other & burst in your room doing considerably more damage than the first but <u>not</u> breaking the mirrors. The pieces were scattered all around & one sticking in the wall which I especially charged Robt. not to take out but to leave in for Aunt Janey's satisfaction to show after the war. The floor upstairs is pretty well torn up & your floor has three or four holes in it. . . . The fire the other day burnt down Bowens Kitchen & half his stables, the brick house on Water St. & partially burnt two or three wooden ones. They had hard work to save 34. The fence between was burnt down but Robt. has patched up a sort of temporary one. No. 36 was not otherwise injured. . . .

Much love to dear Aunt Janey & the girls & much to yourself, Auntie,

From your affectionate boy,
Augustine

St. Michael's Episcopal Church, where Augustine T. Smythe was stationed in the steeple as a signalman. Courtesy of the Library of Congress.

Augustine T. Smythe, St. Michael's Church steeple, Charleston, S.C., to Margaret M. Smyth

31 March 31 1864

My very dear Mother,

Here I am on my lofty perch[1] behind a big telescope looking out for any movements of the Yankees which may be of sufficient importance to send up to Genl. Jordan.[2] My tour of duty to-night is from 1:30 A.M. to 9 A.M. & I have been on duty half the day. . . . The duty is pretty heavy, as I am on every other day & half of every other night. The worst difficulty is the trouble of getting up here for it is not a joke climbing up 150 feet. . . . I have been on now two days & nights in succession, but hereafter it will be regular. Our place is the upper piazza above the clock. We have it boarded in & bunks put there for us to sleep in so that we are tolerably comfortable except the wind which blows thro the cracks of the boards at a great rate & there is always a wind up here. I still eat at home & shall try to fix it so as to sleep there every other night when I am not on duty. Our business up here is merely to keep a close eye on all the movements of the enemy & report them to the Genl. It is quite interesting to watch them as we have a splendid glass. Now it is daybreak & their vessels are moving about & soldiers marching on Morris Isl. at a great rate. Nothing unusual. It is well I am not superstitious up here at night sitting alone. . . .

Good bye with love to all,
From your boy
Augustine

Augustine T. Smythe, St. Michael's Church steeple, Charleston, S.C., to Margaret M. Smyth

Thursday
7 April 1864

My dear Mother,

. . . You must not feel anxious about me up here & never fear my falling down the stairs, tho' there are 170 of them. "High life above Stairs" with a vengeance. . . . It is no joke to walk up 170 winding stairs, I can assure you without trying to run either up or down them. Besides I know all the bad places by this time. There are four of us up here, two on every day. . . . Oh my, there goes that bell (10 o'c) & such a cracking & a shaking as this old steeple gets when ever they ring it is a caution. The first time you experience it, you feel certain that it is going to fall immediately. Now I have got rather used to it, but still it is not the most comfortable feeling I have ever had. It shakes so I can hardly write. . . .

We have a rope ladder outside in case the steeple should be struck for us to descend, but it has passed safely thro' so much that I am in hopes it will go thro' the rest. It seems as if God's providence was specially directed towards this venerable (but shaky) old Spire. . . .

No news at all. The Yanks threw three or four shells into the City yesterday morning apparently trying a new gun but did not keep it up. To-day there has been some little firing down below & another Monitor has arrived. How different to-day from this day twelve month. Then Sumter drove back the Ironclads. Now I am afraid she could not tho' she might help. A David went thro' Wappoo to-night going round to North Edisto I think. Hope she will have better success than the last time, when she struck a boat, but the torpedo wd. not explode. They say several of them (Davids) are to be carried down by R.R. & sent to Port Royal. . . .

Love to all the dear ones at home.
Your boy Augustine

Augustine T. Smythe, St. Michael's Church steeple, Charleston, S.C, to Margaret M. Smyth

15 April 1864

My dear Mother,

Thanks for your letter received the other night. Fields has not yet made his appearance but I suppose will in a day or two. I intended telling you not to send the little Bantam here as she is too pretty to be down here & hope you have not done so. There is no news at all. Yankees very quiet to-day tho' yesterday they were shelling briskly. . . . I have had No. 36 nailed up to prevent any further incursions of the Soldiers. They just roam at will now thro' the whole of the lower portion of the City. Our house & Mr. Middleton's are the only two in Meeting St. below Broad which have not been entered. . . . A shell struck St. Philip's Steeple yesterday & then went on & hit the Pavilion Hotel. . . . The Soldiers the other day to spite me, pulled down all the Wisteria from the brick wall but I have fixed it up nicely again & trained it into both trees. I dont think it will kill them for it has been in a tree in Mrs. Beach's yard a long time & there is no sign yet of it's dying. Our Stores on the wharf have <u>not</u> been seriously injured, but the soldiers have been in there also. They have done three times the damage to the City that the shells have. Tis a shame. Everything is very dull here now except a rumor that we are again to change our officer, this one to go away & Memminger to be sent here. . . . All quiet along the Bar. The Charleston Hotel[3] was struck yesterday. Joe Huger[4] of the Corps was killed on Wednesday by a shell from Gregg which took off half his head. He was in Sumter.

Mail time. Love to all the dear ones, Sis, Janie, Ellen, Father, babies & all & much to Mother from her boy

Augustine

Augustine T. Smythe, Charleston, S.C., to Margaret M. Smyth

18 April 1864

My very dear Mother,

. . . This morning McArthur came to me, just as I finished breakfast to say that Uncle R's house had been broken open & robbed, so I at once went round there & have just returned in time for dinner. This causes my hurry now, to get this to the Office in time. When I got round there I found that they had rifled the house nearly all the lead pipe that was exposed, the copper boiler from the kitchen, the lead from the bathing tubs & pantry all had been torn away. I found fortunately the copper boiler & two large pieces of lead from the tubs hid in the Stable preparatory to being carried off. So I got a waggon & had it brought round here. The pumps also, which by some strange oversight they had left. I cut away & brought here also together with some curtains from the windows. They had entered from the next house breaking open a window in the Stable as I tracked them, & thinking they could not have made way with everything I got the police & had the next house searched where I knew some soldiers slept. There I found about 40 lbs. of the pipe & a number of nick nacks & work boxes etc. from the house. The police carried two women & one soldier to the guard house, but they will do nothing with them except a week perhaps in the house of correction. I have had the house nailed up & think they will hardly come there again just now. They cut all the pipes from & to the cistern & everywhere thro' the house, tearing open the lower part of the bath tubs to get the pipe. It is a shame to see the high handed way in which they bandit over the city. There is hardly a house down town which they have not robbed. They killed poor West as you see in the papers. The coroner's jury is still sitting. It is hardly safe to go about the Streets at night now. In case I should be ordered away tho there is no likelihood of it just now I should most certainly employ Philip to stay in the yard, if for nothing else, to keep the dogs here. I have two now, one a fine bull terrier belonging to Adger. He will be well worth his $15 or $20 pr. month. You have no idea how they do damage a house. Poor Mr. Bowen's house! It makes me sad to go into it. They dogs are invaluable. I should not take $500 for them. The Stuff I have here from Legare St. must be worth 2 or 3000 dollars. In Mr. B's house they have taken down all the gas fixtures. In Mr. Courtney they have ripped up the floor for the pipe & taken the lead from the roof. Tis a shame. So sorry you did not get the box of asparagus & flowers & I sent by the train to Gourdin's. The train was delayed on the road & the waggon must have gone without waiting for it. It is at Gourdin's now I expect. I wrote you a long long letter in it, giving you all the news. . . . The garden is looking finely & there are some really splendid roses in it. . . .

Thanks for the money. It was very acceptable. We have not been paid off yet & now I dont know when we shall be. . . .

Much love to Sis, Janie, Ellen, Father & all & much to yourself dear Mother fromYour boy

Augustine

P.S. I am going to write to Uncles telling them my secret. You think it best & I dont know but what it is. Aunt Janey says so too.

Augustine T. Smythe, St. Michael's Church steeple, Charleston, S.C., to Margaret M. Smyth

8 May 1864

My own dear Mother,

I wrote you on Monday Night & mailed the letter on the cars the next day telling you all about my Virginia plans, since which I have heard nothing from them, & don't know whether I am to go or not. . . .

I did have a very pleasant visit to Col. I staid at the Seminary with Ellison[5] took breakfast with him two mornings & slept with him at night. I spent most of my time with Miss Lou of course & was more satisfied with my choice than ever. I have drawn a prize Mother & you will agree with me when you know her. She is not a fashionable girl at all but a plain, neat loveable one & I know will make me happy as my wife. I was out riding on horse back with her both evenings of my stay. She rides well & a great deal, nearly every day, with Sister. She sings very well indeed. This you know pleases me & will please you too for you are also fond of singing. I am very glad the girls will stay there a day or two on their way down. It will give them a chance to be better acquainted with her & she with them. I know they will find it pleasant there. . . .

With much love
Your own boy
Augustine

Augustine T. Smythe, Charleston S.C, to Margaret M. Smyth

12 May 1864

My dear Mother,

. . . This is a damp rainy disagreeable morn. Been raining all night. The fog is so thick we cant see James Island. Still the Yanks keep up their shelling. They threw one a minute ago which burst just by the Huguenot Church.[6] Am not certain that it did not strike it. Another by Cumberland St. in the Burnt District.[7] What wonders science has wrought that these persons can stay four miles distant and hurl shell into a place they cannot see. Truly man is wonderful in his ingenuity. They struck Mr. Dana's Church[8] on Tuesday not doing much damage tho. Monday they dropped their shells in this neighborhood. Some three or four fell in Church St. between Broad & Tradd & some in Elliott St. Pretty close for a continuance. None came any farther tho. They struck the Court House steps the other day. The shells must have gone over the steeple or gone round it for the Steeple is in a direct line between Morris Isl. & the Court House. This is pretty much all that is going on now. Another Monitor has made its appearance off the Bar, making seven in all. This must be to protect their works on Morris Isl. wh. otherwise might be easily taken. No news here. What glorious tidings from Va. but how dearly bought is that victory. Longstreet[9] wounded & Jenkins[10] killed by our own men, by the same Brigade that shot Jackson.[11] Then the loss among the lower men. What a price we are paying for our liberty. . . .

Augustine T. Smythe, St. Michael's Church steeple, Charleston S.C., to Margaret M. Smyth

13 May 1864

My dear Mother,

. . . Uncle Joe & Adger left on Friday morning as they expected & are by this time well on their way to the Regt. which is at Petersburg or this side with Beauregard, where as you see there is some trouble about the Rail Road which the Yankees hold at present. As they are sending reinforcements to Beauregard however, I hope soon to hear better things from him. News to-day says Col. Pressly[12] wounded, so Maj. Glover[13] will be in command. That is bad. He is not much of an officer. Col. Dargan[14] is killed. Poor Cousin Janie,[15] it will be a sad blow to her. Col. Blake[16] also wounded. There will be trouble for his pretty little wife. What a cruel thing is war, lacerating & breaking so many hearts. God grant I may never witness nor participate in another one. Hagoods Brigade behaved with distinguished gallantry. This is no news tho'. Everyone knew it would do so, whenever it got into a fight. I am very anxious to see the list of casualties in the Brigade among the privates & sub-officers. Oh! how I should like to be with them. Were it not for the orders I expected I should have applied to go with them when they left & even now I feel strongly tempted sometimes to join them. However, I still wait on my orders from which I have heard nothing more. I shall mail my letter to Adger by the mail to-morrow as the one sent to Wilmington will hardly reach him. He will in all probability have passed W. before the letter got there. He may be detained there tho' then will get it. I shall mail yours anyhow. His address now will be Capt. J.E.A.,[17] A.Q.M., 25th S.C.V., Hagood's Brigade, Beauregard's Army, Va. This is the only one I knew that can reach him. (How I wished the other morning I was going on with them! Here everything is so dull & quiet. No news at all.) The Yankees have evidently moved nearly all their troops from this Department & consider the siege nearly raised. One of their Monitors left yesterday & was taken South probably to Port Royal to be overhauled. So the arrival of these new ones instead of pretending an attack, is merely a relief to those that have been on duty here for sometime in order that they may be re-fixed & repaired. They have again begun on Sumter however, as if they thought that if they had to relinquish their hopes of getting Charleston, yet they could have it all their own way with Sumter. Friday & Saturday they were firing at it all day long, not only from the land batteries on Morris Isl. but also from two of their Monitors which came up near the Fort & participated in the bombardment. It was a magnificent sight from the Steeple here, to look at this fierce fight, tho' it was hardly a fight for poor old Sumter could do nothing, going on below us. Sullivan's Isl. opened on the Monitors & hit them several times & yesterday all our batteries on James Isl. fired on Morris Isl. It was really grand. Notwithstanding all this to occupy them there however, the indefatigable Yankees still found time to keep up their shelling of the City as steadily as usual. They can teach us a lesson in energy. During all this firing so far the only casualties have been two or three negroes slightly, but by shells, the severest wound being the loss of a foot. This the effect of over 1000 shells. No serious damage done to the Fort. This will hardly pay.

The shells have been dropping all around our house this last day or two. Two deserters went over to the Yankees on Wednesday night & it is supposed gave them information concerning the state of affairs in Sumter. Hence this sudden & heavy bombardment, to try & injure our battery there. They must also have told them of the troops on the Battery, as since then they seem to have made that their target to aim at. Several have fallen on the Battery itself. One went into Prioleau's yard yesterday & another into Huger's yard on East Battery. Two fell yesterday in Ladson's Court & one in Meeting St. near it. Two went in Church St. near the Battery some where along that neighborhood. In fact nearly all have fallen below the Steeple & mostly below Tradd St. They came popping round the house, sometimes shaking it till you can feel it tremble when they burst near at hand. I had a very narrow escape on Friday A.M. about 5 o'c. as I was going up to the depot to see Adger off. Just at the corner of Tradd & the Bay as I was going to step on one end of a cellar door, a shell fell thro' the other end, not three feet from me & burst down in the cellar covering me with dirt & smoke but leaving me unharmed. Had it burst on level ground it would have killed me, but as it was in the cellar I was fortunate enough to escape. One piece even knocked my pipe from my mouth & so close did it come that I could feel the wind. This is just a little closer than I care to have them come again. On my way back I stopped & dug up a large piece of the shell which I intend to keep. I saw also on Saturday afternoon a narrow miss. I was on the Battery when I heard a shell coming. It passed over us & struck on the pavement across the Street just by a crowd of women & soldiers who were collected there not six feet from them. Fortunately it did not burst & so injured none of them, but if it had burst some one must have been hit. . . .

Augustine

Augustine T. Smythe, Charleston, S.C., to Jane A. Adger

2 June 1864

My dear Aunt Janey,

Many thanks for your kind letter. . . .

I am beginning to fear that my papers must have been lost between this & Richmond as I have heard nothing from them & oh! it is a disappointment. I cannot write this way home for they are all so settled there that I am doing more & better here, in their opinion, than I could anywhere else, & write to me so much to stay that I feel almost as if my hands were tied. I do not want to stay here this summer & did my best to get away & a little while ago hoped I had succeeded. Now I doubt. The papers should have been back. But if it were not for those at home, Mother & Father, who are so very much opposed to my going, thereby doing me I think an injury, I should try again & even return to my company if there was no other way. Aunt Janey you know I am ambitious & it does gall me & cut me to the quick to hear of my companions rising in rank, while I remain here wasting abilities which I know to be naturally good & with no prospect of being any higher than I was when I entered the Corps over 18 months ago. They write to me from home of the comforts I can enjoy here more than in the field, but God knows that when I entered the Army I surrendered myself up willingly & entirely & I do not think anyone ever heard me complain or grumble at any hardships I may have endured. On the contrary in proportion as discomforts increased my spirits rise, so I have always found. Again they write me of the good I am doing in protecting the property! A negro can do that. No Aunt Janey you know that when I entered the Army I selected a company going to Va. but gave it up & went into one which I did not like on Mother's account. It was a trial at the time & the ill effects I have felt ever since. . . . I want to be there & I must confess to almost jealousy when Uncle, Adger, James & even Andrew[18] went & I was left. Still when I get letters from home & see how my parents are worried & troubled at this idea of my going, the question arises. Ought I to sacrifice their comfort & feelings, to my wishes? So I am quiet but unwillingly. But if the orders I have already applied for should come, then there will be no difficulty, for then I shall <u>have</u> to go. I have been waiting patiently, & hoping almost against hope, but now I begin to fear they are mislaid. . . . So you see how I feel about it, how I am not satisfied here, nor am I satisfied with my part in this war, so different from what I hoped or planned. But my O! I really beg your pardon Aunt Janey for writing you all this, which if you skip you will not lose anything. Please remember tho' this letter is to you & dont show it unless to Auntie. I have not opened my heart to anyone else nor is there anyone to whom I could, but I feel that you will understand, & sympathize & advise & I am restless here.

The Yankees continue to shell as usual. Indeed the last two or three days they have been shelling much more rapidly. The other day at a fire in Elliott St. they threw 25 shell in an half hour. Pretty quick. Some came very near the Steeple. One the other night burst just on the Broad St. pavement by the Church, but did not strike it at all. This is the only Church down town that has not been hit. All the rest are marked. Do you know that sometimes when I am up there I almost wish they would strike the Steeple. I should like it & I should not regard a wound as a misfortune. This may be wrong but I cant help it. I do feel so. . . .

Arthur Robinson is killed![19] God help his poor Mother! She was wrapt up in her Arthur & he was as noble a fellow as ever lived. Everybody knew & everybody liked Arthur Robinson. He is a loss, a severe loss to his country & his friends. Dear Arthur! he was one of my most intimate chosen friends, one that it will be almost impossible to replace. I must stop tho' for it is getting late. No news to give, except that it is raining slightly. I have been quite unwell a week ago, but am all right again.

Love to dear Auntie, also to Aunt E., Sallie & all the girls at Rivoli.

Ever
Your boy
Augustine

Augustine T. Smythe, Charleston, S.C.,
to his sister Sarah A. Smyth, Summerton, S.C.

3 June 1864

My dear Sarah Annie

. . . It is quite warm down here to-day, very little breeze. Last night tho' there was quite a severe thunderstorm which made it very pleasant then but does not seem to have helped it any to-day. You must be suffering from the heat up in the country. Poor father, I feel very sorry for him. What will he do without the Battery this summer, tho' for that matter even were he down here he would get but very little good of it for it so cut up "revised & abridged" that there is hardly enough left for a good walk. One great consolation about the Steeple is that we generally have it cool up there for if any breeze at all is stirring, that is the place to catch it. Occasionally tho we do have it very warm up there & then it is horrible.

The Yankees are throwing their shell as usual to-day, but not so fast as for one or two days past. They are using now a very heavy gun & the roar of the shells as they fly on the path of destruction is really awful. One struck quite close to the Steeple this morning just before I left, in Broad St. between King & Meeting . It did make a terrible noise as it flew past the Steeple. Yesterday tho shells fell principally around King & Market St. & in the neighborhood of Trinity Church.[20] One just going over now has burst high up town. Strange that these shells never give me a moments thought now. I hear them coming & it seems all a matter of course. I pay no attention to them at all. But then I have had some little experience now & you remember the old adage, "Familiarity breeds contempt." Well one of these will knock me over some day I expect & thus teach me the respect due them. Yesterday the Yanks had their hands full, shelling the City, Sumter, Sullivan's & James Island at the same time, while our batteries were replying to them. It is beautiful to see from my elevated position these bombardments. The white smoke puffing out in dense clouds from the batteries there the flash & small speck of smoke indicating the bursting shell, but which gradually expands & enlarges until it is lost among the real nebular. It is a sight worth seeing & one to be remembered but seen too oft. why there the beauty was. It may be very grand for a week or so, but when has it before him every day for months the grand vanishes, only the sameness remains. . . .

Now remember you are to write to me soon again & tell me about your visit. Love to brother, Sue, Sis & all the dear ones in Summerton.

Your afft. brother
Augustine

Augustine T. Smythe, Charleston, S.C., to Margaret M. Smyth

9 June 1864

My dear Mother,

. . . Well! the Yankees have succeeded at last in hitting St. Michael's Church, not the Steeple, just at the base of it. The shell entered the South roof of the church on Tuesday but did not burst nor do much damage. So I suppose they would be easier did they, but know it. I do not consider the Church as broken however, until the Steeple itself receives a scratch. They have been throwing their shells very near it for some time however, striking the Court House again & bursting all around in Church, Broad & Meeting Sts. Last night I saw what must have been the celebrated Greek fire. About 8 P.M. a shell fell in Meeting just above the Mills House & burst. As it exploded a piece of fire was thrown a great height in the air & all around the spot were large splotches of fire. Fortunately, it was in the Street & in the Burnt District, so there was nothing to burn. The fire lasted about five minutes. This morning I looked at the cinders. They looked as tho' something had been rolled up & saturated with the liquid. I hope the Yankees think it a failure from seeing no conflagration follow the explosion & that they will no longer regale us with such. . . .

Good bye now it is late. Love to all the dear ones at home. Ever with much love,

Your own boy
Augustine

Another shell gone into No. 36. It went thro' the roof down thro' the drawing room into the East sitting room. Nothing hurt except the door just by the private staircase. It did not burst. All well. 14 shells now gone into No. 36, 4 of them in the house.

Augustine T. Smythe, Charleston, S.C., to Jane A. Adger

13 June 1864

My dear Aunt Janey,

Your kind & sympathizing letter I received on Saturday last & I hasten to reply. But first let me thank you sincerely for your letter comforting as it was for as you say it does help sometimes to unburden the heart & share the load, especially with one on whom you feel you can call at anytime & always receive a ready sympathy. There is one question tho' you ask me & so nicely I want to answer & that is "why should you wish to be promoted?" Now even should the war end in the winter, I hardly dare say fall, still how I should desire it! You must know I am ambitious Aunt Janey, you who have watched over me from my cradle, you must know how I long to rise above the crowd, to get above & leave a name behind me when I go. This has been my spur, always at school, I feared nothing so much as a mistake in my lesson & consequent low mark; at college it was always with pride & joy that I noticed the Professors single me out with one or two, to be always called up when the recitation was difficult. I know that I have abilities above the common & I thank God for them & pray for his grace to assist me in making good use of them. Then feeling as I do in this way you can imagine how I chafe at still remaining here & filling a position which is filled equally well by so many others whom I know are my inferiors in mind & how I long to get into some place where there is more scope. I have mastered this, did that long ago, & it is shallow, now I want more. Hence my request for the Engineers or the Ordnance Bureau, or even a commission somewhere, where one could make more use of mind, where intellect would be required. Therefore even let the war end in winter till then I should like to be promoted. Again, whatever be my course in after life, mercantile or professional, I want to rise to be at the top of the list, at the head of my class, and now dont you see, Aunt Janey the advantage those will have, who have held positions during this war. If heaven so will it, how gladly should I become a public man & go to Congress perhaps

& do you not see how if such should be the case the ground I am losing now in not being there where these stirring scenes are being enacted. . . .

The Yankees have favored No. 36 with the fourteenth shell. It went in thro' the house too, thro' the roof, down thro' the parlor just by the North door, then down thro' the little East sitting room breaking the door, the North door into the entry all to smash & then thro' to the ground. The sitting room you used to use most. It did not burst so the chief sufferer was the plastering & the door. Mirrors unhurt. This is the fourth in the house. One went into Desaussure's big house[21] on the Battery the other day & burst just behind a mirror without breaking it. . . . Oh! how it rained yesterday & last night & to-day. The old Steeple rocked & shook & leaked so that there was hardly a dry place, and then it turned so cold. To-night almost cold enough for fire. By the way we are to have a guard to keep shells from the Steeple & City now in the shape of a number of Yankee officers & men including Gen. Seymour, who are to be put in the Guard house & [Court] House & notification sent to the Yankees of the fact.[22] Wonder how it will act. They will hardly fire on their own men. . . .

Did I tell you that the Hibernian Hall had been struck three times lately & badly & the Court House twice slightly. Plenty of shells round the Steeple. Thirteen fell one day between Queen St. & St. M's Alley in Meeting St. But it is nearly 12 o'c. & I must to bed as I got very little sleep last night & must sit up again to-morrow night. Much love to dear Auntie. This letter to her too. Love to all at Rivoli & much to yourself dear Aunt Janey from

Your affectionate
Augustine

Augustine T. Smythe, Charleston, S.C., to his sister Jane A. Smyth

26 June 1864

My dear Janey,

Your last letter I did not receive until Wednesday owing no doubt to some delay in the mails which are now very irregular. . . .

Well I have no longer a whole roof above my head. Friday week ago, a shell entered thro' the roof, thro' the third story & down into the Study, where it smashed the mantel piece & then fell on the floor without bursting. This was very fortunate. Had it burst, the damage would have been much greater. As it was not even a pane of glass was broken, & the only serious hurt was to the marble mantel. I was down stairs at the time & expecting such a thing, for the shells had been falling all around me the whole afternoon, striking the houses opposite, & dropping in the lot next door. This was the only one tho' that came into my house. Since then, astonished & dismayed no doubt at their temerity, [the] Yankees have carefully avoided our neighborhood & have thrown their shells higher up town. . . .

I came up here yesterday with Miss Anna Frost.[23] Mr. Tom F.[24] & two Miss Harlestons, to show them the Yankees. It is well worth a visit to obtain the view, but one visit is enough. It must not be seen too oft. I have entirely forgotten now where the beauty of the view is except when I am asleep. By the way is Miss Anna to be married soon? I think so but it is only a suspicion on my part. She is looking very pretty. Miss Minnie Hayne[25] is staying with her now on a visit. You have heard of Minnie Whaley's marriage.[26] That was a sort of run away affair. Her parents disapproved the match, so she went one morning at 7 o'c. when they were in the country & got married. None of her family were present but her Sister Miss Josephine. I dont care about things done up in that way myself. . . .

Now I must close as it is time for me to go to dinner. . . . Give the baby[27] a kiss for me. Is it as pretty as ever.

Your affectionate
Gus

Augustine T. Smythe, Charleston, S.C., to Margaret M. Smyth

27 June 1864

My dear Mother,

. . . Everything here as usual. To-day is very hot, but there is a pleasant breeze stealing in this window, by the next yard, which is delightful. Outside tho it is very warm, real summer weather. The least movement brings in profuse perspiration. Clear tho' & bright, & dry. Luckily there is plenty of water in our cistern so I have no stint. Wish the pipes did not leak so that I might use the Bathing tub. I have been at a man nearly a month now to come & fix it but have been unable to get him. . . .

The Yankees are shelling as usual but nearly all their shells have fallen short. Yesterday, only two or three came in & they burst on the Bay. There was also considerable firing at Sumter, & by our batteries on Gregg, one shot carrying away the flag staff. . . . The Yankee prisoners are in Mr. Conner's house[28] at the corner of Broad & Rutledge Sts. It is a splendid house & a delightful situation. They have a large yard & empty lot to walk in & the other day the Govt. sent round & had gas fixtures put up so that they might have light all at the expense of the Confederacy. They are on their parole not to leave the premises but there is also a guard stationed round them. Great many people go round to see them. They are quite a good looking set, & very well dressed. Have plenty of money which they spend for coffee & sugar etc. It seems a shame to treat them so well. As we have now got the credit of putting them in shell range, we ought to do so & not leave them out there where a shell does not drop once in two months. They seem perfectly well contented with their situation & well they may be for they are much better off than in camp. . . .

Now I must stop & carry this to the Office. I dread the walk for it is very hot. Love to Father, Sue, Sis, & all the dear ones at Summerton. Ever with much love dear Mother, Your own boy

Augustine

The O'Connor residence on Broad Street, which housed Union POWs. The ruins around it were caused by the great fire that swept through Charleston in December 1861. Courtesy of the Library of Congress.

Augustine T. Smythe, Charleston, S.C., to Jane A. Smyth

1 July 1864

My very dear Sister

Your letter came duly a mail or two ago, but I have so many to write to in Summerton that you know I must take you by turns. So you must not get inpatient when your letters do not receive immediate attention but be certain that they will be answered as soon as I have replied to those which came before. I wish very much that I could get up to see you all, if only for a little while, but there seems no chance just now. They are not granting furloughs at all, & I even am unable to get a forty eight hour leave to run up to Columbia. It seems that they are expecting an attack or demonstration of some sort against Charleston & therefore are unwilling, as is but right, to weaken the force here by furloughs. . . .

The Yankees as usual are shelling to day & their shells are falling closer to No. 12 than they have done for some days past. None in the immediate vicinity however. There is also a brisk cannonade going on between Battery Gregg & the batteries on James Island, & Gregg is also firing on Sumter. So we have no lack of music. The Yankees have made no reduction of their fire on account of the prisoners in the city, but in retaliation have sent to the North for an equal number of our men, of similar rank, who are to be placed on Morris Island.[29] I doubt if they will be as comfortable as these are. We have them in a fine large house, at the foot of Broad St. with a large open yard for exercise. Yesterday as I passed they were all engaged in a game of cricket & seemed to be enjoying it exceedingly. They have money in abundance, with wh. they purchase sugar, coffee, etc. Our Govt. sent the other day & had gas fixtures put up in the house for them & is now building a Bathing House in which they can swim. In fact they are ten times better off than our men who guard them & I expect many of them are quite willing to be prisoners. There is nothing very hard in their lot, as they are now situated. They have all taken their parole. . . .

How I wish this war would end & we could all be once again re-united in our own house with none to trouble us nor make us afraid. I wish too you could see the grape vines how full & fine they are, promising many a feast & the peach trees too. There is one peach nearly ripe now. . . .

Love to Mother, Father, Sis, Sue, & all the dear ones, & much to Sarah Annie from her affectionate brother

Gus

Augustine T. Smythe, Charleston, S.C., to Jane A. Adger

4 Aug. 1864

My dear Aunt Janey

I am almost ashamed to write after having delayed so long & had I not a good excuse, I should be so in good earnest. But since the receipt of your letter, I got the chance & ran up home for two or three days & being left by the train & consequently having to waste a day at the depot, I was away in all six days. Pretty good when I had leave technically for 48 hrs. My Officers knew of it however so there was no wrong done. I enjoyed my trip exceedingly & was well repaid for my two night rides of 30 miles each. It only made me wish the more earnestly that this cruel war would cease & let us once more enjoy the blessings of peace of home, of an united family circle. But another reason of my delay is that I am studying up to stand an examination for Ordnance Officer, which I hope to get. . . . If I get this position it will be entirely unsought, as I have not done the least thing towards it except write out a formal application for an examination by Col. Yates direction. He, Col. Yates, came to me up town one day, about two weeks or so ago, & asked me how I should like the position of Ordnance Officer, telling me there was great need for one at Fort Johnson there & that Gen. Jones[30] had sent him orders to nominate some young man whom he knew to be a capable & that he should apply to have him appointed. So Col. Y. offered me the nomination, which I accepted & wrote out the application as he directed. Col. Y also said he would try & have me appointed Acting O.O. until they could hear from Richmond, but as I have heard nothing more from him since, I suppose he was unable to effect it. I dont intend doing any thing more. If it comes, well it will come unsought, & if not why I shall not have the unpleasantness of any personal refusal or rebuff. So I am studying up to be ready for it, & as I only got the principal book yesterday, I ought to be hard at it. I find it very dull work, however, studying when there is no certainty of my being allowed the examination. . . .

The Yankees have been doing some very pretty shooting at this part of the City for the past two or three days. Tuesday they commenced attracted no doubt by the sight of carts moving about on the Battery, hauling sand, etc. Several fell on the Battery itself, doing no damage except scaring the darkies who were working there. Two went into the Ladson's house, just below us; one or two in the yard of Prioleau's, opposite; one struck the little wooden house next to Mrs. Courtney's bursting out the whole side. Two women, soldier's wives, were sleeping there, & one of them had just left the room & gone down stairs when the shell passed thro' it. Two fell in the street, exactly in front of our house, between us & Mr. Roper. One of these I had dug up, & as it is a large one, a 100 pdr., have put it by the small one which came in the house, as mementos. All of these thrown were the large size. Col. Ash's house[31] on South Battery was struck twice & so Mr. Russel Middleton's. The old Huger house up the street was struck & set on fire, but it was soon extinguished. One also went in the house where McNeil was staying, in Gibbes St. passing thro' the piazza where he was sitting with his wife, but not hurting them. He moved immediately up to his brother's in Smith St. Yesterday afternoon another struck the house next door, Lowndes' old house, now Wagner's, not a foot from where it was hit before, knocking in a great deal of the wall & some pieces going down into the cellar. Yesterday afternoon also a woman & two men were slightly wounded in King St. The shell passed thro' the room, a small one, where they were, & the splinters flying about struck them on the head & back. They were painfully but not seriously wounded. There is almost more danger from the fragments than the shells themselves. Tuesday several fell in our yard, one even coming into the house & into this room. They fly very far then burst in the lower end of Water St. & a fragment was picked up by the Guard House. To-day they are shelling, but with a range farther up town, about Hayne St. Last night they kept it up steadily & burst several very near the Steeple, in Broad & Chalmers Sts. Yesterday as you see by the papers the exchange of prisoners was made. The Yankees suspended firing until <u>just as our boat reached the city</u>, when they opened anew. They still keep up their heavy fire on Sumter but do no serious damage. This is all. Only the constant firing to relieve the monotony. Robt. McNeil complained yesterday of being sick & as he has not come now this morning I suppose he must still feel badly. He is very much annoyed by the persons stealing fruit from your yard. Twice he has caught them, & handed them to the police when they are fined $25 @ piece & have to give $300 security for good behaviour. The other day he caught a tartar however. There were several soldiers in there, & on his ordering them out, & threatening to have them arrested, they immediately detailed two or three of them as a guard to keep him quiet, while the rest helped themselves to whatever they wanted. We are feeling quite secure here now, having received some reinforcements. An attack is looked for, but with God's help we hope to resist it manfully & well. We have not very much confidence in Jones. They say he was sent here as this was the easiest place, the work being all done, & they had no place else to send him. But we have others, Taliafero,[32] Ripley & Robinson,[33] whom we believe in. So you need not be anxious about Charleston, tho' she was in some danger the other day. I do not think the Yankees will ever get the old City. I wish very much I could see you. I want to have a long talk with you about some matters. Must stop now & send this to the Office. Love to all at Woodburn[34] & much to dear Auntie & yourself from

Augustine

Old Exchange Building. The city post office was located here until the bombardment began in August 1863. Courtesy of the Library of Congress.

Augustine T. Smythe, Charleston, S.C., to Jane A. Smyth[35]

Sunday
2 Sept. 1864

My dear little Sister

. . . Am anxious to hear how you all are in Summerton & if none of the sick have yet reported for duty. You are one of the well ones tho' & must help on the invalids.

You see by the papers that the Post Office[36] has been moved & far enough this time up to the corner of Ashley & Cannon Sts. The shells were falling too closely around the old stand & the Office could not bear the pressure. They are now not very likely soon again to have to move, but it is very inconvenient. The Yankees are very quiet to-day, not a gun has been fired since I came up here this morning, nor any movement taken place outside. They must be all at Church. Yesterday tho' they kept the shells coming in, & one of them struck the Orphan House, just above the portico, making an ugly hole. A colored man also was killed near Citadel Green by a fragment. Casualties now are of daily occurrence, sometimes two or three per day. People are moving down town, several coming in Legare & Tradd Sts. The Yanks will hear of this tho' & then we shall have it down town again. A report is afloat that Gen. Hardee[37] is soon to take command here, & relieve Jones. If he can be spared from out West. I hope he will for Jones is not much of an Officer. I hear rumors also of an expected land attack on Charleston by the Yankees & should not be surprised if they did try us again. Trying & succeeding however, are two very different things. I don't believe they will ever be allowed to take Charleston. If we only give them a good thrashing down here, it will cheer you "blue" people up a little, won't it? Well just let them come on. Charleston was not made for Yankees & under God we shall show them so when they come. I like this new movement out West too. It will rather surprise Sherman & the North, if after all his brilliant success & complete crushing out of the rebellion, he has to retreat. Then how much greater will be our victory & how much more beneficial the results accruing from it, after our late retreat. I think I shall set my period for peace two months sooner when that event comes off, as I firmly believe it will.

Philip had an accident, or adventure rather on Friday afternoon. Coming down town from a message, he had to pass by an encampment, where were a company of reserves. Some of them called at him, & laughed at him, but he took no notice of it all, which so nettled them that one of them threw at him with a brick & hit him on the head inflicting rather a severe tho' by no means serious wound. I went yesterday morning & complained to the Commanding Officer, but he can hardly stop it. Things of this sort occur daily, showing how lawless the once quiet law abiding, peaceable place has become. All the result of the war! I am so glad you are not here exposed to it. . . . Now you must be a good girl & write to me soon again & I shall try to answer you promptly. Love to Mother, Sis & all the dear ones at home.

Ever your brother
Gus

Augustine T. Smythe, Charleston, S.C., to his cousin Jane E. Adger[38]

8 Sept. 1864

My dear Cousin Janey,

. . . I suppose you will hear from home of Mother's sickness. Sue's letter received last night said she was better & up in her chair, but still very weak & with no appetite. Father also on Saturday night had a very severe attack which they almost feared would result in a stroke of paralysis. . . . Wish I could help them.

No news here except that the enemy are shelling the city as usual & principally with time fuze shell which burst in the air & scatter fragments all around. They are much more dangerous to persons tho' they do less a damage to houses. . . .

Well I think the Yankees have got our men on Morris Island at last.[39] They have them in a large pen, a piece of ground surrounded by a high fence, with no shelter, merely the bare sand enclosed by this barricade. It is closely watched by sentinels who are stationed all around it, mounted upon the outside so as to be able to over look the fence, & the whole place inside. This pen has been completed for some little time, but the prisoners were only introduced yesterday & today they seem to have put in quite a number. This is not positive yet, for we have no certain, no official notification of the fact, but it is extremely probable & tallies with the expressed intentions & [ensigns] of the Yankees. Oh! wont it be cold during the piercing winds of this winter on that bleak beach with no shelter! I think they may have as an object, the forcing us to an exchange of officers alone & I trust if they do propose anything of the kind, we shall be firm enough to refuse it. It would be base to desert the poor privates in prison. Their men now must go somewhere, I suppose, either Sullivan's Isl., James Isl., or perhaps Sumter itself.

We are having delightful weather now, cool autumn weather, which is so refreshing after the hot dry days of summer. Up here at nights is already cold & this winter if they do not allow us a fire as they say they will not, it will be almost unbearable. It does seem a shame to waste such fine days as these in this old Church Steeple. I wish I could only get up to the country for a while.

I must bid you good bye now . . . remember me kindly to Mrs. Fleming & Mrs. Parker & also Mr. Warren[40] & believe me ever Your affectionate

Gus

Morris Island stockade prison, 1864. From his steeple post, Smythe observed the Confederate POWs in this enclosure through his telescope. Courtesy of the Library of Congress.

Augustine T. Smythe, Charleston, S.C., to Margaret M. Smyth

8 Sept. 1864

My very dear Mother,

You dont know how anxious I have been about you up in Summerton all day, since the receipt of Sue's letter last night, enclosing your note & telling me of Father's attack. . . . Except for this anxiety about you at home, I am getting on first rate here at home. . . .

No news save the belief & very probable almost certain, that the Yankees have put our prisoners in their hands, on Morris Isl. at last. They erected some time ago in the sand between Wagner & Gregg, a large stockade or fence, about 8 or 10 ft. high enclosing a portion of the Island. We at first supposed it a breakwater to keep out the tides, but two or three days ago a large transport with men on board, crowded, came in from Hilton Head & yesterday & all to-day they have been introducing men into this pen, which is also strongly guarded by sentinels, who march around on platforms or shelves, fastened to the fence, about 4 ft. from the ground so that each sentinel can over see the whole pen at a glance. I can see no sign of shelter, except what looks as tho' it might be a couple of small tents, but I do not think so, & I can see the men in the morning getting their rations & also see the poor fellows looking through the cracks of the fence. How tantalizing to them & us, thus to be within sight of each other, but so out of reach! It will be piercingly cold this winter on that bare beach, exposed to all the fury of the bleak sea winds, but I trust they will not be there then. As soon as it is known officially I suppose Gen. Jones will remonstrate & then retaliate by putting some of the Yankees now crowded in the Roper Hospital, Work House &c. either on Sullivans or James Islds. or perhaps on Sumter itself. Then firing will have to cease. I imagine quite a novel mode of warfare, each party sheltering itself under their prisoners. My own idea is that they wish to force us to an exchange of these officers, but unless they also include privates I trust we shall refuse, for however much we may pity these poor fellows, we should not forget the thousands of private soldiers languishing in the North, & if the Yankees once got their officers back, they do not care for the men. . . .

Now Mother cheer up, & you must not look on the blue side of things; why not see the brighter side? I am still hopeful & trusting that God will soon remove this heavy affliction from us, & grant us peace. I think the next news from Geo. will be good. And at the North if McClellan[41] is elected it will be because we have whipped them into it, & if Lincoln, I believe he only can be by military interference & then for a row.[42] So do not give way yet dear Mother. There are many very many happy days yet in store for you & Father here in Old Charleston, surrounded by the children you have reared to love & honor you. This light is hurting my eyes very much, so I must stop. Love & sympathy to Janey, & to Sis. Hope both Janey & baby are better. Shall be so anxious to hear of Father on Saturday. Love to all the dear ones at home & much to yourself my own dear Mother from your boy

Augustine

Augustine T. Smythe, Charleston, S.C., to Margaret M. Smyth

[12] Sept. 1864

My dear Mother,

Well the examination is over & I am truly glad of it! I never studied harder in my life than I did for it & had the satisfaction of passing well I trust. The result will not be known for a few days, but I wrote everything on the page & Capt. Minor told me that I answered in the oral examination very well. So I think I have passed. . . .

The Yankees are shelling continually now with fuze shells. Tuesday one went corner King & John Sts. another King & Hudson, another in Orphan House yard. There was great excitement up town, women running about with their babies etc. & one colored woman was killed. They have not been up as high as that since. Another the same day went up corner Smith & Calhoun St. They are much more dangerous than the other shells, as they burst in the air & the fragments scattering all about produce quite a scatteration among any crowd of persons around. The pavements all about the city are marked with spots where they have fallen. Strange tho' I have heard of no accidents & yet every shell must break into 10 or 12 pieces. It is miraculous. The firing at Sumter still continues but not very rapidly. The Yankees are tiring of it. . . . You cant imagine how good I feel now that the examination is over. My mind has been on such a stretch the whole time that it rebounds now & I can hardly keep quiet. How I wish I could be with you all to-day instead of by myself. . . .

Love to Father, Sue & all the dear ones at home. Shall write to the girls in time. Hope Sue is well again. Jimmie sends love to all. Please take care of your self dear Mother. Ever your boy

Augustine

Charleston Orphan House, 1865. During the bombardment, the children of the Orphan House were relocated to Orangeburg for their safety. Courtesy of the Library of Congress.

Augustine T. Smythe, Charleston, S.C., to Jane A. Adger

16 Sept. 1864

My dear Aunt Janey,

I have not much time, but I have some good news which I want to tell you. I have passed the examination & stand first on the list! Nine passed out of thirty who applied. I never was so surprised or gratified, for tho' I was almost certain I had got thro' alright, I had no idea I should head the list, especially under the unfavorable circumstances. I know you would like to hear this & so tho' you are in my debt for a long letter, & as note I cant help writing it to you. Now dont accuse me of vanity or conceit, "cause 'taint" but it does give me great satisfaction to know that I was able to study up & beat those fellows. You are the only one in Pendleton to whom I have told it, & to you I know it will be of interest. It is not positively certain yet, as besides the two examiners here, there is a third in Richmond to whom the papers must be sent & who ratifies the decisions of these two; still Capt. Minor,[43] Chief of the Board here, told me that tho' it was possible he thought it extremely improbable that he would put me any lower, as my papers were very satisfactory; & again, there was an oral examination here for the result of which he can only have their report. So I am in hopes of retaining my position, even if I do not get a commission. Nine passed, & there are four to be commissioned. Col. Gorgas[44] has the selection of any four out of the nine. They tell me tho' that I stand a very good chance, & I hope I may get it, as if I do, I most probably shall be ordered into the field & you know well how I want to go there. That is unless Col. Yates chooses to step in now & apply for me at Ft. Johnson, where I shall have all the discomforts of the field & yet remain here. One of his officers yesterday wanted to know if I did not wish to go there, but I said "no to Virginia." So I trust he will not apply for me. This latter examination, he had nothing to do with. The one he spoke of to me I have never heard anything more of, so I do not feel bound to go with him. If he applies to Gorgas for me however I'm afraid I might be ordered there. Only one thing troubles me about going into the field, the want of a servant. They are so short for house-servants at home, I hate to take John, & I shall need one. I am going to run off on Monday for two or three days, & get home. Adger is there & the folks are sick so I want very much to be there. Then I shall see all about it. The being first however pleases me as much as the prospect of a near fulfillment of my wishes. . . . I want very much to see you & Auntie again, as well as the others before I should have to go. All this may be counting chickens however. Good bye again & love to Aunts.

Ever
Your boy
Augustine

Augustine T. Smythe, Charleston, S.C., to Margaret M. Smyth

28 Sept. 1864

My own dear Mother,

While keeping my watch up here, I shall employ my time in writing to you to send by Miss Kezia to-morrow, instead of the mail, as she will go so much more quickly. The Yankees are throwing in their shells at a tremendous rate, one every two or three minutes since 5 o'clock, now it is 10 P.M. & before that all morning at the rate of one every 5 minutes. Since 8 A.M. they have thrown 114 shells up to 9:45 P.M. Now they have stopped but there is no saying for how long the cessation will continue. And the shells too are not dropping down town, & very few in the water, but up they go to Chapel & Ann Sts. & all around there. One an hour or so ago went into Mr. Carr's house in Aiken's Row. The family had just left the parlor & seated themselves at the supper table when the shell went into the room they had left & burst, knocking the chairs about & making havoc all around. One two or three days ago went into Wolfe St.![45] Citadel Green is a command resort.[46] The Citadel Square Church[47] was hit the other day, & very much damaged & the same with Grace Church.[48] Ours as yet is unhurt, but there is no knowing how long it may remain so. Every church now below it except Zion[49] & Bethel[50] have been hit. They have not opened yet. I do hope they will be quiet for the rest of the night. Surely they have done enough for to-day. They are now using some three or four guns, one of them a 200 pdr. & they do have an enormous range. The report comes to us that they are manufacturing them to shoot still farther, so as to command the entire city. Won't we have a jolly time then! As far as <u>we</u> personally concerned, it is a benefit, for now we are only troubled with a time fuze shell every now & then, by far the greater majority go up town. But where are the people to stay is now the question. Some have come down to South Bay as the safest place, & I believe it is well! the war I think has not much longer to run for I do think we shall, with God's blessing have peace in the Spring. But when it does come, there will have to be some bricklaying done in old Charleston. The damage done to the City is beginning to mount up & if they keep on at this rate will be very great. But how much better off are we than the poor citizens of Atlanta,[51] Memphis[52] & so many other of our cities. If they let us off with the shelling we should be thankful. I used to feel very much like grumbling up here, but since they have put our poor fellows in that Pen on Morris Isl. whenever I begin to complain & happen to cast my eye over there it hushes me up at once. Oh Mother! amidst all our troubles & privations how much have we to be grateful for: that we are still an united unbroken family, not one member even maimed, our home, tho' in the reach of Yankee missiles, still out of their hands & so little injured, & you all, tho' not so well placed as you were here, still with a comfortable shelter, where you can at least obtain the necessaries of life & feel secure, as secure as possible, from the invasion of our vandal foes. When I read in the papers,

& especially the late ones, of the sufferings & hardships now undergone by so many, so very many of our fellow citizens, my heart wells up in gratitude to Our Father that those dear to me are so comfortably settled as you are in comparison, for instance to the poor exiles from Atlanta. Truly we should be grateful.

The Yankees have confined themselves entirely to the city to-day, not firing a shot at any other place. There are two reasons assigned for this; that they fear we have their men confined in some of our fortifications, & that they are merely mounting new guns & preparing for a more vigorous bombardment of Sumter than they have ever given it before. This latter I heard from a gentleman just out of Sumter, who says Gregg bristles with guns just mounted, but invisible to us because of traverses. They can amuse themselves however as much as they please with the old Fort, & waste as much ammunition as they think fit, they cannot take Charleston in that way, nor reduce old Sumter to a much worse fix. All the bombarding will never take it. They do not seem as busy preparing for an attack here as they did before I left. I hardly think they have given up the idea, probably have only postponed it. Well when they do come, we shall under God, give them such another thrashing as will make them sick of Charleston. They had better make up their minds to rest quietly content with shelling it. Both the batteries at White Point[53] now, are completely armed, four in one, & two in the other of the heaviest & most efficacious guns we have, & they are busy preparing a chamber in front of the DeSaussure's house for the Blakely gun which was burst last year, but which Eason has fixed up, stronger they say than it was before. They are also working on Castle Pinckney, making it very strong indeed, so we are getting ready to give them a warm reception.

Have been down stairs to get the Sergeant of Police to carry a letter up for me to the Office which Locke, my chum, forgot to mail this afternoon. He tells me that a shell went into Mr. Burckmyer's house in Charlotte St. this afternoon & wounded more or less severely all his family, five in number.[54] He will wish now he had staid with Jack Ragin. Also that again to-day the Citadel Square Church was hit, & Zion very much damaged by one, & St. Joseph's, the old Anson St. church, also struck. Ours yet unhurt. From him I heard also that two shells lately have entered Mass. Joe's house on E. Bay, using it up, especially the basement pretty badly. So the cry is still they come. And as an incentive to matrimonial harmony, (read this to Sis), a man named Burgess had fallen out with his wife, & two evenings ago they were cooking supper, one upstairs & the other in the room below, when a shell came in where he was, struck the fire place & a brick hit him on the head injuring him so badly that to-day he died from the effects of it. They report down stairs several persons hurt this afternoon, but it was only report. (Quite a number are moving down on South Bay but this will only attract the enemy's fire there I think.) . . .

My watch is nearly out so I shall stop, write a line to Adger, & then turn in myself & make Locke turn out. Am going to-morrow to look at a boy for sale. Good bye. Love to all the dear ones at home. Wish so much I could have made my visit longer. In much love to yourself Mother.

Your boy
Augustine

Citadel Square Baptist Church, completed in 1856. Smythe's letter of September 28, 1864, reported that the church had been "very much damaged" by shells. Courtesy of the Library of Congress.

Augustine T. Smythe, Charleston, S.C., to [Margaret M. Smyth]

Friday
30 Sept. 1864

. . . Our church was struck on Wednesday afternoon. Shell went in the roof & thro' the S.S. room not doing very much damage save breaking the windows, but it will put an end to any more service being held there just now. Yesterday & last night, they fired continuously but less rapidly. Saw Mr. Burckmyer yesterday. His daughter Margaret wounded in the head slightly, Miss Margaret Bennet severely in wrist, one of Jno. Moffett's children & the daughter of the Irish woman who stays with them, pretty badly cut. 23 whites in the house at the time. They were all better yesterday. No other news. . . .

Your boy
Augustine

Augustine T. Smythe, Charleston, S.C., to Margaret M. Smyth

5 Oct. 1864

Twenty two to-day Mother! how quickly has this last year flown away. God grant with a better record than any other. But oh! as I look back on the time misspent, the opportunities wasted, the chance of improvement, unimproved, I am saddened & humbled & can only pray that grace may be given me in future to live more worthily, nearer up to my advantages, more in accordance with the will of my Maker, so that if I am permitted to see another return of this day, I may not feel lowered down by the weight of wasted energies & unfulfilled resolutions as I am to-day. God help me! & if he does I shall do better. I am going to turn over a new leaf if I can, & instead of living carelessly & idly as I have so long done, bend all my powers to the improvement of my mind, soul, body, so that in whatever position it may please Him to assign my lot in life, I may be able to act my part for his glory, the good of others & my own happiness. Again may God help me!

But when I do not look back Mother when my mind dwells only on the present & the future, then I cannot realize that I am twenty-two! I feel within me the same, elastic spirit, unbent, unbroken, the same joyous sense of mere existence, the same buoyant hope & trust for the future that animated me at eighteen! Thank God tho' my life has been so misspent, it has been a happy one. He has been very merciful to me Mother, & I trust I feel it, in casting my lines in such pleasant places, & in preserving me so far free & untroubled from all the cares & burdens of life. Tho' I trust I have grown in wisdom & steadiness, I have not grown old. I feel the same happy boy I did when years ago I would march down this street, a proud school boy with a First Certificate to carry home to Mother. Oh those happy days of old! But we shall see as happy yet Mother. 'Ere long God will bless our efforts with success & then how much more keen & exquisite will be our enjoyment of all those old domestic comforts, those family re-unions prized before, but then immeasurably more valued from this temporary loss. And then, Mother dear Mother, it shall be our proud duty & privilege in the evening of your days to watch over you & Father, provide for you comforts & try in some small measure to return the love so lavishly poured out upon us. And never fear. School days may be o'er, but in the broad struggle of life there are yet "Firsts" to be won, & with God's help & blessing Mother I shall still bring them home to you, & receive your approbation.

I am sad & yet joyous to-day. Sad for the past, for the year gone! & yet so little now that I can show for it; yet joyous in my bright anticipation for the future, that glorious future which will open on our country, our own beloved South, when we have established our independence & it will not be now long delayed. Then what a field for action! What occasions to call out all that is in a man, all his energies, all his powers. Oh Mother! can you wonder at my buoyancy when God has as mercifully disposed of everything around me? Can you be surprised at it when this beautiful autumn day I feel so strong, & the young life rushes in my veins & pulsates thro' me, until the mere sense of living is pleasure! Thanks be to God for all his mercies to me & mine. . . .

Did you never Mother have a craving just for one little glance into the future one little peep as it were, to see where & what you will be a year or two hence? I cannot help it to-day. I feel as if I should like barely to raise the veil & find where another birthday will meet me. It is best as it is tho' & wiser far than to have our lives troubled by any such knowledge. But I shall then see, Mother & prophecy that on the next return of this day we shall all be re-united in old No. 12, a happy family! So look up Mother, look up! Things are not so bad as people, some of them, make out, & 'ere long you will see me coming up to escort you all down home, & God grant it may be soon.

And now I must stop Mother. Shall write to Adger to-morrow & give him any news there may be. My love to all the dear ones at home, Ellen, Sallie, Janie, all of them, & much to Father.
God bless & comfort you mother & cheer you up is the prayer of

Your own loving boy
Augustine

Augustine T. Smythe, St. Michael's Church steeple, Charleston, S.C., to his sister Sarah A. Smyth

16 Oct. 1864

My dear Sarah Annie,

. . . I am sorry to tell you that St. Michael's Steeple[55] has been struck at last, this morning at 10 o'clock, a shell entering & bursting in it. Fortunately it came in just by a window, so the wall is little injured, not at all of any account. I was not up here at the time. It came in considerably below where we reside, in the compartment below the clock, just where the works are, & fortunately also not in the staircase so that with the exception of tearing up the floor considerably & making a great litter there is no damage done, save the loss of the old prestige of the Steeple. It had escaped so long, I was in hopes it would have done so entirely. The shell just before that one entered the church, going thro' the S.E. corner of the roof, but not bursting & the one just before that struck the Court House. So you see it was pretty good shooting. Now they are going higher up town, about Hayne St. Not shelling very rapidly however. The other day they opened on our end of town throwing one in Mrs. Lowndes' yard, striking Wilkinson's & Spears' on the Battery but not hitting us. So they have not entirely given us up yet. . . . This Church, St. M's, has now had two shells in it, besides one in the Steeple, & has been hit several times by fragments. Did I tell you that a shell had gone thro' the Steeple of the Citadel Square Church, entirely thro' it, but only knocking out some bricks. Now all the high Steeples have been hit, & all the churches below ours. . . .

Write soon again to your brother Gus.

Augustine T. Smythe, Charleston, S.C., to Margaret M. Smyth

20 Oct. 1864

My dear Mother

. . . I got down safely from Columbia after a very pleasant visit, nothing at all happening to mar it, save the disappointment of not meeting Adger, Sue & Aunts. . . . I have come back to my duty, irksome as it is with my heart lightened, & my mind invigorated. These little trips to see you & to Columbia help me beyond measure. And Mother, the more I see of Miss Lou, the more pleased am I, the more satisfied with my choice, & the more confident that she is one to make me happy. I like her in toto, her temper, her disposition & her education. She is a girl who without being a blue, is still intellectual, one who enjoys reading & being read to, one who will stir me up, & make me study & read & one with whom I can read & study, in fact an agreeable, accomplished companion. It always wakes me up to be there & talk with Mrs. McCord, she is herself so well-read that I have all I can do to keep up with her. Miss Lou is of course nothing like her Mother in this, not so much I mean, but still she shows the effects of it, in her fondness for books & reading. I spoke to you of Mrs. McCord once offering me a place to put my books which were being injured by being kept in those boxes, from which the covers were torn & the books thus exposed, not only to dust & dirt, but also to being removed when I went in the Store house this last time I was so sorry to see them fine books, thus being ruined, that I accepted Mrs. McCord's offer which before I declined & moved my books down to her house. They were somewhat hurt & several missing, so I am very glad now that I did so. She admired some of them very much, & she might well do so, for there are some very pretty ones. I think I have inherited Fathers fondness for books per se. I do love to have a nice book. So now they are there under Miss Lou's charge & she promised to read some of them too. I know Mother you will be pleased with her. One thing I like is that tho' like other girls of her age, fond of a novel, she can read other books with pleasure. The first she chose from mine, tho' there were one or two of the genus novel, was Macaulay's Essays. So you see I must study up now & not be behind. Mrs. McCord as very kind to me, treating me almost as if I was her son already. . . .

The Yankees have not shelled the City for two days, tho' they keep up an occasional fire on Sumter & the Island. It has been quite cold & I am suffering with a slight sore throat caught up here in the Steeple. It is much better however to-night, & I am very careful with it. Am on duty every day & night now till Sunday. After Sunday I go on regularly. I heard to day that there is a chance of my appointment coming on soon, as there is great need of Ordnance Officers, & they have applied for some. I do hope I shall. The danger will not be as great as here, & the exposure less. I do dread the winter in this cold bleak place. Already it is chilly, we have to muffle up in blankets, even in the day sometimes. (And the mice up here are horrible!) . . .

This light is miserable so I must stop. Love to all the dear ones at home. Ever my own dear mother, Your boy

Augustine

This 1865 photograph depicts shell damage to the Circular Congregational Church graveyard. Courtesy of the Library of Congress.

Augustine T. Smythe, Charleston, S.C., to his sister Jane A. Smyth

27 Nov. 1864

My dear Annie

Such a pleasure to me just now to receive by the courier from the Bathing House a batch of letters, among them two from home, one of which should have come last Wednesday. They are doubly welcome to me up here alone as I have been all morning. I was beginning to get anxious, as I had not heard from you for over ten days, & I generally hear so regularly. . . . The weather has moderated extremely, it is quite pleasant to-day, so he will not have to start in that bitter cold weather. It was horribly cold here form two or three days last week. One day I almost froze up here in the Steeple. Now we have the stove fixed. Yesterday it was done. Now we shall be more comfortable tho' it is so windy & bleak up here, that we cannot be entirely so. But how many are then much worse off than we are. This thought should make us contented, Annie, in all our discomforts.

Everything here going on pretty much the same. The Yankees are shelling quite rapidly this morning, one shell about every 10 minutes. They are falling from Queen St. to Society, none very near here. Nothing else of news, that I can hear. Sherman I believe is all right. Reinforcements have been pouring out to Georgia & I shall be very much disappointed if they do not whip him badly. Such too is the general belief here. . . . I see by the Northern papers, that they think there if Grant can be held in check till Christmas, & Sherman routed, Lincoln will be unable to raise another army to take the field in the Spring. God grant it may be so. I am tired of this war, but not willing to give up yet, "by a jug full." And I am still bright & cling to our eating dinner at No. 12 on my next birthday, certain.

I wish I could be at the Major's to get some of his hog fixings. I have rather a weakness that way you know. Here I live on beef, beef, until I can almost feel the horns coming out of my head. There! the smoke from the last guns at Battery Gregg has been blown all the way across the harbor up to the City. Uncle obliged to the Yanks for it. I am all alone now you know, my chum went off two or three days ago, having been transferred at his request to a Rgt. in Va. where he expects a commission. I find it rather desolate in the house at night, especially, & as the gas does not give light enough to read by, I have to retire very early. I am going to try & rig up a lamp however. There is still coal there enough to do me a while, so I sit then by the fire & think of the happy moments when we were all there together & long for their return. Oh that this war may soon end! I am glad you were amused with Macaria.[56] Tis not a book I admire very much tho' I read half & did not finish. Sue asks about "Joseph II & his Court." I have not seen it but know no reason why she should not read it. . . .

Must stop. I wrote to Sue the other day. Hope she received it. Love to brother, Sue & Ellen, & all the dear ones.

Your brother,
Gus

CHAPTER 5

Sherman Targets South Carolina
December 1864–March 1865

Augustine T. Smythe, Charleston, S.C., to Margaret M. Smyth

19 Dec. 1864

My very dear Mother,

After spending four or five days tramping along the Savannah River, here I am back again in old No. 12 safe & hearty. Our objective going was to establish a line of signals from Hardeeville to Savannah, but it was impossible to be done. The Islands in the River, Argyle & Hutchinson's[1] were & are in the hands of the enemy, & of course not to be used for signal posts, while all the headlands along the bank which would have answered for that purpose are in such close proximity to the enemy that if we raised our flag there, they could run over in the night & take us without the least trouble, there only being at those points picquets of two or three men. So we have had to return unsuccessful, much to my regret, for I did wish the thing done. It was not possible tho'. The Yankees holding the Islands in the River & the Georgia Shore, we could not have kept the line up, as the only places from which we could signal would be the large rice mills on the banks of the river & they are so isolated, only connected with the mainland by long dams that the Yankees could with no trouble cut us off, & thus break up the line. We got back last night, late in the night, pretty tired for we have done a great deal of walking. So sorry I did not meet Joe here, but I shall see him on his return for of course he will stay with me.

There is little news there. Persons from Savannah[2] talk pretty blue, some of them, of its chances of holding out. The Yankees have formed a complete cordon around the city, from the Savannah River round to the Ogeechee at Ft. McAlister[3] & from there to the sea. This is only broke at one place, Scriven's Ferry,[4] which is now the only way left us of communicating with Savannah. But I don't believe they will take the city, & so many from there say. Hardee has a large army, & abundance of provisions, so there is no danger of his being starved out, & the fortifications around the city are excellent. Still it is a ticklish position. There are a great many troops on this side of the River, & the country is despoiled, Wheeler is in command & is there with his cavalry & the people say that it is a question which they should prefer, Wheeler's cavalry or the Yanks.[5] In truth they do act most shamefully, robbing every house they meet, stealing the horses & mules & leaving emptiness behind them. The planters there are in a great state of alarm.[6] Many of them have had all their negroes taken from them & their crops burnt by Yankees; while others have saved their servants, but then know not where nor how to send them for safety, nor how even to feed them. At Pocotaligo things seem quiet. The Yankees still shell every train passing along the road. Going down we got thro' scot-free, but coming up they struck one of the cars in front, a horse car, fortunately not injuring any of the running gear. So we got up all right. Ellison can tell you more about that place however than I can. . . . Tell Adger I am afraid I shall not be able to meet him in Columbia, but to write me & if possible, he may be sure I shall be up. They are very strict about persons going out of the city. Just think! Next Sunday will be Christmas. Oh how differently do we look forward to it now from what we did in the good old times. Oh dear. Well, the war must end before very long, it cannot last always. Beautiful day, soft & pleasant as a Spring morning & as I sit with the windows open & look out on your rose bushes I long so much to see you all again. But cheer up. You have two of your sons any how with you this Christmas & the third will be with you in spirit. Must stop. Feel stiff still. Love to Sue, Sis, Annie & all the dear ones & to Father & Adger. The Yankees have not opened fire yet. I do not believe they have men to man their batteries, all down at Pocotaligo. In a day or two tho' we shall have it again. Good bye.

Ever dear mother your boy Augustine.

Augustine T. Smythe, Charleston, S.C., to Margaret M. Smyth

25 Dec. 1864

Christmas night Mother, but oh how different from what it used to be! This has been a sad, lonely day for me. I could not but recall the past days of joyous festivity & compare them with my Christmas. As I passed No. 36 this morning, I had to stop & feel how changed it was so desolate

& lonely, riddled by shells, & threatened by the enemy, from the old times when Christmas found it filled with good cheer & crowded with smiling faces & happy hearts, now separated and far distant from each other! How soon will it be 'ere we can once more assemble together. I was on duty all last night alone, the third in succession that I have spent thus in the Steeple & also all morning until 3 o'clock. Then I came home to dinner, not exactly like Aunt Janey's Christmas dinner, by myself & as it was raining hard & I could not go to church, I sat here by the fire & thought of you at home & wished I could be with you all. How many times I have wished that wish to-day! Then I went down to the Bathing House to hear the news & chat a while & determined to have a good supper at any rate in honor of the day, my bill of fare for dinner was cold beef, rice & potatoes. I brought a friend up with me & we have just finished a hearty supper of sausages, eggs, bread & butter, & a cup of coffee which he furnished as I had none parched. We cooked it ourselves here at the grate. Philip asked leave to spend Christmas with his children & as he has served me well, I let him go yesterday to return Tuesday morning. A boy from Middleton's cooks my breakfast & dinner till he returns. This accounts for my dinner to-day. The box came splendidly & was a most acceptable Christmas present. . . .

Savannah has gone! Now we are planning to try & rescue Charleston from the same fate, as she is in much danger. God grant us his aid now! . . . There is no sign yet of this city being given up, but it is well to be prepared, & we must fight hard to retain it & where are the troops? These Reserves & Militia are not worth a fig! I am not giving up yet tho'. Our turn will come presently, the Yankees have had a pretty long run of luck. Perhaps, very probably, I overrate our danger. . . . Provisions can hardly be bought here now & it is going to be worse soon. Nothing in the shape of provisions is allowed to leave the city. It is very late, nearly 12 o'c & my light dim. Good night. Love to all the dear ones, Sue, Annie, Sis, Father, Adger, Ellen & all

Ever Mother
Your boy,
Augustine.

Augustine T. Smythe, Charleston, S.C., to Margaret M. Smyth

2 Jan. 1865

Happy New Year to you Mother! & to all (the dear ones) at home! & may we all be spared to spend the next one together in No. 12 Meeting St. or better still all together at Uncle Robert's.

The New Year has opened clear & cold. I was on duty all night Saturday night, & saw the old year out & the new one in. Oh but it was cold! The coldest night I have ever yet felt up here. I had a fire but the wind was so high & keen that it did me precious little good. I had to wrap up in a blanket, head & all to try & keep warm. Yesterday I went to church, & it was cold I can assure you. I almost froze to death. It & to-day however are without exception the coldest days we have had this year. Saturday was rainy & bleak, but it cleared off during the night. Heard a fine sermon yesterday morning rather political, but it was too cold to enjoy it comfortably. I am up in the Steeple this morning but shall be relieved at 3 o'clock & then go home to a good dinner. Yes I have a turkey! A box came on Saturday from Mrs. McCord as I knew her writing, tho' Miss Lou said nothing of it, with a turkey, ham, some sausages, cake etc. on which with Ellen's pickles & some of your potatoes & rice, I expect to enjoy a fine New Year's dinner. . . .

All quiet outside. The Yankees opened on Friday night & threw three shells into the city. One of them fell just before Mrs. Comer's house but I knew nothing of it till next morning when Philip waked me to ask if I had heard it. Again Saturday night three were thrown in, one going into Scotch Churchyard. Since then they have again quieted down. The James Adger[7] has just left off the Bar & gone North. Many rumors afloat but there is no knowing what to believe. One says Presdt. Davis has for sworn any farther interference with military affairs & turned that entire Department over to Gen. Lee, and that by him Gen. Joe Johnson has been re-instated in command of Division of West in place of Beauregard. All this however lacks confirmation. A gentlemen just from Richmond told me yesterday that there were serious thoughts there of putting 300,000 negroes into the Army, & that the question was very favorably discussed.[8] I almost hope they will not. Sherman keeps quiet. No movements at all from his Army. So the question about Charleston is still undecided. . . .

Getting late—must stop. Am quite well & hearty & enjoying the Steeple. Love to Sue, Sis, Annie & all the dear ones & in much love to yourself Mother I am Your boy

Augustine

Augustine T. Smythe, Charleston, S.C., to Margaret M. Smyth

9 Jan. [1865]

My dear Mother,

I must write in haste as I have to go down to Sullivan's Isl. presently & do not know if I shall be back in time to get my letter in the mail. On duty all last night, & it was cold I assure you. Now I have just finished breakfast, feel much better. Quite well & hearty & getting along very well. . . . No news. Sherman keeps quiet. As for Columbia I should not attempt to move anything. That place will be defended at all hazards, even Charleston will be given up to hold it & I don't see how you can move the things nor where. No one there to attend to it. Ellison would not have time, & if I could get off of which I see no chance it would be only for a day or two. No Mother they are there & there let them stay. If they are lost we cant help it, & must submit. About this place I don't know what to think. Hermes says what I have heard several times from other sources that Lee's army will be sent here & Richmond left rather than allow Sherman to devastate this State as he has done Georgia. So I am hoping for the best. The man from Gas Co.[9] has just come to remove the metre, which will be injured by not being used. Did the Gas Co. furnish it? I told him we bought it, but he says no, so I have told him to go ahead. No gas down town now. . . . If Columbia should go of which I see hardly any chance, I think Mrs. McC. would go to Abbeville. The City here is in a very lawless condition, robberies & assaults every night. It is horrible & dangerous to go out after dark, especially down town where there is no light in the streets. . . . Love to all the dear ones at home & much to yourself Mother

from your boy
Augustine

Augustine T. Smythe, Charleston, S.C., to Jane A. Adger

23 Jan. 1865

My dear Aunt Janey,

. . . We are jogging along here now pretty well. A week ago tho' we were expecting to evacuate every day & were all ready for it. But now that the roads are open & re-inforcements on the way, we feel easier. Butler's division[10] is en route for this place & Longstreet's Corps they say. Gentlemen from Richmond tell me that the talk there is to give up Richmond to save Charleston & such is I suppose the case. I hear sad accounts from North Carolina however. A gentleman who passed thro' Raleigh a day or two ago, says the Legislature is in secret session there & many of the leading men openly avow the wish that they would call a Convention & let the people say whether they wish to return or no. Georgia too is whipped. The only two States who are really in it heart & soul are Virginia & South Carolina they say. Hurrah for the Palmetto! God grant we may never be brought low! Here we are quiet. The fleet outside has lately been increased & there are nine Monitors now, but they know too well to attempt to come in here. We only wish they would, it would not be a Ft. Fisher[11] affair. We sustained a heavy loss the other day tho'. The new Ironclad "Columbia"[12] the finest in the Confederacy so considered, was just coming down from the dry dock to go on duty. At one place in the creek, tide was too low so they anchored over what they supposed a mud bank to wait the next tide, but found at half tide that they were just over a wreck on which she grounded & breaking her back, sunk & is now a complete loss, tho' the iron off of her may be recovered. Such is luck! Our best boat! Robbers plentiful as usual & despite all my endeavors, No. 36 has suffered severely. As fast as I would put up the fence or nail the windows, they would break them down. All the lead, etc. has now been taken out, & worse than that three of the mirrors. I found it out the next day & then they had one of the large ones from over the fire places, down by the window ready to carry off that night. So I had it & the other brought home, & then going to the Guard House got a guard & searched several houses in the neighborhood which I suspected but could not find them. The three narrow ones have been taken. I have notified the police of their loss, & shall offer a reward of say $100 or $200 for them, if you think best. I hesitated doing so on my own responsibility as I did not know whether you would think it worth while. It is useless almost to attempt to stop those fellows. They live all around & as soon as night comes, they knock down the fence, cut open a window & go to work. No law down in this part of town now. Assaults every night or so. The other night they robbed a man here just at our door & another night pulled our courier off his horse, robbed him & then put him on again & sent him off. It is horrible, the lawless state now of all Charleston formerly so orderly. No shelling tho'. A sharp bombardment at Sumter from Gregg the other day produced quite an excitement until it was explained that one of our steamers had got aground off the fort & the Yanks were amusing themselves knocking her to pieces. Not much of a boat but we could ill spare her. My! but people do curse Jeff Davis now! And the Mercury![13]. . . With the Mercury everybody prays from Gen. Bragg[14] deliver us. Why does Davis persist in keeping him in command. And Hood too? They say is coming here. You will hear all these rumors in Columbia however, & as it is very late 2 A.M. I must stop. . . . In much love to Auntie & with renewed thanks to you & her.

Yours affectionately
Augustine

Augustine T. Smythe, Charleston, S.C., to Margaret M. Smyth

9 Feb. 1865

My very dear Mother,

Your letter of Thursday last I received to-day on my return from the N.E. R.R.[15] where I had been waiting from 8 to 12 o'c for the train which was delayed. . . .

At the same time I recd. a few lines from Mrs. McCord merely to tell me that Miss Lou was a little better to-day & free from fever but that it would probably be a week yet at least 'ere she is able to be up or to write. She says her returns of fever lately are entirely new ones & she is slowly conquering them. She cannot get well fast. I do hope & pray she may soon be well. Miss Hannah is also down with a little fever, but was getting well when Mrs. McCord wrote. I do not think the young ladies will leave Columbia. Everyone advises against it, & really to me it seems almost the best thing is to remain. Better there at home if the Yankees should come than in a strange place, among strangers & have them around. Oh! it is horrible! these times are enough to make one gray! But I try to hope Sherman will not reach Columbia. They are fortifying there, & reinforcements are on the way, they say. Ewell's Corps Report also has it that Gen. R.E. Lee is to come on here for a while. His presence would alone be of great aid to us, if only to inspire confidence. We can hardly hear anything satisfactory from Sherman relative to his movements. It is almost certain that he has cut the Rail Road & yet the report has not been officially confirmed. Of this however there is I think very little doubt. It also appears that he is heading for Augusta. He will then meet with resistance I hear. Gen. D. H. Hill commands the city & has strongly fortified it. I hope they will show fight & at any rate detain Sherman until reinforcements can come on. So here we are waiting for orders. I wish I were in the field near him. But I don't want to go back to Hagoods' Brigade in North Carolina. We are quiescent here just now. May have to evacuate but not at all so decided. Government needs the port & will strain every nerve to keep it open & to hold it. So as far as the city itself is concerned, I am much more sanguine. Well our commissions have received a slap. It is better so unless they would have given us our terms. The good effects are already apparent here. Men see that they must fight, that there is no alternative, & they are making up their minds to it. While the matter was only in agitation the idea was that peace would soon be made & every man wanted to live through what he considered his last fight. Hence they ran. I have heard many so express themselves. One fellow I overheard saying he "was glad the Yankees had sent back that answer, cause now those fellows who wanted to holler" & were getting ready for it would find out that they couldn't. A Regt. of Reserves from here went up to-day to Santee bridge on N.E.R.R. to guard it. No, no, Mother we are not whipped yet! And by 4th March, the old Pope or some nation may want to say something. Hope on! hope ever! This the best way. Heard from Joe a few days ago, & wrote to him just now. He is quite well & has been promoted. It is quite an honor & shows he stands well both in his class & in the estimation of his officers. Mrs. McCord mentioned a day or two ago that he had not been there on Sunday, & wondered if he had been sick, & said she would see about it, but in the letter to day, she says she could not get out herself, but had found out that he was on guard. She is a kind lady Mother, & should Joe be sick, you may feel assured that he will be well attended to. Don't send me any of his provisions tho'. He may require them before long. Bitter, bitter cold. I thought awhile back it would snow, but it seems to be clearing off now. Am up here in the Steeple all to-night. It is so cold & windy. I am all crouched down by my stove, which on account of the wind will not burn, trying to keep warm (but it is so windy & so many cracks that it is worse than a fire in the open-air.). . . .

You have several times asked me what I shall do if Charleston is given up & I don't remember if I answered you. Of course I leave & most probably, nay certainly almost with the corps. It will be needed in the field & tho' "1" will be reduced a good deal, I am marked down as one of the last to be sent back only in case they break it up. Already some 11 have been returned, as the junction of the Savannah Corps with ones renders it rather large. I think I shall leave Philip with the house, Coz. Liz wrote me to bring him out if I though him able to attend Adger in camp. I do not so judge him fit, & therefore unless he begs, shall not urge him to come & I do not think he will. If he does I shall try to make some arrangement with McNeil to stay there & if I can't do that then we must just let the matter rest with Providence. I trust tho' the necessity for any such fixings is far off.

Too dark. Must stop awhile & then finish when I can light my lamp. . . . Good bye my Mother. Love, much love to all the dear ones at home

Augustine T. Smythe, Charleston, S.C., to his sister

13 Feb. 1865

My dear Annie,

. . . Miss Lou is much better than she was, tho still unable to leave her room, & only allowed to sit up at intervals for a short time. Still she is clear of fever, & if that continues her strength will gradually increase. So I hope it will not be very long now before she is quite well again. Mrs. McCord has had bolts put on all her window & doors in preparation for Sherman who is expected up there before long. To-day I hear the Rail Road is cut at Orangeburg,[16] & I suppose it will not be long before they reach Kingsville & then all communication will be stopped. I sincerely trust not however. Sherman's plan seems to be to destroy as much Rail Road as possible in his rear & then push on for Lee's army, getting start of our troops behind him. May God aid us to frustrate him.

Another assault against Charleston has been made & repulsed. Last night the Yankees attacked Ft. Johnson with a large force in barges but were decidedly & handsomely repulsed, with the loss of but one man on our side.[17] As it was dark & they effected no landing at all, it is impossible to say how much they suffered, tho' as Sullivan's Isl. & the gunboats both opened on the barge the presumption is that it must have been severely. So out of spite they commenced shelling the city this afternoon, but as most of them fell short, they gave it up after throwing nine & are now firing on Ft. Johnson. The attack on James Isl. is also given up. They landed there on Friday morning about 3000 men & after some brisk skirmishing in which we lost some eight or ten, killed, wounded & missing, including Maj. Manigault killed they say, others that he is a prisoner but wounded, they evacuated Friday night. The two movements were both evidently feelers to see whether or no all our troops had been sent away. So there is one more trial thro' which our old city has triumphantly passed. God grant she may remain unscathed till the end.

Weather still quite cold. It has been really bitter cold for some days. To-day tho' is rather warmer . . . Went to church this morning & heard a fisherman. Tell Father Mr. Peck[18] has gone back to the North—very treasonable, disloyal letter of his was intercepted while he was off on leave, & on his return he was sent off to Yankee land. 'Most dark. I can hardly see so must bid you good night & ask you to write again soon. Love to all the dear ones at home, Mother, Sue, Sis & all. Kiss to babies.

Your own brother
Gus

Louisa R. McCord, Columbia, S.C., to Susan D. Smyth[19]

Tuesday
21 March [1865]
Excuse the appearance of the telegram, it fell in the fire.

Dear Sue

Having got through our tribulation[20] we are very anxious to hear how you people are getting on but before proceeding farther please to look at the enclosed telegram which I received this morning & send you thinking that Mrs. Briggs[21] may not have heard from her husband, even if the rest of you are not glad to hear that "A.T.S. is well." It is the first word I have heard for six weeks so you may believe I was glad to get it. Yesterday telegraphic communication was re-opened a great thing for us unfortunately who have been shut up here for so long, but I should not grumble to you who must be as badly off. As soon as this telegram came Han and I rushed off to the post office (our favorite haunt) to enquire if it were possible to get a letter to Summerton. He, the post master, tells me to write it & it shall go by the first opportunity, though when that will be neither he nor I knows. I may give you very old news but still run that risk. A dispatch was received today, Gen. Lee's report to the secretary of war. Johnston had attacked the enemy on the nineteenth near Bentonsville, routing him & capturing three guns. He, the enemy, retreated slowly but meeting reinforcements again assumed the offensive but was resisted without difficulty. He is now entrenched. Our loss very small. That is our latest news, announced in the very first number of the Col. Phoenix & charming looking little paper about as big as my two hands which began its career today.[22]

Had I been able to write to you four weeks ago I would have given you a most glowing account of Yankee performances but now the excitement has passed off & with it all my spirit for telling adventures. Besides it is hard to write knowing so little of what you have gone through. But I am sure the Yankees cannot have been raiding up near you, we surely would have heard of it. I do trust you may be spared that for you may be assured it is not pleasant. Never did I spend three such perfectly disgusting days. Except for a little while I was too much excited to feel fright or distress or any thing but disgust and a sort of boiling over feeling, a feeling that I was decidedly dangerous to Yankees. I did feel as if I would like to put an end to some of them, as if I could do it if I got them in a nice little dark corner.

I wrote to you just before they came, two days after I think the shelling began during all that time we were listening to the cannons and musketry.[23] You can't think how exciting it was. I used to sit up in bed, listening for every sound until I felt alf wild. The shelling was really a relief, it seemed as if we were beginning to share the danger a little. The shells did one good thing for me, got me down stairs for our house being directly in range several officers advised us to move down to the basement which we did though we spent most of the time in the yard & street. I flew around in style considering they thought me hardly able to walk. The evacuation began that day but we could not believe it. Kept hoping for reinforcements from Charleston. That night was too absurd, we all spent it down here in the parlour as best we could. It looked just like a steam boat cabin, unfortunate females lying about on every side. Minna Cheves[24] & I had mattresses in consideration of being invalids. I never shall forget Hannah's appearance lying on a sofa, with her night cap peeping from under a pile of blankets. I just lay there & laughed. My tune changed the next day, it was horrid work dressing down here. Hannah & I grumbled like two old cats & you may imagine the pitch our scolding reached when suddenly in flew an old Mauma, banging & bolting in all the shutters, slamming doors, & generally putting the house in proper darkness shouting out that "de Yankee in de town." We were incredulous. Maum Rache[25] having the character of an alarmist & after the first rush, we got a little day light in order to finish our elaborate toiletries. Then followed some two or three hours of contradictory rumours, the shelling slacked, greatly to our distress but we knew nothing certainly until we saw their horrid old flags on the state house. It was not a pleasant side [*sic*], one that I hope & pray never to see again. We bolted up upstairs ready for them & well it was we did, for in a short time the yard was crowded with these vile creatures on foot & on horseback, kicking open doors, picking locks & altogether tearing up the place about as effectually as it could well be done. They stole everything, literally everything that could be carried, actually stuffing lard into their pockets. Everything not be be carried was smashed. It was horrid to look at them, they were the most disgusting looking creatures I ever saw. After a while I was so worn out that I left my peep hole & went back to lye [*sic*] down by Minna. Han & Aunt Rachel Cheves[26] had gone down stairs. Presently I heard one of them call out "bolt the doors!" & in came Hannah flying to report that the Yankees had attacked the house a fact of which our ears soon convinced us for such a kicking & pounding you never heard. Then my dear was the time I was frightened. Knowing that they would kick the door down in no time, Mamma unbolted it & then they just over ran the house she just following them to keep them from the stairs. Aunt Rache retreated to our hiding place looking as if she were going to faint & there we all sat bolted in listening to the up roar down stairs. Such banging! You can't imagine what a half hour that was to us, we did not know what they might be doing to Mamma besides the pleasant little idea that they might soon get up stairs & then much good our bolts would do us. Aunt Rache said she would have made us jump out of the window & I know we would have done it. A fine sight it would have been to passing Yankees. Four distracted females sliding down the trunk of the Magnolia & alighting on the ground with broken limbs not to mention scratches & such small wounds. We might have done it though, those who were so fortunate as to reach the ground in safety, carrying off the wounded. But we did not quite get to this. Just in the midst of all the fuss down stairs, while Mamma was having a nice time, one of the men having pushed her up against the wall and dragged her watch off, while another flourished a handful of stolen knives in her face, and all the rest behaved themselves in somewhat the same way, stealing & smashing & were at last beginning to look up stairs, some one rang the bell & in walked Gen. Howard[27] & his staff come to look for quarters. My dear, when we poor things up stairs heard them Minna just bounced up out of bed & threw one arm round Hannah & the other me, we all joined in a regular dance of rejoicing, round & round the room. Mamma in the meanwhile received the general as coldly as possible in spite of feeling somewhat relieved at his arrival. We did not adopt the plan some people thought necessary of entertaining the officers as visitors, on the contrary we left them the lower story entirely. The first evening they sent up a message hoping that we would make use of the parlour as usual but we declined. We never left our rooms except for a little while after dark when we walked in the upper piazza. We girls were geese enough to imagine that all was quiet for the night but one of the first things we knew the house was on fire. I then went out to look at the fire, it was a fearful sight worse than Charleston. We seemed almost surrounded by the flames and with the wind blowing so furiously we thought it impossible than any house should escape.[28] Early in the evening we had seen fires in every direction but I was so exhausted & stupefied as not to realize how it was until I was roused by the announcement of the house on fire. Had we been burnt out we would have been in the condition of many others, with nothing whatever saved for we attempted nothing, only put on our bonnets and took our seats quietly in the parlour, evidently astonishing the Yanks by our coolness & composure. In truth I felt perfectly indifferent & except for the boiling over rage as quiet as I ever was in my life. There we sat quietly talking until about two o'clock. I know they thought us a hard headed set. The house caught twice but was put out, the general to do him justice trying to save it, though his men did their best to let it burn & vowed in the yard that it should burn the next night. That was an awful night, not that I was frightened or even distressed at the time, but it was a horrid feeling to be so at the mercy of the these men when you could see how they rejoiced at all their work. The whole night long there was the most horrid confusion. Yells & curses & worse than all their horrid laughter & jokes & then by way of adding to it they were throwing shells & hand grenades about the whole night. Crowds of women and children gathered in the park & the Yankees actually stood on the hill above & threw the hand grenades among them.[29] We had an encampment right in these pines which gave us the full benefit of their performances, during the day that was our special aggravation. Saturday night was pretty quiet though we did not dare to go to bed. Sunday the same. Monday they left, oh it was a blessing. But they left a nice crowd & as one of the two guards the general left us got drunk our position became rather disagreeable. The other said the house was going to be pillaged, we overheard him but nevertheless they announced their intention of going & then we were let with the place just swarming with men, so took some bundles on our backs & went over to the Reynoldses[30] where we spent the night on the said bundles & returned the next morning hardly expecting to see the house standing. This performance was repeated for several nights until at last they told us we could stay at home & then you cant imagine how delightful it was to get to bed again though it was by no means delightful to look around us. You never saw anything like it. Fortunately we had some bacon and corn hidden in the garden along with the silver so they left that & we have it to live on. There is great scarcity of provisions but they give out rations to every one who can squeeze through the crowd to get them. Those who can pay buy them but the crowd is awful. For two weeks we heard not even a rumour. It was dreadful after all the excitement. I felt half crazy sometimes. Most of that time I had to spend on the sofa & it was a long time before I could leave the house again & that made it all the harder to bear. It was a relief even to get out to look at the ruins.

Eighty six squares, four fifths, I believe of our poor little town is gone but fortunately so many houses were left vacant that people found places to go to. After a while we began to come to life, couriours [*sic*] came in one by one, bringing however very little news, but it was delightful to see a grey coat again, we used to attack every one that passed for news. Now to [*sic*] we have a post office & a telegraph which is something fine though I wish between them they would bring me some news. It is so hard to be patient. Have you heard anything of Ellison. I have asked about the cadets but cannot hear of their whereabouts. Somebody said they had been furloughed for a few days so I am hoping that he may have got home.

I must hurry to the office with my letter for fear the opportunity should turn up before I am ready. Goodbye. Do write to me as soon as you can. I am a horrid girl not to have said before that I received a note from Miss Janey Adger inquiring after you. I had to answer her as I did Major Briggs[31] that I had heard nothing. Mamma & Han send love. With a great deal from myself to all of you believe me

Yours most affectionately
L.R.McC.

I hope you may get this for such dreadful reports seem to be spread of the condition of Columbia. I doubt if there is now suffering from want of food but they do say that the provisions may not last many days but then wagons come in from the country. It is dreadful for those who have literally nothing. We are among the fortunate having still a house & good for a little while at least & I know things will get better. Any how I for one would rather trust to that than go away. At first there was nothing for those who had lost all but contributions were given by the more fortunate & now the worst must be over.

Louisa R. McCord, Columbia, S.C., to Margaret M. Smyth

23 March 1865

Dear Mrs. Smythe,

I have just this moment received the enclosed dispatch & thinking it would be as welcome to you as it was to me will make another effort to get a letter to you in order to send it. I wrote to Sue a tremendously long scratch only two days ago. This telegram has made me feel happy, it was so long since I had heard, not since the evacuation of Charleston & I was beginning to feel very anxious when Maj. Briggs' dispatch came. That was a great help but this is splendid. Now I shall persecute the poor man at the post office more than ever. He hates us already I think. Our post office is a very fine establishment in a kitchen on one of the burned squares where every [*sic*] goes and sticks their heads through the window to inquire for letters. At first the arrival of a letter caused a great excitement. One afternoon coming out of church five people including the minister informed us that there was a letter waiting for us. I had some terrible disappointments in that way for all proved to have come from Abbeville. I wish you could see our poor little town, it is too pitiful. You can scarcely look in any direction without seeing these rows of ruined houses looking so melancholy and deserted in the midst of their burned gardens. But anything is better than to have it left to the Yankees as they have been obliged to do [*sic*] poor old Charleston. That was hard for us all but it must have been particularly so to you who have lived there. We were dreadfully [*sic*] the Yankees might be going to garrison this place, if they had we would have left if we had starved on the road. The night of the fired [*sic*] I firmly expected to be tramping along the Winnsboro road before daylight & at the time in my excitement rather liked the idea, it seemed rather a relief to have every gone, nothing to take care but yourself. No doubt I might have changed my mind had the experiment been tried. It was a queer state of affairs after we were left, people walking into any vacant house they took a fancy to which of course no one thought of objecting to. In some cases Gen. Sherman was so kind as to make presents of houses to friends of his, they I am happy to say were turned out. The college, new State House[32] & Seminary were not burned. To our surprise the college library was not injured. Sherman left it to us with the request to make use of it as had we read more, we never would have been in this rebellion. He also left what they called liberal supplies for the town, a few of the leanest stolen cows which they shut up in the camps without food or water until they nearly died. Oh the hypocrisy of those Yankees! It was wonderful to see how the officers tried to make us think the fire accidental as if we had no eyes & ears to find out for ourselves.[33] I could scarcely keep my countenance. When a piece of cotton was found burning in our entry, the General Howard commenced speaking of the dreadful wind & the strange way in which cotton had been blowing about all day.[34] He tried his hand too to humbug us about the shelling & kept referring to it though we assured him it had not inconvenienced us, which was a delightful satisfaction as he had just said we were in one of the hottest places. When I get on the Yankee subject it is hard to stop, but I must not cross[write]. With love to all

Yours very affectionately
Louisa R. McC.

Louisa R. McCord, Columbia, S.C., to Augustine T. Smythe

31 March [1865]

My own dear Gus

I wish you could know how delighted I was to get your letter this morning. I had thought myself very fortunate to have received one & had no idea another could possibly reach here so soon. It came very quickly though. I don't think Mr. Edgerton brought it for it is post marked Raleigh. It is too bad that you should have received none of mine for I have written constantly. I think this is the fifth letter since they have begun sending off mail & before that I wrote by every possible opportunity, at least five or six times. The address must have been the difficulty though. I adopted many suggestions and made several variations in it in hopes that one might be right. But now that you have told me how to direct I do hope at least one of the letters may reach you. As for the telegram, I cannot help hoping that when you sent into Raleigh that day you must have found it there for I sent it as soon as I received yours. I told you in my last two letters that I had heard from Summerton at last. The Yankees had not been to them although they had had several alarms. They were all well except your sister in law who had been feeling badly for a day or two.

This last letter of yours was much more satisfactory than the first, it told me a little more of what you were doing & intended to do though even now I am in a horrid state of ignorance on that important subject. You speak of trying to get a transfer & I have not the remotest idea of where you want to be transferred to. Now I do hope I may not hear some of these days that you have been transferred without hearing where to. This losing of my letters is horrid. I don't think anyone who has not lived through this war can appreciate the full value of letters or know what a loss one can be. But as regards letters, our condition as begun to improve & I know will continue to do so. . . . It is too bad that you should not at least know that we are not starving, not by any means. You must believe it now though for I assure you I am telling no fibs. Of course we live in rather rough style but we are very fortunate to be no worse off and as for me the only consequence of the fever left me is a very fine appetite so I am by no means particular as to the quality of the fare. I only wish you were as well off as we are. I was just now trying to remember how long it is since you were here last but all my ideas of time are in such a jumbled up state that it is perfectly impossible. I only know it seems a long, long time. And do you remember your promise then to come back in three weeks. I used to be there and count the days, wondering if I would be well by that time. I would have been better satisfied to let the time pass slowly had I known what was coming. And then when Frank Miller came up here & told me he thought you must be on the cars & would be here the next day. I was almost wild with impatience. I wanted so much to see you if it was only for an hour & I did not give up hope until the town was actually in Yankee hands. Afterwards we found that you had not passed near here. I wrote to you only this morning but determined to hurry this off before the mail closes as I am impatient to try the new direction. Love from Mamma & Han & a great deal from

Your darling

NOTES

Introduction

1. A. T. Smythe to J. A. Adger, 2 June 1864, Augustine Thomas Smythe Papers, 1209.03.02.04, South Carolina Historical Society, Charleston, South Carolina.

2. Some confusing variations of surname spellings mark Smythe's paternal genealogy for several generations. Thomas Smyth was the son of Samuel Smith, who had inexplicably changed the spelling of his name from Smyth to Smith. Thomas changed the spelling of the family name back to Smyth, to avoid being confused with another man by the same name, and eventually his son Augustine added an "e" to the name for the same reason. Augustine's father, Thomas Smyth, left a valuable record of his life and times in a book published many years after his death as *Autobiographical Notes, Letters and Reflections.* His granddaughter, Louisa Cheves Smythe Stoney, arranged and annotated "three bulky volumes" Smyth had compiled, she surmised, "with the evident intention of some day writing the full story of his eventful and unusual life." Smyth, *Autobiographical Notes,* Prefatory Note, 8, 14, 509.

3. Ibid., 8, 14–15, 18, 28, 39–40.
4. Ibid., 40, 59–62, 65, 76–78.
5. Ibid., 55, 65–66, 78.
6. Ibid., 79–81.
7. Ibid., 212; O'Brien, *Conjectures of Order,* 65.
8. Smyth, *Autobiographical Notes,* 65, 68.
9. Ibid., 509.
10. Martin, *The Mind of Frederick Douglass,* 43; Smyth, *Autobiographical Notes,* 374.
11. Smyth, *Autobiographical Notes,* 65, 68.
12. Foner, *Life and Writings of Frederick Douglass,* 1:181.
13. Smyth, *Autobiographical Notes,* 194.
14. Adger, *My Life and Times,* 165–67.
15. Ibid., 170–73.
16. Smyth, *Autobiographical Notes,* 195.
17. Adger, *My Life and Times,* 174–75.
18. Smyth, *Autobiographical Notes,* 733.
19. Ibid., 736–37.
20. *Journal of the Proceedings of the Seventieth Annual Convention,* 30–35.
21. Adger, *My Life and Times,* 162–63.
22. Smyth, *Autobiographical Notes,* 238.
23. Ibid., 244.
24. Stephens, *Science, Race, and Religion in the American South,* 170–73.

25. Smyth, *Autobiographical Notes,* 554.
26. Smyth, *The Sin and the Curse,* 13.
27. Ibid., 8.
28. Adger, *My Life and Times,* 179–80.
29. Farmer, *The Metaphysical Confederacy,* viii.
30. Smyth, *Autobiographical Notes,* 563.
31. Ibid., 565.
32. Ibid., 575.
33. Vile, *Encyclopedia of Constitutional Amendments,* 118.
34. Smyth, *Autobiographical Notes,* 737.
35. Ibid., 675.
36. Ibid., 684.
37. *In Memoriam: Rev. Thomas Smyth, D.D.,* 9.
38. Smyth, *Autobiographical Notes,* 716.
39. *In Memoriam: Rev. Thomas Smyth, D.D.,* 3–24.
40. Hagy, ed., *On the Eve of the Civil War,* 151; Bailey, *Biographical Directory of the South Carolina Senate,* 1523; J. Adger Smyth to Gus Smythe, 23 December 1860, South Carolina Historical Society, Charleston, South Carolina (hereafter SCHS).
41. "Excerpts from the Wartime Correspondence of Augustine T. Smythe," *South Carolina Historical Magazine,* 27.
42. Ibid; A. T. Smythe to M. M. Smyth, June 1862, SCHS; A. T. Smythe to J. A. Adger, 17 June 1862, SCHS.
43. A. T. Smythe to J. A. Adger, 5 February 1863, SCHS; Orvin, *In South Carolina Waters,* 113–16.
44. "Excerpts from the Wartime Correspondence of Augustine T. Smythe," *South Carolina Historical Magazine,* 27.
45. Snowden, *History of South Carolina,* 833.
46. Ibid., 840–41.
47. Ibid., 842–44.
48. Ibid., 845.
49. "The Signal Corps in the Confederate States Army," 104.
50. Ibid.
51. Ibid., 105.
52. A. T. Smythe to J. A. Adger, 23 April 1863, SCHS.
53. "The Signal Corps in the Confederate States Army," 105.
54. A. T. Smythe to M. M. Smyth, 19 December 1864, SCHS.
55. Major General Samuel Jones, the Confederate departmental commander at Charleston, later wrote that "Charleston was General Gillmore's objective point, which he proposed to gain by way of Morris Island. . . . For the complete success of his plan it was exceedingly important that he should, with the least possible delay, demolish Fort Sumter and silence Fort Moultrie and other batteries on the west of Sullivan's Island, the accomplishment of which formed a part of his plan, and thus open the gate to Charleston for the entrance of the fleet before his adversary could prepare other works to bar his approach to the city." Jones, *The Siege of Charleston,* 249.

56. The Confederate engineer John Johnson also described Gillmore's strategy in the summer of 1863: "The Union commander decided to make [Folly Island] his base, and concentrated here a force of ten thousand infantry, 350 artillery, and six hundred engineer troops, forming a total of nearly eleven thousand men, for a descent from Folly Island upon the southern end of Morris Island, with the design of advancing on Fort Sumter for its reduction, with the closest possible co-operation of the navy." Johnson, *Defense of Charleston Harbor,* 86.

57. Ibid., 144.

58. According to General Jones, "While approaching Wagner and preparing to demolish Sumter, General Gillmore had made other preparations. . . . He had with difficulty and at much cost constructed a battery known as the 'Swamp Angel,' in the marsh between Morris Island and the Confederate works on James Island, from which Charleston could be bombarded." Jones, *Defense of Charleston Harbor,* 260.

59. Roman, *The Military Operations of General Beauregard in the War between the States,* 2:140.

60. Fitzgerald Ross, a foreign newspaper correspondent in Charleston at the time, wrote about the ultimatum sent to General Beauregard and the initial shelling of the city, which began in the middle of the night: "Next morning we heard of the 'fair warning' General Gilmore [sic] had given of his intention to shell the city. It seems that at nine o'clock in the evening a note had been sent to the commanding officer at Fort Wagner to forward to General Beauregard, in which it was demanded that Fort Wagner, Fort Sumter, and the other defences of the harbour, should be immediately given up to the Yankees; if not, the city would be shelled. Four hours were graciously given to General Beauregard to make up his mind, and to remove women and children to a place of safety. The note was entirely anonymous, no one having taken the trouble to sign it. It reached General Beauregard about midnight, and was of course returned for signature and without an answer. At half past-one the shelling commenced. No doubt General Gilmore wished that the effects of the bombardment should have their influence on General Beauregard before it was possible that he should give an answer to the summons. . . . It is rather an extraordinary proceeding, to say the least of it, to bombard the city because the harbour defences, which are three and four miles distant, cannot be taken; and the attempt to destroy it by Greek fire is very abominable; but the spite of the Yankees against Charleston, 'the hotbed of the rebellion,' is so intense that they would do anything to gratify it." Ross, *A Visit to Cities and Camps of the Confederate States,* 120–21.

61. General Samuel Jones protested to General Foster that the bombardment of Charleston served no military purpose and that the indiscriminate shelling was carried out simply to destroy the city, not to disable military targets. Stokes, *Immortal 600,* 39–40.

62. Ibid.; *Official Records of the War of the Rebellion,* series 1, v. 35, part II, 163.

63. A. T. Smythe to M. M. Smyth, 27 June 1864, SCHS.

64. A. T. Smythe to J. Smyth, 1 July 1864. Smythe might have mistaken "cricket" for the game of baseball, which was becoming popular in the Union army.

65. Stokes, *Immortal 600,* 43.

66. A. T. Smythe to M. M. Smyth, 15 April 1864, SCHS.

67. A. T. Smythe to J. A. Adger, 23 January 1865, SCHS.

68. A. T. Smythe to M. M. Smyth, 20 November 1863, SCHS; A. T. Smythe to T. Smyth, 25 November 1863, SCHS; A. T. Smythe to M. M. Smyth, 2 December 1863, SCHS.

69. *Official Records of the War of the Rebellion*, series 1, vol. 28, 682–83; Phelps, *The Bombardment of Charleston*, 10. Phelps's book is a good source of information on the civilian evacuations of Charleston. He wrote, "As far as the official Confederate records indicate, the actual tallying of casualties stopped in January 1864, when the war's focus shifted from Charleston. At that point only five people had been killed and six wounded. As recorded in the newspaper articles and personal accounts presented in this book, however, the casualties continued to mount until the end of the bombardment." Ibid., 150.

70. Ibid.

71. A. T. Smythe to J. A. Adger, 4 August 1864, SCHS; A. T. Smythe to J. Smyth, 2 September 1864, SCHS; A. T. Smythe to M. M. Smyth, 28 September 1864, SCHS.

72. McCord, *Louisa S. McCord: Political and Social Essays*, 1.

73. Fought, *Southern Womanhood and Slavery*, 165.

74. Smythe, "Recollections," 60.

75. Ibid., 60–61.

76. Sarah Smyth to A. T. Smythe, 10 February 1864, SCHS.

77. J. A. Adger to A. T. Smythe, 16 February 1864, SCHS.

78. A. T. Smythe to M. M. Smyth, 17 February 1864, SCHS.

79. Smythe, "Recollections," 3.

80. Ibid., 64.

81. McCord, *Louisa S. McCord: Poems, Drama, Biography, Letters,* 245.

82. L. R. McCord to M. M. Adger, 23 March 1865, SCHS.

83. Smythe, "Recollections," 69–70.

84. McCord, *Poems, Drama, Biography, Letters,* 20; Fought, *Southern Womanhood and Slavery,* 170–73, 178–79.

85. McCord, *Louisa S. McCord: Poems, Drama, Biography, Letters,* 21.

86. Bailey, *Biographical Directory of the South Carolina Senate,* 1523.

87. McCord, *Louisa S. McCord: Selected Writings,* 9–10; McCord, *Louisa S. McCord: Poems, Drama, Biography, Letters,* 35.

88. Bailey, *Biographical Directory of the South Carolina Senate,* 1523.

89. Ibid., 1524.

90. Ibid.

91. *History of the United Daughters of the Confederacy,* 157–58.

CHAPTER ONE: A TASTE OF WAR AND NEW DUTIES

1. The Battle of Secessionville took place on June 16, 1862, on James Island near Charleston.

2. John H. Taverner, a native of England, served in the Washington Light Infantry and was a member of Second Presbyterian Church of Charleston, where he is

buried. Smyth, *Autobiographical Notes,* 644; Thompson, *The Charleston South Carolina Second Presbyterian Church at 200,* 62.

3. Fleetwood Lanneau Jr. held the rank of First Sergeant in Company B (Washington Light Infantry), 25th South Carolina Infantry Regiment. He was twenty-two years old at the time of his death and was a member of Second Presbyterian Church. Smyth, *Autobiographical Notes,* 644; Thompson, *The Charleston South Carolina Second Presbyterian Church at 200,* 62.

4. Jane Ann Adger (1822–99), the daughter of James Adger (1802–58) and Sarah Elizabeth Ellison Adger. Law, *Adger-Law Ancestral Note-Book,* 15.

5. Richard Walsh Greer was a second lieutenant in Company B, 25th South Carolina Infantry Regiment. He died on June 16, 1862, and is buried at First Scots Presbyterian Church in Charleston. Kirkland, *Broken Fortunes,* 138.

6. Joseph Ellison Adger (1824–98) served as an assistant quartermaster in the 25th South Carolina Infantry Regiment. His wife was Susan Cox Johnson Adger (1829–1905). Smyth, *Autobiographical Notes,* 649; Law, *Adger-Law Ancestral Note-Book,* 15.

7. Goat Island is located in the Stono River near James Island and adjacent to Cole Island.

8. Colonel Clement Hoffman Stevens (1821–64) of the 24th South Carolina Infantry Regiment. He was later a brigadier general. Warner, *Generals in Gray,* 291–92.

9. Hannah Cheves McCord (1843–72) was the older sister of Lou McCord (later Mrs. Augustine T. Smythe). Hannah married John Taylor Rhett (1836–92) in 1869. *South Carolina Genealogies,* 4:30.

10. There was a J. H. Houston who served in Company A, 25th South Carolina Infantry Regiment. Hewett, ed., *South Carolina Confederate Soldiers,* 510.

11. Joseph Manigault (1827–1911) was a captain and assistant adjutant general in the Confederate Signal Corps. Smyth, *Autobiographical Notes,* 663; *Works Progress Administration Cemetery Index.*

12. Private Robert E. Pennal (1831–73). Hewett, ed., *South Carolina Confederate Soldiers,* 379.

13. John Gotea Pressley (1833–95), who was probably "the youngest signer of the Ordinance of Secession," was a native of Williamsburg District, South Carolina. He graduated from the Citadel in 1851 and became a lawyer in Kingstree, South Carolina. After the war he moved to California and became a prominent judge in Sonoma County. He is buried in Santa Rosa, California. May, *South Carolina Secedes,* 194–5.

14. George H. Moffett (1829–75) was an adjutant of the 25th South Carolina Infantry Regiment and a relation of the Adger family. Dillingham, "Genealogical Notes," 80.

15. Robert Adger (1814–91). Law, *Adger-Law Ancestral Note-Book,* 15.

16. A "bathing pavilion" for "salt water bathing" was located off the Battery and became the headquarters for the Confederate Signal Corps in Charleston. Sparkman, *Through a Turnstile into Yesteryear,* 43; Thomson, *Charleston at War,* 88.

17. This is Caroline Gilman Glover (1823–77), the widow of John Wilson Glover (1823–46). She was the daughter of the Reverend Samuel Gilman and Caroline Howard Gilman. Mrs. Glover married Lewis Jervey in March 1864. *South Carolina Genealogies,* 3:43; Glover, *Col. Joseph Glover,* 126–7.

18. Wappoo Creek, or Wappoo Cut, is a body of water connecting the Ashley and Stono Rivers, which had strategic importance in the defense of Charleston. Burton, *Siege of Charleston,* 118, 121.

19. General Pierre Gustave Toutant Beauregard (1818–93) was the Confederate commander of the Department of South Carolina, Georgia, and Florida from 1863 to 1864. The department was headquartered at Charleston. Warner, *Generals in Gray,* 22–23.

20. This is Laurence Massillon Keitt (1824–64) of Orangeburg District, South Carolina. Keitt was a signer of the Ordinance of Secession, a lawyer, and a delegate to the Provisional Confederate Congress. In January 1862 he raised the 20th South Carolina Infantry Regiment, which served more than two years at Charleston, during which time Colonel Keitt was the commander of forces on Sullivan's Island. May, *South Carolina Secedes,* 168–9; Allardice, *Confederate Colonels,* 224.

21. This is Joseph Atkinson Yates (1829–88). An article titled "Unique Fight in the Stono," published in the *New York Times* in 1920, recounts the capture of the USS *Isaac P. Smith* and states that Yates "was the only officer of land forces who succeeded in the attempt to make a war vessel surrender to land batteries." According to the article, Colonel Yates devised the idea of using concealed batteries along the Stono River to capture the ship. Yates File, SCHS.

22. The Marion Light Artillery was an independent artillery organization, which became part of the 1st South Carolina Artillery Regiment. Kirkland, *South Carolina C.S.A. Research Aids.*

23. Legareville was a place of summer residence for about twenty-five planter families. Built around 1838, it was situated along the Stono River on John's Island. Jordan and Stringfellow, *A Place Called St. John's,* 115.

24. The term "floating-batteries" is possibly soldiers' slang for hardtack either floating or cooking in a liquid substance to soften it.

25. The Federal gunboat *Isaac P. Smith* went up the Stono River in late January 1863 and anchored at "Tom Grimball's plantation." It received fire from a Confederate battery on James Island and returned fire, but its crew was surprised when more shelling came from another battery opposite on John's Island. Caught in a deadly crossfire, the damaged gunboat moved downriver, where it lost engine power and began to drift. The *Isaac P. Smith* then received fire from even more Confederate batteries until its commander was forced to surrender. Orvin, *In South Carolina Waters,* 113–16.

26. Brigadier General Roswell Sabine Ripley (1823–87) was a native of Ohio who married into the Middleton family of South Carolina in 1852 and soon afterward settled in Charleston. He was on duty in South Carolina in 1863 and 1864, and after the war he lived in England for a period. Warner, *Generals in Gray,* 257.

27. William F. Nance of Newberry, South Carolina, was assistant adjutant general to General Ripley. Pope, *History of Newberry County,* 228.

28. Named in honor of Brigadier General Barnard Elliott Bee Jr. (1824–61) of the Confederacy, who was mortally wounded at the First Battle of Bull Run (Manassas), Battery Bee was located on Sullivan's Island. It was designed by the South Carolina

engineer and architect Captain George E. Walker (1828–63), "who was careful to build his works with especial reference to the effects of modern artillery." Johnson, *Defense of Charleston Harbor,* 20.

29. The Federal ironclad vessel *Keokuk* was severely damaged by fire from Fort Sumter in this engagement. "Kept afloat with difficulty that night, she sank at her anchorage off the southern part of Morris Island early the next morning." Johnson, *Defense of Charleston Harbor,* 53–54.

30. The *Thistle,* the second blockade runner by this name, was built in Scotland and purchased by Fraser, Trenholm & Company. Wise, *Lifeline of the Confederacy,* 324.

31. In 1863 the Chicora Importing and Exporting Company of South Carolina purchased an English paddlewheel steamer named *Havelock,* which became the blockade runner *General Beauregard.* Wise, *Lifeline of the Confederacy,* 115, 304.

32. James Hillhouse Alexander (1840–1902) of Washington, Georgia, was the brother of General Edward Porter Alexander and served in the 9th Georgia Infantry Regiment until January 1862, when he was detailed for duty in the Signal Corps in Charleston. "He was then commissioned as captain in the signal service, for which, by order of the government at Richmond, he proposed a manual, remaining in that city until this task was completed." He served at Wilmington, North Carolina, for a period and then again at Charleston until July 1863. He eventually obtained the rank of major. *Confederate Military History,* 7:464–65.

33. John Marshall Otey (1839–83), a native of Virginia, was assistant adjutant general to General P. G. T. Beauregard in 1863. He rose to the rank of lieutenant colonel. Roman, *Military Operations,* 409.

34. Pocotaligo, South Carolina, was the site of a small community and an important rail station on the Charleston and Savannah Railroads. Federal troops attempted to capture the station in May and October 1862 but failed in both attempts. Emerson, "Lowcountry Rail Line Threatened," 93–103.

Chapter 2: Aboard the CSS *Palmetto State*

1. The *Juno,* a fast side-wheel steamship, was a privately owned blockade runner, which the Confederate Navy purchased and used as a torpedo boat. Its service as a torpedo boat was brief, however, and it returned to blockade running in 1864. Campbell, *Engineer in Gray,* 76–82; Wise, *Lifeline of the Confederacy,* 152–53.

2. Captain Philip Johnstone Porcher (1835–64) was the commander of the *Juno.* Porcher, "Porcher," 177.

3. The *New Ironsides* was one of three experimental Union ironclads produced to counter the threat of the CSS *Virginia* and is considered to be the most powerful Union vessel of the Civil War. Tucker, ed., *The Civil War Naval Encyclopedia,* 473.

4. Smythe is referring to Captain Stephen Clegg Rowan (1808–90) of the United States Navy, commander of the USS *New Ironsides,* a wooden hulled ironclad vessel used as a blockader at Charleston and Wilmington, North Carolina. In 1866 Rowan was promoted to the rank of admiral. Sifakis, *Who Was Who in the Civil War,* 558.

5. Major General Quincy Adams Gillmore (1825–88) was the Union commander of the Department of the South and directed the siege operations against Charleston in 1863. Disputes between Gillmore and Rear Admiral John Adolphus Bernard Dahlgren (1809–70), the local naval commander, led to a "professional and personal feud" between the two officers. Sifakis, *Who Was Who in the Civil War,* 165, 249; Wise, *Gate of Hell,* 211.

6. Smythe is writing from the CSS *Palmetto State,* an ironclad gunboat constructed in Charleston at the shipyard of Marsh & Son and launched in October 1862. Its first commander was Lieutenant John Rutledge. Orvin, *In South Carolina Waters,* 85–90.

7. The Smyth family left Charleston in August 1863 and took refuge in Clarendon District, South Carolina, where they resided in a rented house near the village of Summerton. For the remainder of the war Thomas Smyth continued his ministry in several local Methodist churches. Smyth, *Autobiographical Notes,* 658.

8. William H. Ward of Virginia was a lieutenant commander on the CSS *Palmetto State.* Orvin, *In South Carolina Waters,* 93.

9. Marshall P. Jordan of Virginia. Orvin, *In South Carolina Waters,* 92.

10. Brigadier General John Henry Winder (1800–65) was the Confederate provost marshal of Richmond, Virginia. Warner, *Generals in Gray,* 340–41.

11. Louisa Susanna Cheves McCord (1810–79) was the future mother-in-law of Augustine T. Smythe. She was a noted author and intellectual, and during the war she was well known for her tireless work on behalf of Confederate soldiers in Columbia, South Carolina. *South Carolina Genealogies,* 3:85.

12. Mrs. McCord is referring to the loss of her son, Captain Langdon Cheves McCord, who died as a result of wounds received at the Battle of Second Bull Run (Second Manassas). He was twenty-one years old at the time of his death in January 1863. *South Carolina Genealogies,* 3:85; Kirkland, *Broken Fortunes,* 244.

13. The baby is Langdon Cheves McCord, born on February 3, 1863, the daughter and only child of Captain Langdon Cheves McCord and his wife, Charlotte Reynolds (1842–1923). She later was Mrs. Henry C. Cheves, and she died in 1940. *South Carolina Genealogies,* 3:85.

14. Formerly a blockade runner named the *St. Johns,* the *Spaulding* was captured in October 1863 near St. Andrews Bay, Georgia, on its way to Charleston. Wise, *Lifeline of the Confederacy,* 321.

15. John Randolph Tucker (1812–83) took command of the ironclad CSS *Chicora* in 1862. In March 1863 he became the commander of the Confederate naval forces at Charleston. *Appleton's Cyclopedia,* 6:176.

16. A martello tower was a fortified cylindrical structure that resembled a silo. The one on James Island was located close to Fort Johnson and was built for the defense of Charleston Harbor sometime between 1806 and the end of the War of 1812. Robinson, "North American Martello Towers," 162–63.

17. "Castle Pinckney, built of brick and rough-cast, in 1810, on a low, marshy island known as Shute's Folly, was distant one mile from the city. It was a complete little casemated work of that period, but on so small a scale and so near to the city to be

of little value in the defense of the harbor. Its casemates were disarmed, its front wall covered with an exterior slope of sand, well sodded, and its ramparts furnished with merlons and traverses." Johnson, *Defense of Charleston Harbor,* 21.

18. Construction on the gunboat *Charleston* began in December 1862. The boat went into service nine months later, bearing twenty-four inches of armor plating, four Brooks rifles (cannons), and two nine-inch smooth-bore guns. Orvin, *In South Carolina Waters,* 99.

19. The "machine" to which Smythe refers is the submarine CSS *H. L. Hunley,* which sank for the first time on August 29, 1863. It was recovered a few days later. A newspaper in Charleston, the *Courier,* reported on August 31, 1863: "On Saturday last, while Lts. Payne and Hasker, of the C.S. Navy, were experimenting with a boat in the harbor, she parted from her moorings and became suddenly submerged, carrying down with her five seamen, who were drowned. The boat and bodies had not been recovered up to a late hour on Sunday. Four of the men belonged to the gunboat Chicora, and were named Frank Doyle, John Kelly, Michael Cave, and Nicholas Davis. The fifth man, whose name we did not learn, was attached to the Palmetto State."

20. Built in Charleston by James M. Eason & Brothers and by Jones Brothers, the *Chicora* was an ironclad ram commissioned in November 1862. In 1863 some of its crew members volunteered for the first test mission of the submarine *H. L. Hunley.* Orvin, *In South Carolina Waters,* 95–96, 156.

21. The British blockade runner *Sumter,* also known as *Gibralter,* was chartered as a transport vessel while awaiting a cargo of cotton in Charleston. On August 31, 1863, while carrying Confederate troops, the *Sumter* was mistaken for an enemy vessel and fired upon from Fort Moultrie on Sullivan's Island. Orvin, *In South Carolina Waters,* 145–46; Johnson, *Defense of Charleston Harbor,* 140.

22. Battery Gregg was a Confederate fortification built on the north end of Morris Island. Wise, *Gate of Hell,* 61.

23. Smythe is referring to one of two six-hundred-pound, 12.75-inch imported Blakely rifled guns that Charleston's defenders received without instructions for loading or firing them. The gun to which he refers was mounted at Battery Ramsey at White Point and was damaged during a test firing in early September 1863. See *Official Records of the War of the Rebellion* 28, no. 2: 387–88.

24. The British-built blockade runner *Antonica* (formerly the *Herald*) was owned by the Chicora Importing and Exporting Company of Charleston. Wise, *Lifeline of the Confederacy,* 304.

25. Frederic Fraser Warley (1830–76) of Darlington, South Carolina, began his military service with the Darlington Guards and later became a major in the 1st South Carolina Artillery Regiment and commanded Battery Wagner on Morris Island. "He was wounded . . . while being conveyed to Charleston in General Ripley's boat, was captured and carried to Hilton Head." After being exchanged, Warley was placed in command of a prison camp at Florence, South Carolina, and later returned to active field service. United Daughters of the Confederacy, *Treasured Reminiscences,* 66–67.

26. A "sap" is a covered trench or tunnel.

27. Battery Wampler was located on James Island near Fort Johnson. Wise, *Gate of Hell,* 212–13.

28. Battery Glover was located on James Island. Ibid., 225.

29. The Charleston Battalion, also known as the 1st Battalion, South Carolina Infantry Regiment, or "Gaillard's Battalion," was organized in the spring of 1862. The members of this unit distinguished themselves in the Battle of Secessionville in 1862 and at Battery Wagner in 1863. Phelps, *Charlestonians in War,* 12.

30. Thomas Abram Huguenin (1839–97) of Beaufort District, South Carolina, entered military service as a lieutenant in Company A, 1st South Carolina Infantry Regiment. He was promoted to captain in July 1861 and later held the rank of major. Huguenin was in command of Fort Sumter from July 1864 until the end of the war, succeeding Captain John C. Mitchel. Hewett, ed., *South Carolina Confederate Soldiers,* 240; Burton, *Siege of Charleston,* 298.

31. Robert J. Bowen (1834–94) was a lieutenant on the CSS *Palmetto State.* He was a native of Mississippi. Orvin, *In South Carolina Waters,* 92.

32. Smythe is referring to the *Palmetto State*'s armor plating.

33. This refers to the CSS *David,* a steam-propelled torpedo boat designed by St. Julien Ravenel of Charleston. According to an essay written by Augustine T. Smythe Jr., Ravenel "designed a torpedo boat, which he felt sure would be effective, but which for lack of means, he was unable to build. Mr. Theodore Stoney, of Charleston . . . gave his check for $20,000 and within a very few days, she was under process of construction at Stoney Landing, on Cooper River. Within two months she was completed . . . and on the night of the 5th of Oct., 1863, she set out on her famous expedition against the Ironsides." The cigar-shaped boat, which carried a torpedo at the end of an iron shaft fourteen feet long, was dubbed the "David" perhaps because of its small size in comparison to the much larger enemy vessels that it opposed. Its engineer David C. Ebaugh claimed that it was named after him. Smythe, "Torpedo and Submarine Attacks," 56–57; Orvin, *In South Carolina Waters,* 102.

34. "Man proposes but God disposes."

35. Ellen A. Crawford (1828–92) was a Smyth family servant. Thomas Smyth took her from the Charleston Orphan House as a young girl, and she became a nurse to his children. "She lived as their staunch and loyal friend, and ended her days among them." Smyth, *Autobiographical Notes,* 380.

36. This apparently refers to Dr. Edward North, a Charleston physician who died on May 26, 1863. Otto, *Family of Captain Edward North,* 20.

37. This is a quotation from Henry Wadsworth Longfellow's poem "A Psalm of Life," first published in 1838. The full stanza reads: "Trust no Future, however pleasant! / Let the dead past bury its dead! / Act, —act in the Living Present! / Heart within, and God o'erhead!"

38. On October 5, 1863, the CSS *David* exploded a torpedo against the unarmed quarter of the USS *New Ironsides.* The larger ship suffered severe damage and was towed to Port Royal, an area of South Carolina under Union control. Luraghi, *History of the Confederate Navy,* 261–62.

39. Smythe is referring to Lieutenant William Thornton Glassell (1831–79) of Virginia. Luraghi, *History of the Confederate Navy,* 260–62.

40. Camp meetings, which began to take place in the South about 1800, were outdoor religious gatherings, or revivals, that lasted for days. In South Carolina they eventually they became associated almost exclusively with the Methodist denomination. Attendees who had to travel long distances to the meetings would bring tents and provisions. Betts, *History of South Carolina Methodism,* 160–62.

41. "Aunt E" is Elizabeth Keith Shrewsbury Adger (1812–90), the wife of the Reverend John B. Adger (1810–99), a Presbyterian minister, educator, and missionary. During the war she lived at a plantation near Pendleton in Anderson County, South Carolina. Gist, *Presbyterian Women,* 271–73.

42. Anderson's Brigade, composed of several Georgia regiments, was under the command of General George Thomas ("Tige") Anderson (1824–1901). The brigade arrived in Charleston in September 1863. Its next major engagement was at Knoxville, Tennessee. Wise, *Gate of Hell,* 212; Warner, *Generals in Gray,* 6–7.

43. The Union Bank of South Carolina was located on East Bay Street. An 1860 *Charleston City Directory* gives its address as 125 East Bay, but it also occupied a building at 139 East Bay sometime afterward. During the war the bank moved its operations to Anderson, South Carolina. Clark, *History of Banking Institutions,* 66–68; Hagy, ed., *On the Eve of the Civil War,* 162.

44. The wharves owned by James Adger & Company were located off East Bay Street. Poston, *Buildings of Charleston,* 53.

45. Rivoli was an Adger family plantation located near Pendleton in Anderson County, South Carolina. Stevenson, *Diary of Clarissa Adger Bowen,* 11.

46. Jefferson Davis, the president of the Confederacy, was plagued with eye problems for much of his life. He eventually lost sight in his left eye, the eyelid of which was sometimes closed. Allen, *Jefferson Davis,* 243, 652.

47. Smythe means *cereus,* a flowering cactus.

48. Robert McNeill (or McNeal) was an Irish gardener and a member of Thomas Smyth's congregation at Second Presbyterian Church. Smyth, *Autobiographical Notes,* 654.

49. Smyth family servants.

50. The Central Wharf was located off East Bay Street, at the end of Cumberland Street.

51. "Greek fire" was a mixture of incendiary chemicals that were loaded into artillery shells. Many of the first shells of this type sent into Charleston were defective. In early 1865, General John G. Foster, the Union commander of the Department of the South, was informed of an improved version of Greek fire by O. S. Halsted Jr., who recommended it for the burning of "that hotbed of rebellion Charleston." Foster replied that if Halsted would send him some, he would "fire them on Charleston with pleasure." Burton, *Siege of Charleston,* 255, 260.

52. Calcium floodlights, or limelights, were used by the Federals to illuminate areas targeted for shelling for artillery fire. They were first located on batteries near Cummings Point but were later placed on boats. Wise, *Gate of Hell,* 148.

53. An "oyster plantation" of about twenty acres was owned by the heirs of its original owner, David Truesdale. Burrell, *South Carolina Oyster Industry,* 3.

54. The "Episcopal one" was Grace Church. Its services were suspended during the war and never resumed. "When the United States forces established their batteries on Morris Island, the Church then came in reach of their shells, which riddled roof and floor, and consumed the wood work." *Report on the Destruction of Churches,* 11.

55. The "Catholic one" on Sullivan's Island was St. John the Baptist Church, a frame building erected in 1845. Preservation Society, *Churches of Charleston,* 65.

56. The Moultrie House was an elegant hotel on Sullivan's Island, a place of summer resort for many Charlestonians. It had luxurious accommodations and opened for business in 1850. The hotel was located just east of Fort Moultrie. Miles, *Writings of the Islands,* 95–98.

57. Battery Marshall was located on Sullivan's Island near Breach Inlet. Rosen, *Confederate Charleston,* 94.

58. Long Island is now known as the Isle of Palms, adjacent to Sullivan's Island.

59. Daniel Heyward Hamilton (1816–68) was formerly the U.S. marshal for South Carolina. Allardice, *Confederate Colonels,* 179.

60. According to the 1860 Charleston directory, Crane, Boylston & Co. was a dry-goods store located at the corner of Meeting and Hayne Streets.

61. The *General Moultrie,* formerly a Charleston dredge boat, did not run the blockade to Nassau until early March 1864. Wise, *Lifeline of the Confederacy,* 302.

62. Charles Macbeth (1805–81), a Charleston attorney, was first elected mayor of the city in 1857 and was re-elected in 1859, 1861, and 1863. Four of his sons served in the Confederate army. In 1860 his residence was located at the corner of Gibbes and Legare Streets. *Year Book (Charleston, S.C.),* 251–53; Hagy, ed., *On the Eve of the Civil War,* 131.

63. The Charleston Orphan House, the first municipal orphanage in America, was located at the corner of Calhoun and St. Philip Streets. During the bombardment of Charleston, the orphaned children were sent to Orangeburg, South Carolina, for their safety. King, *History and Records of the Charleston Orphan House,* 6.

64. Smythe probably means James A. Duffus. There was a James A. Duffus (born 1812) who was the deputy secretary of state in South Carolina. A *Charleston City Directory* of 1860 lists a man by the same name as a clerk in the office of the Secretary of State, but he is likely the same person. Hagy, ed., *On the Eve of the Civil War,* 107.

65. This refers to 36 Meeting Street, the residence of Augustine's uncle James Adger (1812–81). Smyth, *Autobiographical Notes,* 747.

66. Fort Ripley, or Battery Ripley, was a fortification in Charleston Harbor. According to John Johnson, it was "a small work, built in 1862 on the middle ground or shoal between Castle Pinckney and Fort Johnson." Johnson, *Defense of Charleston Harbor,* 21.

Chapter 3: Duty at Fort Sumter and an Engagement

1. Lieutenant Thomas L. Swinton of the Quartermaster Department was in charge of the mail boat at Fort Sumter. Johnson, *Defense of Charleston Harbor,* 184.

2. Smythe is referring to Edmund Ruffin (1794–1865) of Virginia, a prominent agriculturalist and publisher and an ardent secessionist. He sometimes visited Charleston "to 'aid' in her defense." *Dictionary of American Biography,* 16:215–16.

3. Fort Putnam, formerly known as Battery Gregg, was on Morris Island. After the Federals took possession of the battery, they renamed it in honor of Colonel Haldimand S. Putnam (1835–63), who was killed in the second assault on Battery Wagner. Little, *7th New Hampshire Volunteers,* 125, 189.

4. The Charleston residence of former governor Robert F. W. Allston (1801–64) was at 51 Meeting Street. He purchased the house in 1857. Today it is designated a National Historic Landmark and is known as the Nathaniel Russell House. Poston, *Buildings of Charleston,* 262.

5. Captain M. Henry Sellers of the 25th South Carolina Infantry Regiment was from Orangeburg District, South Carolina. Johnson, *Defense of Charleston Harbor.*

6. This is probably Captain Nathaniel Broughton Mazyck (1831–1907) of the 25th South Carolina Infantry Regiment. Woodruff, "Dr. Tucker Harris," 237.

7. Located at 115 Meeting Street, the Mills House was a five-story hotel, constructed in 1853. It was later known as the St. John Hotel. The building was demolished in the 1960s, and a reproduction of the original Mills House was built to replace it. Poston, *Buildings of Charleston,* 189–90.

8. This is Captain I. Frank Markoe (1840–1914) of the Confederate Signal Corps. "The Signal Corps in the Confederate States Army," 92.

9. This refers to the home of Smythe's uncle Robert Adger (1814–91). According to the 1860 *Charleston City Directory,* he lived at the corner of Tradd and Legare Streets. His house number, listed in the 1861 tax census records, was 18 Legare Street. The present address of this property, known as the Sword Gate House, is 32 Legare. From 1819 to 1858, Madame Talvande operated a school for young ladies here. Smyth, *Autobiographical Notes,* 748; Hagy, ed., *On the Eve of the Civil War,* 86.

10. This refers to the graveyard at First Scots Presbyterian Church.

11. This is probably St. John's Lutheran Church on Archdale Street. Legerton, *Historic Churches,* 38–39.

12. According to the 1860 *Charleston City Directory,* the business of Harrall, Nichols & Company, a saddlery and warehouse, was located at the corner of Meeting and Hasell Streets.

13. The house at 12 Meeting Street was the home of Thomas Smyth. It was once owned by Thomas Heyward, a signer of the Declaration of Independence, and was later purchased by James Adger, who bequeathed it to Smyth. The house is now numbered as 18 Meeting Street and is known as the Thomas Heyward House. Poston, *Buildings of Charleston,* 255; 18 Meeting Street File, SCHS; Thompson, *The Charleston South Carolina Second Presbyterian Church at 200,* 49.

14. Louisa S. McCord, the mother of Smythe's fiancée, was characterized by many of her contemporaries as "masculine" because of her powerful intellect and commanding appearance. Lounsbury, ed., in McCord, *Louisa S. McCord: Poems, Drama, Biography, Letters,* 416.

15. Some of the buildings on the campus of South Carolina College (now the University of South Carolina) in Columbia were used as hospitals during the war. Mrs. McCord's home was adjacent to the campus. Hollis, *South Carolina College,* 227.

16. This may refer to Brigadier General John Hunt Morgan (1825–64) of the Confederacy. Warner, *Generals in Gray,* 220–21.

17. This is likely Charles Scott Venable (1827–1900) of Virginia, an educator and, during the war, aide de camp to General Robert E. Lee. Venable was Smythe's mathematics professor at South Carolina College. Sifakis, *Who Was Who in the Confederacy,* 290.

18. There was a Sergeant A. Hart in the Signal Corps.

19. The brigade was under the command of Major General James Ewell Brown Stuart (1833–64), a famous Confederate cavalryman.

20. The submarine *H. L. Hunley* went out on its first mission against an enemy vessel on the evening of February 17, 1864. The *Hunley* embedded and detonated a spar torpedo in the USS *Housatonic,* sinking this sloop-of-war and becoming the first submarine to be used successfully in warfare. The *Hunley* also sank with all eight crewmen aboard. Faust, *Historical Times Illustrated,* 363–64.

Chapter 4: A Lofty Perch in St. Michael's

1. Augustine's new post was in the arcade level of the steeple of St. Michael's Episcopal Church, located on the corner of Meeting and Broad Streets in downtown Charleston. The steeple is 186 feet high and "is braced by heavy timbers that give rather than break in high wind." The steeple was also used as an observation post during the Revolutionary War. *A Guide to St. Michael's Church,* 11–12.

2. Brigadier General Thomas Jordan (1819–95) of Virginia was General Beauregard's chief of staff. In May 1864 Jordan took command of the Third Military District in South Carolina. *Confederate Military History,* 4:618–19; Warner, *Generals in Gray,* 167–68.

3. The Charleston Hotel, established in 1838, was a "magnificent Greek Revival structure" located at 200 Meeting Street. It was demolished in 1960. Poston, *Buildings of Charleston,* 405.

4. Private Joseph Proctor Huger (1846–64) died on April 13, 1864. He was seventeen years old and a member of the Signal Corps. *South Carolina Genealogies,* 2:77.

5. Joseph Ellison Adger Smyth (1847–1942), Augustine's younger brother. Smyth, *Autobiographical Notes,* 743.

6. The French Protestant (Huguenot) Church, located at 140 Church Street, was built in 1845. Poston, *Buildings of Charleston,* 85.

7. The "Burnt District" was a large section of downtown Charleston that was destroyed by the Great Fire of December 11–12, 1861. Burton, *Siege of Charleston,* 258.

8. William Coombs Dana (1810–80) was the pastor of Central Presbyterian Church (also known as Third Presbyterian), which was located at 275 Meeting Street. The building now houses Trinity Methodist Church. Poston, *Buildings of Charleston,* 456; Howe, *History of the Presbyterian Church,* 2:596.

9. Lieutenant General James Longstreet (1821–1904) of the Confederate army, a native of South Carolina, was seriously wounded by friendly fire at the Battle of the Wilderness in Virginia on May 6, 1864. Warner, *Generals in Gray,* 192–93.

10. Brigadier General Micah Jenkins (1835–64) of Edisto Island, South Carolina, was a member of the Confederate army. He was killed by friendly fire at the Battle of

the Wilderness on May 6, 1864, in the same incident that wounded General Longstreet. Warner, *Generals in Gray,* 155.

11. Lieutenant General Thomas Jonathan (Stonewall) Jackson of the Confederate army. Warner, *Generals in Gray,* 151–52.

12. Colonel John G. Pressley of the 25th Regiment South Carolina Infantry. Hewett, ed., *South Carolina Confederate Soldiers,* 391.

13. This is Major John Vinyard Glover (1833–64) of Orangeburg District, South Carolina. Culler, *Orangeburgh District,* 168.

14. Alonzo T. Dargan (1839–64) of Darlington, South Carolina, a lieutenant colonel of the 21st South Carolina Infantry Regiment, was killed at Petersburg, Virginia, on May 7, 1864. Ervin and Rudisill, *Darlingtoniana,* 349–50.

15. Jane Ann Quigley Dargan (1843–1936), the wife of Alonzo T. Dargan, was the daughter of Kyle Quigley and Mary Adger Quigley. Law, *Adger-Law Ancestral Note-Book,* 20.

16. Lieutenant Colonel Julius A. Blake (1830–1903) was wounded while serving as an officer in the 27th South Carolina Infantry Regiment. Kirkland, "CSA Research Aids."

17. Joseph Ellison Adger.

18. Andrew Moffett Adger (1846–1915), Smythe's cousin, was the son of Margaret Hall Moffett Adger (1820–1915) and William Adger (1816–53). Law, *Adger-Law Ancestral Note-Book,* 17.

19. Arthur Robinson (1842–64) held the rank of corporal in the Charleston Light Dragoons (Company K, 4th South Carolina Cavalry Regiment). He was killed at the Battle of Hawes Shop in Virginia on May 28, 1864. Smyth, *Autobiographical Notes,* 664; Emerson, *Sons of Privilege,* 72.

20. Trinity Methodist Church, dedicated in 1839, was located on Hasell Street at Maiden Lane. Guy, *History of Trinity,* 21.

21. This refers to a large Greek Revival–style house at 1 East Battery, built by Louis D. DeSaussure (1824–88) just before the war. Poston, *Buildings of Charleston,* 217.

22. Fifty captive Union officers, including Brigadier General Truman Seymour (1824–91) and four other generals, were brought to Charleston by the Confederate commander Major General Samuel Jones, who hoped to deter the continued shelling of the city by placing these prisoners in the downtown area. Stokes, *The Immortal 600,* 39–40.

23. Anne Branford Frost (1845–1935), the daughter of Judge Edward Frost (1801–68) of Charleston, married Thomas Pinckney Lowndes (1839–99). Wood, *Gaillard Genealogy,* 189.

24. Thomas Frost (1829–99), a son of Judge Edward Frost (1801–68). Works Progress Administration Cemetery Index.

25. This is Mary E. Hayne (1845–68), daughter of Isaac W. Hayne (1809–80), attorney general of South Carolina. *South Carolina Genealogies,* 2:324–25.

26. Mary (Minnie) Mitchell Whaley (ca. 1844–1902) eloped with Bartholomew R. Riordan (d. 1897), editor of the *Charleston Mercury* newspaper. Patey, *Whaley Family,* 35.

27. The baby is likely one of the infant children of Smythe's brother James Adger Smyth and his wife, Anne Ransom Briggs Smyth (1838–1901). Sarah Ragin Smyth was born on November 10, 1861, and her brother, Ellison Adger Smyth, was born on October 26, 1863. In a letter of November 19, 1861, Augustine wrote of his newborn niece Sarah, "The baby is an ugly little critter but all at home say it is the loveliest little animal that ever existed."

28. This was the residence of Michael P. O'Connor (1831–81), a prominent Charleston attorney, located at 180 Broad Street. The house still exists and is known as the Cooper-O'Connor House. O'Connor, *Life of M. P. O'Connor,* 24; Poston, *Buildings of Charleston,* 302.

29. After Major General Samuel Jones of the Confederate army placed fifty Union prisoners of war in the O'Connor house on Broad Street, Major General John G. Foster (1823–74), commander of the Federal Department of the South, retaliated by asking for fifty Confederate prisoners of war, all officers, to be sent to Charleston. Within weeks of their arrival, an agreement of exchange was reached by the two governments, and the groups of prisoners were freed and exchanged. Joslyn, *Immortal Captives,* 17–22.

30. Major General Samuel Jones (1819–87) of Virginia succeeded General P. G. T. Beauregard in command at Charleston. Warner, *Generals in Gray,* 165–66.

31. There were two houses on South Battery owned by Colonel John A. S. Ashe (1796–1868), Nos. 26 and 32. Poston, *Buildings of Charleston,* 270–72.

32. Brigadier General William Booth Taliaferro (1822–98) of Virginia, a Confederate officer. Warner, *Generals in Gray,* 297–98.

33. Smythe probably means Brigadier General Beverly Holcombe Robertson (1827–1910) of Virginia, of the Confederate army. Warner, *Generals in Gray,* 269–60.

34. Woodburn Plantation, located near Pendleton, South Carolina, was owned by Augustine's uncle Joseph Ellison Adger (1824–98), who purchased it from his brother John Bailey Adger (1810–99) in 1858. According to John B. Adger's autobiography, Woodburn later became the property of his nephew Augustine T. Smythe. Adger, *My Life and Times,* 210–11, 338.

35. This is Augustine's youngest sister, Jane Anne Adger (1849–1914). Smyth, *Autobiographical Notes,* 743.

36. For most of the nineteenth century the Charleston post office was located in the Old Exchange Building at 122 East Bay Street. It was removed from that site in late August 1863 and "functioned at various locations in the city for the remainder of the war." Miller, *Witness to History,* 45.

37. Lieutenant General William Joseph Hardee (1815–73) of Georgia assumed command of the Department of South Carolina, Georgia and Florida, which was headquartered in Charleston, in October 1864. Warner, *Generals in Gray,* 124–25; Hughes, *General W. J. Hardee,* 248–50.

38. This is likely Jane Eliza Adger (1841–1925), the daughter of Robert Adger (1814–91) and Jane Eliza Fleming (1815–71). Smyth, *Autobiographical Notes,* 748; *Works Progress Administration Cemetery Index.*

39. In August 1864 six hundred Confederate prisoners of war, all officers, were taken out of Fort Delaware at the request of Major General John G. Foster of the Union army and transported to South Carolina by steamship. On September 7, 1864, 560 of these men arrived at Morris Island in Charleston Harbor and were placed in a stockade pen located between Batteries Wagner and Gregg, where they were exposed to Confederate artillery fire. Major General Samuel Jones, the Confederate commander at Charleston, had been ordered to temporarily accept and incarcerate a large number of captive U.S. officers at several locations in the city, including Roper Hospital and the city jail. Because Federal officers were quartered in residential parts of the city and exposed to the continued Federal shelling, General Foster retaliated by placing an equally large number of Confederate prisoners directly in harm's way. This group of Confederate prisoners later became known as "The Immortal Six Hundred." Stokes, *The Immortal 600,* 43–47.

40. Probably William Dalton Warren (1839–93), who married Smythe's cousin Sarah E. Adger. Smyth, *Autobiographical Notes,* 620; *Works Progress Administration Cemetery Index.*

41. In 1864 Major General George B. McClellan (1826–85) was nominated by the Democratic Party for the U.S. presidency on a peace platform. Warner, *Generals in Blue,* 290–92.

42. The vote of soldiers was very important in the presidential election of 1864. The platform of the party that nominated Lincoln at the Union National Convention at Baltimore, Maryland, "praised the soldiers and sailors of the North, and declared that the nation owed them some permanent recognition for their services; and ample permanent provision for their widows and orphans." By 1864, nineteen Union states had made it possible for their soldiers to vote in the field. For those states without absentee voting, thousands of soldiers were sent home on furlough to cast their votes. Charges of voter fraud and intimidation were made by the parties of both Lincoln and McClellan. McPherson, *Battle Cry of Freedom,* 804–5; Winther, "The Soldier Vote in the Election of 1864," 440–58.

43. Charles Landon Carter Minor (1835–1903) became an ordnance officer in Virginia, and, after promotion to the rank of captain in 1864, he was appointed chief ordnance officer in the Department of South Carolina, Georgia and Florida. After the war he was a lawyer, educator, and writer. Tyler, *Encyclopedia of Virginia Biography,* 3:88.

44. Josiah Gorgas (1818–83), a native of Pennsylvania and a graduate of West Point, served in the Ordnance Department during his career in the United States Army. He was appointed chief of ordnance of the Confederate States in 1861 with the rank of major. In 1864 Gorgas was promoted to the rank of brigadier general. He promoted blockade-running efforts to bring in foreign war materiel. Warner, *Generals in Gray,* 112.

45. Wolfe Street was located six blocks north of Calhoun Street.

46. Now known as Marion Square, the Citadel Green was an open area adjacent to The Citadel (South Carolina Military College). Poston, *Buildings of Charleston,* 393.

47. Formed in 1854, Citadel Square Baptist Church is located on Meeting Street just north of Calhoun Street. Poston, *Buildings of Charleston,* 610.

48. Located at 100 Wentworth Street, Grace Episcopal Church was constructed in 1848. The church closed in January 1864 because of the continued bombardment of the city. A shell that struck Grace Church "crushed one of the central columns and cracked the superincumbent walls up to the roof, tore away twelve pews, and cut the interior in many places." Poston, *Buildings of Charleston,* 571–72; *Report of the Committee on the Destruction of Churches,* 10.

49. Zion Presbyterian Church was located at 123 Calhoun Street, near Meeting Street. It originally was established for the benefit of the black members of Second Presbyterian Church of Charleston. Built at a cost of $25,000, contributed by Charleston citizens, the large church building was dedicated in 1859. It was demolished in 1959. Simms, *A History of Zion,* 2–3; Adger, *My Life and Times,* 175.

50. Bethel Methodist Church is located on Pitt Street, near Calhoun Street. Poston, *Buildings of Charleston,* 546.

51. During the Atlanta Campaign, Major General William T. Sherman's army shelled the city for several weeks, beginning the bombardment without prior notice and killing a number of civilians. After the city surrendered on September 2, 1864, General Sherman came to conclusion that he could not hold the city, protect his supply lines, and also pursue offensive operations. He therefore ordered all of Atlanta's remaining citizens (roughly three thousand people) to evacuate the city, a measure that the Confederate general John B. Hood called "an act of ingenious cruelty." Most of Atlanta was burned in November 1864. Grimsley, *The Hard Hand of War,* 190–91.

52. In July 1862, after Confederate troops were forced to evacuate Memphis, Tennessee, General Sherman assumed command of the city. Angered by the actions of guerrilla fighters in the area, he issued an order stating that for every hostile act against Federal boats on the Mississippi River, ten citizens would be expelled from Memphis. In mid-October 1862, in response to continuing fire upon Federal vessels, he ordered forty families to move twenty-five miles outside the city limits. Royster, *The Destructive War,* 107.

53. White Point Garden began in 1848 as a "public pleasure ground" beside Charleston Harbor. A five-gun earthwork battery was constructed there and named Battery Ramsay in honor of Major David Ramsay (1830–63), who died from wounds received in the battles on Morris Island in July 1863. Poston, *Buildings of Charleston,* 291; Thomson, *Charleston at War, 84.*

54. John Adams Burckmyer was a Charleston commission merchant and a business partner of John R. Moffett (Burckmyer & Moffett). His nephew Cornelius L. Burckmyer (1822–77) wrote of this incident in a letter dated October 14, 1864: "Uncle John with his family including John Moffett's . . . was living in a house in Charlotte Street near the water which he supposed, when he went into it, to be out of range. For two or three nights during the heavy shelling he was forced to move the whole concern and spend the night in the open air in some less exposed position. One evening, however, they were all assembled in the dining room, and a large party it was . . . when a large Parrott shell entered the house and exploded right among them and yet, strange to say, not one was killed." In a letter written in September 1864, Cornelius L. Burckmyer reported that the shelling had "killed some five or six negroes, who were caught

in the streets." Snowden, *History of South Carolina,* 5:133; Burckmyer and Holmes, *The Burckmyer Letters,* 428–31.

55. St. Michael's Episcopal Church was pierced by several shells and its graveyard and monuments seriously damaged. *Report of the Committee on the Destruction of Churches,* 9.

56. *Macaria, or, Altars of Sacrifice* was a popular novel by Augusta Jane Evans, published in Richmond, Virginia, in 1864.

Chapter 5: Sherman Targets South Carolina

1. There was a earthwork fortification on Hutchinson Island with "three 32-pounder guns." Jones, *The Siege of Savannah,* 101.

2. After a destructive march through Georgia, General Sherman approached the coastal city of Savannah and demanded its surrender. In a letter to Lieutenant General William J. Hardee, commander of the Confederate forces in Savannah, dated December 17, 1864, Sherman wrote: "I have already received guns that can cast heavy and destructive shot as far as the heart of your city, also I have for some days held and controlled every avenue by which the people and garrison can be supplied, and I am therefore justified in demanding the surrender of the city of Savannah. . . . Should you entertain the proposition, I am prepared to grant liberal terms to the inhabitants and garrison, but should I be forced to resort to assault, or the slower and surer process of starvation, I shall then feel justified in resorting to the harshest measures, and shall make little effort to restrain my army." The city of Savannah surrendered on December 21, 1864. Jones, *The Siege of Savannah,* 139–40.

3. Fort McAllister was a Confederate earthwork fortification protecting the Ogeechee River in Georgia. Federal forces under the command of Brigadier (later Major) General William B. Hazen captured the fort on December 13, 1864. Durham, *Guardian of Savannah,* 140–67.

4. Screven's Ferry was located on the Savannah River, in what is now Jasper County, South Carolina.

5. Major General Joseph Wheeler (1836–1906) of Georgia unsuccessfully opposed General Sherman's advance to Savannah, Georgia. His soldiers came under criticism for a lack of discipline in their foraging, and civilians accused them of plunder. In a letter to Jefferson Davis dated January 8, 1865, Lieutenant General William J. Hardee defended Wheeler, stating: "Wheeler's cavalry has been reorganized under my direct supervision. . . . It is a well organized and efficient body. The reports of its disorganization and demoralization are without foundation, and the depredations ascribed to his command can generally be traced to bands of marauders claiming to belong to it." In letters written after the war, Union general James H. Wilson, revealed that "the invading army had hundreds of their men distributed through the country, representing themselves as 'Wheeler's cavalry,' sent out on their work of theft and insult." Dyer, *From Shiloh to San Juan,* 161–66; DuBose, *General Joseph Wheeler,* 421.

6. Federal forces under the command of General Sherman destroyed a number of Savannah River plantations. The overseer of Gowrie Plantation on Argyle Island wrote to his employer, Louis Manigault, to inform him that "your House, Servant

House and Barn and Contents were all burned; and I was informed by the Federalists that they intended to burn the Threshing Mill, as soon as they got the rice out of it." Wheeler, *Savannah River Plantations,* 8; Batson, *Louis Manigault,* 138.

7. Formerly a sidewheel steamship operating between Charleston and New York, the USS *James Adger* was seized in New York and pressed into U.S. military service in Charleston, where it enforced the blockade. The ship had been the property of Augustine's grandfather, James Adger (1777–1858) of Charleston. Law, *Adger-Law Ancestral Note-Book,* 23–25; Horner, *The Blockade-Runners,* 140.

8. By early 1864 a group of Confederate officers, led by Major General Patrick Cleburne, were advocating for the emancipation of slaves in the Confederacy and enlistment of former slaves in the Confederate army. By early 1865 General Lee had added his voice to those who favored using black soldiers, who would be emancipated, with their families, in return for their service. In March 1865 the Confederate Congress authorized the enlistment of black soldiers. Only a few companies of former slaves were placed into service before the war ended. Boritt, *Why the Confederacy Lost,* 159–60; Gallagher, *The Confederate War,* 81–85.

9. The Charleston Gas Light Company was incorporated in 1846, and its first gas plant, located on Church Street, was completed in 1848. "Except for a short period gas was kept on throughout the war, although the quality of light was so inferior as to bring forth this comment from a newspaper editor, 'The light of the street lamps is distinctly visible to the naked eye.'" Pogue, *South Carolina Electric and Gas,* 4–6.

10. A division of cavalry under the command of Major General Matthew Calbraith Butler (1836–1909) in Virginia was detached to South Carolina and arrived in Columbia by train around February 1, 1865. Martin, *Southern Hero,* 133–36.

11. A Federal amphibious expedition captured Fort Fisher, which was located on the Cape Fear River near Wilmington, North Carolina, on January 15, 1865. Its loss meant the end of Wilmington as the Confederacy's last remaining seaport. Faust, *Historical Times Illustrated,* 273.

12. The engines of the ironclad CSS *Columbia* were built in 1864 at the Confederate Naval Iron Works in Columbus, Georgia. The ship arrived in Charleston in mid-January 1865, but "during her first trial in the harbor she struck a submerged wreck and was now half sunk." Luraghi, *History of the Confederate Navy,* 289; 336.

13. The *Charleston Mercury* newspaper, edited by Robert Barnwell Rhett (1830–76) and his son Robert B. Rhett Jr. (1828–1901), was well known for its criticisms of Confederate president Jefferson Davis. *Dictionary of American Biography,* 15: 526–28.

14. Confederate general Braxton Bragg (1817–76) of North Carolina Warner, *Generals in Gray,* 30–31.

15. The Northeastern Railway depot was located on East Bay Street in Charleston. Poston, *Buildings of Charleston,* 601.

16. General Sherman's army destroyed railroads during its movement to Columbia. Sherman's army arrived in Orangeburg on February 12, 1865, and much of the town, including the courthouse, was burned by the time it departed. Stokes, *South Carolina Civilians,* 36–38.

17. Smythe possibly is referring to an action that occurred at Battery Simkins on February 11, 1865, instead of February 12. Burton, *Siege of Charleston,* 315.

18. The Reverend T. R.G. Peck was the pastor of the French Protestant (Huguenot) Church in Charleston. In October 1864 Confederate military authorities in Charleston examined a letter that Peck had attempted to send to his brother in the north via a blockade runner and found "objectionable" content. Peck wrote of the shelling of his church: "I am determined to have a long, jolly vacation, as soon as this war is over. Every shell which strikes our Church adds a week to it as will take so much longer to repair it. Let Foster fire away." After the letter became known to church officials, Peck resigned, and in December 1864 he was given a passport "to run the blockade to Nassau." Smyth, *Autobiographical Notes,* 594; Howe, *History of the Presbyterian Church,* 2:591; French Protestant Church Records, SCHS.

19. Susan Dunlap Smyth (1844–86) was the sister of Augustine Thomas Smythe.

20. Louisa R. McCord is referring to the sack and destruction of the city of Columbia by Federal forces on February 17–18, 1865.

21. Elizabeth M. Caldwell Briggs (1842–1910) was the wife of Major Richard R. Briggs.

22. About a month after General Sherman's army left Columbia, the noted South Carolina author William Gilmore Simms (1806–70) partnered with the newspaper editor Julian A. Selby to produce a triweekly newspaper called the *Columbia Phoenix.* Each issue, measuring six by eighteen inches, was folded into six small pages. In 2005 the University of South Carolina Press published Simms's account of the burning of Columbia as recorded in the *Columbia Phoenix.* Edited by David Aiken, the volume was the first reprint of Simms's account. Simms, *A City Laid Waste,* 1–2.

23. In the *Columbia Phoenix,* William Gilmore Simms wrote that the city was shelled without notice from General Sherman's forces. "No summons for surrender had been made; no warning of any kind was given." Simms, *A City Laid Waste,* 53.

24. Mary Elizabeth Cheves (1844–1915), daughter of Rachel Susan Bee Cheves and John Richardson Cheves, later married Joseph Cheves Haskell (1843–1922). She was Lou's first cousin.

25. Maum Rache was a McCord family servant, described by Lou McCord Smythe as "being tall, very fat and perfectly black." Smythe, "Recollections," 6.

26. Rachel Susan Bee Cheves (1821–88) was the sister-in-law of Louisa S. McCord. She was the wife of John Richardson Cheves (1815–69). In late 1864, while in Savannah, Georgia, she was warned by O. M. Poe, one of Sherman's generals, not to go to Columbia, South Carolina. "Don't go there," he advised her, "of all places, we are going there." *South Carolina Genealogies,* 1:386; West, "Statement."

27. Major General Oliver Otis Howard (1830–1909), Generals Sherman's second in command, used the McCord home as temporary headquarters while the Federal forces occupied Columbia. On several occasions, he caught some of his own soldiers attempting to set fire to Mrs. McCord's house. Stokes, *South Carolina Civilians,* 53.

28. The day of General Howard's arrival, Mrs. McCord received a note from an unnamed "Yankee soldier" that warned her about the "the horrors to come" and advised her to leave the city. "This was written in the morning; the fires were in the evening

and night," she recorded. McCord, *Louisa S. McCord: Poems, Drama, Biography, Letters,* 245.

29. In notes he kept about the burning of Columbia, Daniel H. Trezevant, a physician, similarly reported of the soldiers: "They threw fireballs among the women & girls who had sought shelter in the park." Trezevant, "Notes on the Burning of Columbia," South Caroliniana Library, University of South Carolina, Columbia.

30. This likely refers to the family of the Reverend James Lawrence Reynolds (1814–77), a Baptist minister and a professor at South Carolina College. His daughter Charlotte Reynolds McCord was Lou's sister-in-law. The family of the Reverend A. Toomer Porter also took refuge with "old Dr. Reynolds," whose house on the campus survived the fires. King, *A History of South Carolina Baptists,* 204; McCord, *Louisa S. McCord: Poems, Drama, Biography, Letters,* 204; Porter, *Led On! Step by Step,* 152–64.

31. Richard Ragin Briggs (1839–1910) of Clarendon District, South Carolina. Smyth, *Autobiographical Notes,* 667–68; Works Progress Administration Cemetery Index.

32. A new state house was still under construction at the time of the city's occupation and destruction. Although it suffered some damage, it was not burned down. The old state house, however, was completely destroyed. Simms, *A City Laid Waste,* 66.

33. General Sherman attempted to blame the burning of Columbia on the Confederate general Wade Hampton, claiming that Confederate soldiers under Hampton's command had set fire to bales of cotton in the streets as they evacuated the city. Sherman later admitted that he had made this false charge against Hampton "to shake the faith of his people in him." The historian Joseph T. Glatthaar wrote: "Just as Sherman's troops burned a dozen towns en route to Columbia, so they torched the capital of South Carolina. . . . The vast majority of the men . . . admitted that if Sherman's troops entered Columbia, they would burn it." Sherman, *Memoirs,* 2: 287–88; Glatthaar, *The March to the Sea,* 143–44.

BIBLIOGRAPHY

MANUSCRIPTS AND ARCHIVAL SOURCES

Dillingham, George Moffett. "Genealogical Notes on Andrew Moffett I and His Descendants." Moffett Family History and Papers, 1830–92. # 1078, Container 11/306. SCHS.

File on 18 Meeting Street, SCHS.

File on Yates Family, SCHS.

French Protestant (Huguenot) Church (Charleston, S.C.). French Protestant Church records, 1846–1945 (bulk 1864–1898). 1030.00. SCHS.

National Archives. War Department Collection of Confederate Records. RG 109. Compiled Service Records of Confederate Soldiers Who Served in Organizations from the State of South Carolina. First (Charleston) Battalion S.C. Infantry (Gaillard's Battalion). Microcopy 267, roll 150.

National Archives. Compiled Service Records, General and Staff Officers, Corps, Division and Brigade Staffs, Non-com. Staffs and Bands, Enlisted Men, Staff Departments, C.S.A. Microcopy 818, roll 25.

Smythe, Augustine Thomas. Augustine Thomas Smythe Papers. 1209. SCHS.

Smythe, Louisa McCord. "Recollections of Louisa McCord Smythe." Stoney Family Papers, South Carolina Historical Society.

Trezevant, Daniel Heyward. "Notes on the Burning of Columbia." Manuscript Volume, 1865, Daniel Heyward Trezevant Papers, South Caroliniana Library, University of South Carolina.

West, Mary Cheves. "Statement in Reference to the Burning of Columbia." Manuscript held by the South Carolina Historical Society.

Woodruff, Caldwell, comp. "Dr. Tucker Harris and His Descendents." South Carolina Historical Society.

Works Progress Administration. Cemetery Index. Unpublished card files at South Carolina Historical Society.

PRINTED PRIMARY SOURCES AND REFERENCE WORKS

Adger, John B. *My Life and Times, 1810–1899.* Richmond, Va.: Presbyterian Committee of Publication, 1899.

Alexander, Edward Porter. *Fighting for the Confederacy: The Personal Recollections of General Edward Porter Alexander.* Chapel Hill: University of North Carolina Press, 1989.

Allardice, Bruce S. *Confederate Colonels: A Biographical Register.* Columbia: University of Missouri Press, 2008.

Allardice, Bruce S. *More Generals in Gray.* Baton Rouge: Louisiana State University Press, 1995.

Appleton's Cyclopaedia of American Biography. Edited by James Grant Wilson and John Fiske. New York: Appleton, 1888.

Bailey, N. Louise, ed. *Biographical Directory of the South Carolina Senate, 1776–1985.* Columbia: University of South Carolina Press, 1986.

Bennett, Susan Smythe. "The McCords of McCord's Ferry, South Carolina." *South Carolina Historical and Genealogical Magazine* 34 (October 1933): 188–89.

Burckmyer, Cornelius L. *The Burckmyer Letters: March 1863–June 1865.* Columbia, S.C.: The State Company, 1926.

Campbell, R. Thomas, ed. *Engineer in Gray: Memoirs of Chief Engineer James H. Tomb, CSN.* Jefferson, N.C.: McFarland, 2005.

Charleston (S.C.) City Council. *Census of the City of Charleston, South Carolina, for the Year 1861.* Charleston: Evans and Cogswell, 1861.

Confederate Military History, Extended Edition. Wilmington, N.C.: Broadfoot, 1988.

Confederate Veteran. Nashville, Tenn.: S. A. Cunningham, 1893–1932.

Conyngham, David P. *Sherman's March through the South, with Sketches and Incidents of the Campaign.* New York: Sheldon, 1865.

Cyclopedia of Eminent and Representative Men of the Carolinas. Vol 1. Spartanburg, S.C.: Reprint Company, 1972.

Dictionary of American Biography. New York: C. Scribner's Sons, 1928–36.

DuBose, John Witherspoon. *General Joseph Wheeler and the Army of Tennessee.* New York: Neale, 1912.

Emerson, W. Eric. "Lowcountry Rail Line Threatened: The Battles of Pocotaligo and Coosawhatchie, October 22, 1862." In *The Civil War in South Carolina,* edited by Lawrence S. Rowland and Stephen G. Hoffius. Charleston, S.C.: Home House Press, 2011

"Excerpts from the Wartime Correspondence of Augustine T. Smythe." *South Carolina Historical Magazine* 62 (January 1961): 27–32.

Faust, Patricia L. *Historical Times Illustrated Encyclopedia of the Civil War.* New York: Harper and Row, 1986.

Fennell, C. A. M. *The Stanford Dictionary of Anglicised Words and Phrases.* Cambridge: Cambridge University Press, 1892.

Foner, Philip Sheldon. *The Life and Writings of Frederick Douglass.* 5 vols. New York: International Publishers, 1975.

Glover, James Bolan. *Colonel Joseph Glover (1719–1783) and His Descendants: Thirteen Generations of the Glover Family.* Marietta, Ga.: Glover Family Association, 1996.

Hagy, James W., ed. *On the Eve of the Civil War: The Charleston S.C. Directories for the Years 1859 and 1860 with Additional Information from the City Census of 1861.* Baltimore, Md.: Printed for Clearfield Company by Genealogical Publishing Company, 2000.

Hart, James D., and Phillip W. Leininger. "Russell's Bookstore Group." *The Oxford Companion to American Literature.* New York: Oxford University Press, 1995.

Hewett, Janet B., ed. *South Carolina Confederate Soldiers, 1861–1865. Name Roster, Vol. 1.* Wilmington, N.C.: Broadfoot, 1998.

In Memoriam. Rev. Thomas Smyth, D.D. Charleston, S.C.: Evans and Cogswell, 1874.

Journal of the Proceedings of the Seventieth Annual Council of the Episcopal Church in the Diocese of South Carolina. . . . Charleston, S.C.: A. E. Miller, 1859.

Kirkland, Randolph W. *Broken Fortunes: South Carolina Soldiers, Sailors, and Citizens Who Died in the Service of Their Country and State in the War for Southern Independence.* Charleston: South Carolina Historical Society, 1995.

Kirkland, Randolph W. *South Carolina C.S.A. Research Aids.* Pawleys Island, S.C. : Randolph Kirkland, 1992.

"Langdon Cheves." *South Carolina Historical and Genealogical Magazine* 41 (April 1940): 96–97.

Law, John Adger. *Adger-Law Ancestral Note-Book.* Salem, Mass.: Higginson Book Company, 1997.

Long, E. B. *The Civil War Day by Day: An Almanac, 1861–1865.* Garden City, N.Y.: Greenwood Press, 1977.

Luraghi, Raimondo. *A History of the Confederate Navy.* Annapolis, Md.: Naval Institute Press, 1996.

May, John Amasa. *South Carolina Secedes.* Columbia: University of South Carolina Press, 1960.

McCord, Louisa S. *Louisa S. McCord: Poems, Drama, Biography, Letters.* Edited by Richard C. Lounsbury. Charlottesville: University Press of Virginia, 1996.

McCord, Louisa S.. *Louisa S. McCord: Political and Social Essays.* Edited by Richard C Lounsbury. Charlottesville: University Press of Virginia, 1995.

McCord, Louisa S. *Louisa S. McCord: Selected Writings.* Edited by Richard C. Lounsbury. Charlottesville: University Press of Virginia, 1995.

O'Connor, Michael P. *The Life and Letters of M. P. O'Connor.* New York : Dempsey and Carroll, 1893.

Omni Gazeteer of the United States of America. Detroit, Mich.: Omnigraphics, 1991.

Otto, Olaf North. *The Family of Captain Edward North and His Wife, Elizabeth Tucker: In Bermuda, America, England, Canada, British India, New Zealand, Australia, and South Africa.* Adana, Turkey: O. N. Otto, 1996.

Patey, James Garner. *The Whaley Family and Its Charleston Connections.* Spartanburg, S.C.: Reprint Company, 1992.

Pickett, Otis Westbrook. "We Are Marching to Zion": Zion Church and the Distinctive Work of Presbyterian Slave Missionaries in Charleston, South Carolina, 1849–1874." *Proceedings of the South Carolina Historical Association* (2010): 91–104.

Porcher, Catherine Cordes, comp. "Porcher, a Huguenot Family of Ancient Lineage." *Transactions of the Huguenot Society* 81 (1976): 90–186.

Porter, A. Toomer. *Led On! Step by Step.* Columbia: University of South Carolina Press, 2010.

Report of the Committee on the Destruction of Churches in the Diocese of South Carolina during the Late War: Presented to the Protestant Episcopal Convention, May, 1868. Charleston, S.C.: J. Walker, 1868.

Richards, Miles S. "Langdon Cheves." In *The South Carolina Encyclopedia,* edited by Walter B. Edgar. Columbia: University of South Carolina Press, 2006.

Robinson, Willard B. "North American Martello Towers." *Journal of the Society of Architectural Historians* 33, no. 2 (May 1974): 158–64.

Ross, Fitzgerald. *A Visit to Cities and Camps of the Confederate States.* London: W. Blackwood & Sons, 1865.

Sherman, William Tecumseh. *Memoirs of General William T. Sherman.* 2 vols. New York: D. Appleton and Company, 1875.

Sifakis, Stewart. *Who was Who in the Civil War.* New York: Facts on File, 1988.

Sifakis, Stewart. *Who Was Who in the Union.* New York: Facts on File, 1988.

Sifakis, Stewart. *Who Was Who in the Confederacy.* New York: Facts on File, 1988.

"The Signal Corps in the Confederate States Army." *Southern Historical Society Papers* 16 (1888): 92–107.

Simms, William Gilmore. *A City Laid Waste: The Capture, Sack, and Destruction of the City of Columbia.* Edited by David Aiken. Columbia: University of South Carolina Press, 2005.

Simms, William Gilmore. *Sack and Destruction of the City of Columbia, S.C.* Columbia, S.C.: Power Press of Daily Phoenix, 1865.

Smyth, Thomas. *Autobiographical Notes, Letters and Reflections.* Edited by Louisa Cheves Stoney. Charleston, S.C.: Walker, Evans, and Cogswell, 1914.

Smyth, Thomas. *The Sin and the Curse; or, the Union, the True Source of Disunion, and Our Duty in the Present Crisis. A Discourse Preached on the Occasion of the Day of Humiliation and Prayer Appointed by the Governor of South Carolina, on November 21st, 1860, in the Second Presbyterian Church, Charleston, S.C.* Charleston, S.C.: Steam-Power Presses of Evans and Cogswell, 1860.

Smythe, Augustine Thomas. "Torpedo and Submarine Attacks on the Federal Blockading Fleet of Charleston during the War of Secession." *Year Book, City of Charleston* (1907): 53–64 (appendix).

South Carolina Genealogies: Articles from the South Carolina Historical (and Genealogical) Magazine. Spartanburg: Published in association with the South Carolina Historical Society by Reprint Company, 1983.

Stevenson, Mary. *The Diary of Clarissa Adger Bowen, Ashtabula Plantation, 1865: with Excerpts from Other Family Diaries and Comments by Her Granddaughter, Clarissa Walton Taylor, and Many Other Accounts of the Pendleton Clemson Area, South Carolina, 1776–1889.* Pendleton, S.C.: Research and Publication Committee, Foundation for Historic Restoration in Pendleton Area, 1973.

Tucker, Spencer C., ed. *The Civil War Naval Encyclopedia.* Santa Barbara, Calif.: ABC-CLIO, 2011.

Tyler, Lyon Gardiner. *Encyclopedia of Virginia Biography.* New York: Lewis Historical Publishing Company, 1915.

United Daughters of the Confederacy. *Treasured Reminiscences: Including Accounts of the 1st, 6th, 8th, 9th, and 21st Regiments, South Carolina Volunteer Infantry, the 6th South Carolina Cavalry Regiment, and the 1st, 15th, and Pee Dee Volunteer Artillery Battalions, Confederate State Army, 1861–1865.* Darlington, S.C.: Darlington County Historical Society and the John K. McIver Chapter of the United Daughters of the Confederacy, 1911.

Vile, John R. *Encyclopedia of Constitutional Amendments, Proposed Amendments, and Amending Issues, 1789–2002.* Santa Barbara, Calif.: ABC-CLIO, 2003.

Wakelyn, Jon L. *Biographical Dictionary of the Confederacy.* Westport, Conn.: Greenwood Press, 1977.

Warner, Ezra J. *Generals in Blue: Lives of the Union Commanders.* Baton Rouge: Louisiana State University Press, 1992.

Warner, Ezra J. *Generals in Gray: Lives of the Confederate Commanders.* Baton Rouge: Louisiana State University Press, 1987.

Warner, Ezra J., and W. Buck Yearns. *Biographical Register of the Confederate Congress.* Baton Rouge: Louisiana State University Press, 1975.

War of the Rebellion: The Official Records of the Union and Confederate Armies. 70 vols. Washington, D.C.: Government Printing Office, 1880–1901.

Winther, Oscar O. "The Soldier Vote in the Election of 1864." *New York History* 25 (1944): 440–58.

Wood, Dorothy MacDowell. *Gaillard Genealogy.* Columbia, S.C. : R. L. Bryan, 1974.

Year Book (Charleston, S.C.). Charleston: News and Courier Book Presses, 1881.

Secondary Sources

Allen, Felicity. *Jefferson Davis, Unconquerable Heart.* Columbia: University of Missouri Press, 1999.

Batson, Annie Jenkins. *Louis Manigault: Gentleman from South Carolina.* Roswell, Ga.: Wolfe, 1995.

Betts, Albert Deems. *History of South Carolina Methodism, 1882–1958.* Columbia, S.C.: Advocate Press, 1952.

Boritt, Gabor S., ed. *Why the Confederacy Lost.* New York: Oxford University Press, 1992.

Burrell, Victor G., Jr. *South Carolina Oyster Industry: A History.* Unknown: V. G. Burrell Publishing, 2003.

Burton, E. Milby. *The Siege of Charleston, 1861–65.* Columbia: University of South Carolina Press, 1970.

Clark, Sylvia H. *Shadows of the Past: An Illustrated History of Clarendon County, South Carolina.* Virginia Beach, Va.: Donning, 2005.

Clark, W. A. *The History of Banking Institutions Organized in South Carolina Prior to 1860.* Columbia, S.C.: The State Company, 1922.

Culler, Daniel Marchant. *Orangeburgh District, 1768–1868: History and Records.* Spartanburg, S.C.: Reprint Company, 1995.

Donald, David Herbert. *Lincoln.* New York: Simon and Shuster, 1995.

Durham, Roger S. *Guardian of Savannah: Fort McAllister, Georgia, in the Civil War and Beyond.* Columbia: University of South Carolina Press, 2008.

Dyer, John P. *From Shiloh to San Juan: The Life of "Fightin' Joe" Wheeler.* Baton Rouge: Louisiana University Press, 1992.

Emerson, W. Eric. *Sons of Privilege: The Charleston Light Dragoons in the Civil War.* Columbia: University of South Carolina Press, 2005.

Ervin, Eliza Cowan, and Horace Fraser Rudisill, eds. *Darlingtoniana ; A History of*

People, Places, and Events in Darlington County, South Carolina. Spartanburg, S.C. : Reprint Company, 1976.

Farmer, James Oscar, Jr. *The Metaphysical Confederacy: James Henley Thornwell and the Synthesis of Southern Values.* Macon, Ga.: Mercer University Press, 1999.

Fetters, Thomas. *The Charleston & Hamburg: A South Carolina Railroad and an American Legacy.* Charleston, S.C.: The History Press, 2008.

Fought, Leigh. *Southern Womanhood and Slavery: A Biography of Louisa S. McCord, 1810–1879.* Columbia: University of Missouri Press, 2003.

Gallagher, Gary W. *The Confederate War: How Popular Will, Nationalism, and Military Strategy Could Not Stave Off Defeat.* Cambridge, Mass. Harvard University Press, 1997.

Gist, Margaret A., ed. *Presbyterian Women of South Carolina.* Columbia: Women's Auxiliary of the Synod of South Carolina, 1929.

Glatthaar, Joseph T. *The March to the Sea and Beyond: Sherman's Troops in the Savannah and Carolinas Campaign.* New York: New York University Press, 1985.

Greene, Jack, and Alessandro Massignani. *Ironclads at War: The Origin and Development of the Armored Warship, 1854–1891.* Cambridge, Ma.: Da Capo Press, 1998.

Grimsley, Mark. *The Hard Hand of War: Union Military Policy toward Southern Civilians.* Cambridge: Cambridge University Press, 1995.

Guide to St. Michael's Church, Charleston. Edited by Alberta Lachicotte Quattlebaum and Elise Pinckney. Charleston, S.C. : Vestry of St. Michael's Church, 1979.

Guy, Yvette Richardson. *A History of Trinity United Methodist Church: From Dissension to Unity.* Charleston, S.C. : Trinity United Methodist Church, 1991.

Hayes, James P. *James and Related Sea Islands.* Privately printed by the author, 2001.

History of the United Daughters of the Confederacy. Vols. I and II. Orlando, Fla.: United Daughters of the Confederacy, 1993.

Hollis, Daniel Walker. *University of South Carolina.* Vol. 1: *South Carolina College.* Columbia: University of South Carolina Press, 1951–56.

Horner, Dave. *The Blockade-Runners: True Tales of Running the Yankee Blockade on the Confederate Coast.* New York: Dodd, Mead, 1968.

Howe, George. *History of the Presbyterian Church in South Carolina.* Columbia: Synod of South Carolina Presbyterian Church, 1965.

Hughes, Nathaniel Cheairs. *General William J. Hardee: Old Reliable.* Wilmington, N.C.: Broadfoot, 1987.

Johnson, John. *The Defense of Charleston Harbor Including Fort Sumter and the Adjacent Islands, 1863–1865.* Charleston, S.C.: Walker, Evans, and Cogswell, 1890.

Jones, Charles Colcock. *The Siege of Savannah in December, 1864, and the Confederate Operations in Georgia and the Third Military District of South Carolina during General Sherman's March from Atlanta to the Sea.* Albany, N.Y.: J. Munsell, 1874.

Jones, Samuel. *The Siege of Charleston and the Operations on the South Atlantic Coast in the War Among the States.* New York: Neale, 1911.

Jordan, Waylon Layne, and Elizabeth H. Stringfellow. *A Place Called St. John's: The Story of John's, Edisto, Wadmalaw, Kiawah, and Seabrook Islands of South Carolina.* Spartanburg, S.C.: Reprint Company, 1998.

Joslyn, Mauriel Phillips. *Immortal Captives: The Story of the Six Hundred Confederate Officers and the United States Prisoner of War Policy.* Shippensburg, Pa.: White Mane, 1996.

King, Joe Madison. *A History of South Carolina Baptists.* Columbia: General Board of the South Carolina Baptist Convention, 1964.

King, Susan L. *The History and Records of the Charleston Orphan House.* Columbia, S.C.: South Carolina Magazine of Ancestral Research, 1984–94.

Legerton, Clifford L. *Historic Churches of Charleston, South Carolina.* Edited by Edward G. Lilly. Charleston, S.C.: Legerton, 1966.

Little, Henry F.W. *The Seventh Regiment New Hampshire Volunteers in the War of the Rebellion, 1861–1865.* Concord: Seventh New Hampshire Veterans Association/Ira C. Evans, Printer, 1896.

McPherson, James. *Battle Cry of Freedom: The Civil War Era.* Oxford: Oxford University Press, 1988.

Martin, Samuel J. *Southern Hero: Matthew Calbraith Butler, Confederate General, Hampton Red Shirt, and U.S. Senator.* Mechanicsburg, Pa.: Stackpole Books, 2001.

Martin, Waldo E. *The Mind of Frederick Douglass.* Chapel Hill: University of North Carolina Press, 1984.

Miles, Suzannah Smith. *Writings of the Islands: Sullivan's Island and the Isle of Palms.* Charleston, S.C.: The History Press, 2004.

Miller, Ruth M. *Witness to History: Charleston's Old Exchange and Provost Dungeon.* Orangeburg, S.C.: Sandlapper, 1986.

A New Guide to Modern Charleston. Charleston, S.C.: Walker, Evans, and Cogswell, 1912.

O'Brien, Michael. *Conjectures of Order: Intellectual Life and the American South, 1810–1860.* Vol. I. Chapel Hill: University of North Carolina Press, 2004.

Orvin, Maxwell Clayton. *In South Carolina Waters, 1861–1865.* Charleston, S.C.: Nelsons' Southern Printing and Publishing, 1961.

Phelps, W. Chris. *The Bombardment of Charleston.* Gretna, La.: Pelican, 2002.

Phelps, W. Chris. *Charlestonians in War: The Charleston Battalion.* Gretna, La.: Pelican, 2004.

Pogue, Nell Coleman. *South Carolina Electric and Gas Company, 1846–1964.* Columbia: South Carolina Electric and Gas Company, 1964.

Pope, Thomas H. *The History of Newberry County, South Carolina.* Columbia: University of South Carolina Press, 1973–1992.

Poston, Jonathan. *The Buildings of Charleston: A Guide to the City's Architecture.* Columbia: University of South Carolina Press, 1997.

Preservation Society of Charleston. *The Churches of Charleston and the Lowcountry.* Columbia: University of South Carolina Press, 1994.

Roman, Alfred. *The Military Operations of General Beauregard in the War between the States, 1861–1865.* New York: Harper and Brothers, 1884.

Rosen, Robert N. *Confederate Charleston: An Illustrated History of the City and the People during the Civil War.* Columbia: University of South Carolina Press, 1994.

Royster, Charles. *The Destructive War: William Tecumseh Sherman, Stonewall Jackson, and the Americans.* New York: Vintage Books, 1991.

Simms, Lois Averetta. *A History of Zion, Olivet, and Zion-Olivet Churches, 1850–1985.* Unknown: L. A. Simms, 1987.

Simms, William Gilmore, ed. *War Poetry of the South.* New York: Richardson, 1867.

Snowden, Yates, ed. *History of South Carolina.* Vol. II. Chicago: Lewis, 1920.

Sparkman, Mary A. *Through a Turnstile into Yesteryear.* Charleston, S.C.: Walker, Evans, and Cogswell, 1966.

Stephens, Lester D. *Science, Race, and Religion in the American South: John Bachman and the Charleston Circle of Naturalists, 1815–1895.* Chapel Hill: University of North Carolina Press, 2013.

Stokes, Karen. *The Immortal 600: Surviving Civil War Charleston and Savannah.* Charleston, S.C.: The History Press, 2013.

Stokes, Karen. *South Carolina Civilians in Sherman's Path: Stories of Courage amid Civil War Destruction.* Charleston, S.C.: The History Press, 2012.

Stoney, Samuel Gaillard. *The Story of South Carolina's Senior Bank.* Charleston: South Carolina National Bank, 1955.

Thompson, William Murry. *The Charleston South Carolina Second Presbyterian Church at 200: A History.* Charleston, S.C.: William Murry Thompson, c. 2009.

Thomson, Jack. *Charleston at War: The Photographic Record, 1860–1865.* Charleston, S.C.: Thomson, 2000.

Wheeler, Frank T. *Savannah River Plantations.* Charleston, S.C.: Arcadia, 1998.

Wise, Stephen R. *Gate of Hell: Campaign for Charleston Harbor, 1863.* Columbia: University of South Carolina Press, 1994.

Wise, Stephen R. *Lifeline of the Confederacy: Blockade Running during the Civil War.* Columbia: University of South Carolina Press, 1988.

INDEX